A MURIEL RUKEYSER READER

Poetry

Theory of Flight (1935)
U.S. 1 (1938)
A Turning Wind (1939)
Wake Island (1942)
Beast in View (1944)
The Green Wave (1948)
Elegies (1949)
Orpheus (1949)
Selected Poems (1951)
Body of Waking (1958)
Waterlily Fire: Poems 1935–1962 (1962)
The Outer Banks (1967)
The Speed of Darkness (1968)
29 Poems (1972)
Breaking Open (1973)
The Gates (1976)
The Collected Poems of Muriel Rukeyser (1978)

Prose

Willard Gibbs (1942)
The Life of Poetry (1949)
One Life (poetry and prose) (1957)
The Orgy (1965)
The Traces of Thomas Hariot (1971)

Plays

The Middle of the Air (1945)
The Colors of the Day (in celebration of the Vassar·Centennial) (1961)
Houdini (1973)

Translations

Octavio Paz: Selected Poems *and* Sunstone (1963)
Gunnar Ekelöf: Selected Poems (with Leif Sjöberg) (1967)

Children's Books

Come Back, Paul (1955)
I Go Out (1961)
Bubbles (1967)
Mazes (1970)
Uncle Eddie's Moustache (Poems for children by Bertolt Brecht,
    translated by Muriel Rukeyser) (1974)

Screenplays

All the Way Home (documentary filmscript) (1958)

EDITED BY

JAN HELLER LEVI

WITH AN INTRODUCTION BY

ADRIENNE RICH

A · MURIEL RUKEYSER · READER

W. W. NORTON & COMPANY

NEW YORK LONDON

The text of this book is composed in 10/13 Garamond Light,
with the display set in Optima. Composition and manufacturing by
The Maple-Vail Book Manufacturing Group.
Book design by JAM DESIGN.

Library of Congress Cataloging-in-Publication Data

A Muriel Rukeyser reader / edited by Jan Heller Levi : with an
introduction by Adrienne Rich
p.   cm.
I. Levi, Jan Heller.
PS3535.U4A6   1994
811'.52—dc20   93-5786

ISBN 0-393-03566-2

W. W. Norton & Company, Inc., 500 Fifth Avenue, New York, N.Y. 10110
W. W. Norton & Company Ltd., 10 Coptic Street, London WC1A 1PU

1 2 3 4 5 6 7 8 9 0

CONTENTS

INTRODUCTION

To enter this book is to enter a life of tremendous scope, the consciousness of a woman who was a full actor and creator in her time. But in many ways Muriel Rukeyser was beyond her time—and seems, at the edge of the twenty-first century, to have grasped resources we are only now beginning to reach for: connections between history and the body, memory and politics, sexuality and public space, poetry and physical science, and much else. She spoke as a poet, first and foremost; but she spoke also as a thinking activist, biographer, traveler, explorer of her country's psychic geography.

It's no exaggeration to say that in the work of Muriel Rukeyser we discover new and powerful perspectives on the culture of the United States in the twentieth century, "the first century of world wars," as she called it. Her lifetime spanned two of them, along with the Spanish Civil War, the trial of the anarchists Sacco and Vanzetti, the Depression, the New Deal, the Holocaust, the Cold War and McCarthy years, the Vietnam War, the renewal of radicalism in the 1960s, the women's liberation movement of the late '60s and '70s, and, throughout, the movements of African-Americans and other working people for survival and dignity. All these informed her life and her art, as did other arts—film, painting, theater, the music of the blues and jazz, of classical orchestras, popular song. From a young age she seems to have understood herself as living in history—not as a static pattern but as a confluence of dynamic currents, always changing yet faithful to sources, a fluid process which is constantly shaping us and which we have the possibility of shaping.

The critic Louise Kertesz, a close reader of Rukeyser and her context, notes that "No woman poet makes the successful fusion of personal and social themes in a modern prosody before Rukeyser."[1] She traces a North American white women's tradition in Lola Ridge, Marya Zaturenska and Genevieve Taggard, all born at the end of the nineteenth century and all struggling to desentimentalize the personal lyric and to write from urban, revolutionary, and working-class experience.[2] In her earliest published poetry, Rukeyser writes herself into the public events unfolding from the year of her birth, and into the public spaces of a great, expansive city. "The city rises in its light. Skele-

---

[1] Louise Kertesz, *The Poetic Vision of Muriel Rukeyser* (Baton Rouge: Louisiana State University Press, 1980), p. 84.

[2] Ibid., pp. 78–84.

tons of buildings; the orange-peel cranes; highways put through; the race of skyscrapers. And you are part of this."[3]

Rukeyser grew up on Riverside Drive in an upwardly mobile Jewish family—her mother a bookkeeper from Yonkers who counted the poet-scholar-martyr Akiba among her legendary forebears, her father a concrete salesman from Wisconsin who became partner in a sand-and-gravel company. Both loved music and opera, but the house was sparsely supplied with books—"except in the servants' rooms: what do you hear there? *The Man with the Hoe, The Ballad of Reading Gaol.* The little five-cent books . . . read and reread."[4] Rukeyser was sent to Ethical Culture schools and to Vassar, but her father's financial difficulties forced her to leave college. "I was expected to grow up and become a golfer," she recalled—a suburban matron. "There was no idea at that point of a girl growing up to write poems."[5] But she was writing poetry seriously by high school. She was also leading a secret life with the children in her neighborhood, playing in the basements and tunnels beneath the apartment buildings, and noting "the terrible, murderous differences between the ways people lived."[6]

Rukeyser was twenty-one when her *Theory of Flight* received the Yale Younger Poets Prize. Two crucial motifs of her life and work were already unmistakable: the book's title suggests how early she embraced the realm of the technological and scientific imagination; and the opening "Poem out of Childhood" points to her lifelong project of knitting together personal experience with politics. "Knitting together" is the wrong phrase here; in her words, she simply did not allow them to be torn apart.

Any sketch of her life (and here I have space for the merest) suggests the vitality of a woman who was by nature a participant, as well as an inspired observer, and the risk-taking of one who trusted the unexpected, the fortuitous, without relinquishing choice or sense of direction. In 1933, having left Vassar, she went to Alabama and was arrested while reporting on the Scottsboro case (nine African-American youths unjustly convicted of raping two white women, a conviction later overturned by the Supreme Court, and a landmark issue for radicals). In the years to come she traveled as a journalist to Spain on the eve of the Civil War; to Gauley Bridge, West Virginia, for hearings on a silicon mining disaster; to the opening of the Golden Gate Bridge; to North Vietnam and to South Korea on political journeys. She was disinherited by her family, had a two-months'–long, annulled marriage, bore

[3] Muriel Rukeyser, *The Life of Poetry* (New York: William Morrow & Company, Inc., 1974), see p. 170.

[4] Ibid., see p. 172.

[5] Janet Sternberg, ed., *The Writer on Her Work,* vol. 1 (New York: Norton, 1980), p. 221.

[6] Ibid., p. 221.

a son by a different man and raised him in single motherhood. She worked in film and theater, taught at Vassar, the California Labor School, and Sarah Lawrence College, and was a consultant for the Exploratorium, a museum of science and the arts in San Francisco. A wealthy California woman, out of admiration for her work and recognition of her struggles to earn a living as a single mother, provided an anonymous annual stipend, which Rukeyser gave up after seven years when she once held a steady teaching job. She edited a "review of Free Culture" called *Decision,* was hunted as a Communist, was attacked both by conservative New Critics and "proletarian" writers, continued productive as writer and filmmaker, underwent a stroke but survived to write poems about it, and to see her poetry rediscovered by a younger generation of women poets and her *Collected Poems* in print. In 1978 she agreed to speak on a "Lesbians and Literature" panel at the annual convention of the Modern Language Association, but illness precluded her appearing.

Rukeyser's work attracted slashing hostility and scorn (of a kind that suggests just how unsettling her work and her example could be) but also honor and praise. Kenneth Rexroth, patriarch of the San Francisco Renaissance, called her "the best poet of her exact generation." At the other end of the critical spectrum, for the *London Times Literary Supplement* she was "one of America's greatest living poets." She received the Copernicus Prize of the American Academy and Institute of Arts and Letters, and wrote "The Backside of the Academy," celebrating "my street . . . the street I live and write in," its raw urban vitality and human potentialities unencouraged by the locked doors and formal rituals of the Academy. In her lifetime she was a teacher of many poets, and readers of poetry, and some scientists paid tribute to her vision of science as inseparable from art and history. But, in fact, she has largely been read and admired in pieces—in part because most readers come to her out of the very separations that her work, in all its phases, steadfastly resists. We read as feminists, or as literary historians, or we are searching for a viable Left tradition, and we sift her pages for our concerns; or we are students of poetry who assume a scientific biography is irrelevant to us; or we are trapped in ideas of genre that Rukeyser was untroubled by: what are passages of poetry doing in a serious political biography? (She called her life of Wendell Willkie "a story and a song.") Or, meeting her only in anthologies, we meet only the shorter poems of a great practitioner of the long poem, and meet her prose not at all. We call her prose "poetic" without referring to her own definitions of what poetry actually is—an *exchange of energy,* a *system of relationships.*

Rukeyser was unclassifiable, thus difficult for canon-makers and anthologists. She was not a "left-wing" poet simply, though her sympathies more often than not intersected with those of the organized left, or the various lefts, of her time. Her insistence on the value of the unquantifiable and unverifiable ran counter to mainstream "scientific attitudes" and to plodding forms of materialism. She explored and valued myth but came to recognize that mythologies can rule us unless we pierce through them, that we need to criticize them in order to move beyond them. She wrote at the age of thirty-one: "My themes and the use I have made of them have depended on my life as a poet, as a woman, as an American, and as a Jew."[7] She saw the self-impoverishment of assimilation in her family and in the Jews she grew up among; she also recognized the vulnerability and the historical and contemporary "stone agonies" endured by the Jewish people. She remained a secular visionary with a strongly political sense of her Jewish identity. She wrote out of a woman's sexual longings, pregnancy, night-feedings, in a time when it was courageous to do so, especially as she did it—unapologetically, as a big woman alive in mind and body, capable of violence and despair as well as desire.

In a very real sense, we learn to read Rukeyser by reading her. She "scatters clews," as she wrote of the charismatic labor organizer Anne Burlak, "clews" that take light from each other, clews that reunite pieces of our experience and thought that we have mistrusted, forgotten, or allowed to be torn from each other. Much that we are taught, much that we live, is of this description. When Rukeyser said that she wrote the biography of the physicist Willard Gibbs because it was a book she needed to read, she could have been speaking of her work as a whole. She wanted to be able to read the life and research of a physicist against the background of the slave trade, of nineteenth-century industrial expansion and urban violence, of the lives of women—intellectuals and factory hands—of Emily Dickinson's poetry and Edison's invention, of Gibbs's own resonances with Melville and Whitman. She wanted to be able to write her own poems in full recognition of the language and imagery of the scientific imagination, the "traces" of the splitting she deplored. Her work was always a process of testing, by the written word and in the most concrete and risk-taking ways, her instincts, making their foundations and meanings visible, first to herself, then to the world.

When Rukeyser is, or appears, "difficult," this may be partly due to resistances stored in us by our own social and emotional training. But it's also true that while she can be direct and linear, she often builds on a nonlogical accumulation of images, glimpses, questions, a process resembling the way our apparently unrelated experiences can build into insight, once connected. This can be an accumulation within a given poem or book of poems, within a prose book, or in the undivided stream of her poetry and her prose. She

[7] "Muriel Rukeyser, 1913–1979: 'Poet . . . Woman . . . American . . . Jew,'" in *Bridges: A Journal for Jewish Feminists and Our Friends,* vol. 1, no. 1 (Spring 1990). Rukeyser's words are quoted from her essay in a series called "Under Forty: A Symposium on American Literature and the Younger Generation of American Jews," in *Contemporary Jewish Record,* vol. 5, no. 7 (February 1944).

isn't a writer with a few "gems" that can be extrapolated from the rest; of all twentieth-century writers, her work repays full reading.

I myself first read Rukeyser in the early 1950s. Like her, I had won the Yale Series of Younger Poets prize at the age of twenty-one, and I was curious to see what a woman poet, at my age, now ahead of me on the path, had written in her first book. I remember the extraordinary force of the first poem in *Theory of Flight,* how it broke over me, and my envy of the sweeping lines, the authority in that poem. But I was not yet ready to learn from her. *The Life of Poetry* had been published in 1949, the year I began to take myself seriously as a poet, or at least as an apprentice to poetry. No one in the literary world of Cambridge, Massachusetts, where I was a student, spoke of that book as an important resource; young poets were reading Empson's *Seven Types of Ambiguity,* Eliot's *Tradition and the Individual Talent,* I. A. Richards's *Practical Criticism.* Of my professors, only the brilliant and volatile F. O. Matthiessen spoke of Rukeyser, but the poets he taught in his seminar were Eliot, Pound, Williams, Stevens, Marianne Moore, e.e. cummings. I came to Rukeyser in my maturity, as my own life opened out and I began to trust the directions of my own work. Gradually I found her to be the poet I most needed in the struggle to make my poems and live my life. In the past quarter-century, as many silenced voices—especially women's voices—began to bear witness, the prescience and breadth of her vision came clearer to me—for it is a peculiarly relevant vision for our lives on this continent now.

In the 1960s and early seventies Rukeyser and I, together with other poets, often found ourselves on the same platform at readings for groups like RESIST and the Angry Arts Against the War in Vietnam. I never came to know her well; New York has a way of sweeping even the like-spirited into different scenes. But there was an undeniable sense of female power that came onto any platform along with Muriel Rukeyser. She carried her large body and strongly molded head with enormous pride, and stood with presence behind her words. Her poems ranged from political witness to the erotic to the mordantly witty to the visionary. Even struggling back from a stroke, she appeared inexhaustible.

It's to be hoped that more of her books will soon be back in print, and still-unpublished writings collected for the first time. She was, in the originality of her nature and achievement, as much an American classic as Melville, Whitman, Dickinson, W. E. B. Du Bois, or Zora Neale Hurston.

In the limited space of a single volume, in an act of extraordinarily creative editing, Jan Heller Levi has gathered here some "clews" to Muriel Rukeyser's legacy to us.

ADRIENNE RICH

1993

EDITOR'S INTRODUCTION

I have told this story before:

In 1978, I stood at the door of an apartment on East 50th Street in New York City. I had come to apply for a position as personal assistant to Muriel Rukeyser. I was twenty-four. My mother had died a month before. Jane Cooper, the friend and former teacher who had sent me here, had warned that Rukeyser was ill—another stroke, and laser surgery on the eyes. "If she's too sick, Jane, I won't be able to take the job," I said.

The door opened.

One of the most important poets of the twentieth century ("Muriel, mother of everyone," Anne Sexton called her) wobbled there for a moment. She was very sick. There was something lionlike about her; something monumental, but about to topple.

Muriel Rukeyser tugged her red bathrobe tighter, and ran her fingers through her gray hair. She looked half confused, half irritated. Then she backed up like a Mack truck with serious gear shift problems (how could those ridiculously thin legs possibly support her?) and invited me in. She was, as I recall, sucking on a cigarette, the ash dangerously long.

Yes, she remembered I was coming; yes, she was happy to meet me; yes, we must talk, come sit here. Her eyes were unsteady. She relied on a metal walker to get from here to there. Her words came out like they'd been rolled through rubber. *If she's too sick, Jane, I can't—*

But of course, I was going to. From the moment she opened that door, I was hers; my choice dropped away. (Well, it wasn't exactly choice that dropped away. I think of something she wrote in *The Life of Poetry*: "I think there is choice possible at any moment to us, as long as we live. But there is no sacrifice. There is a choice, and the rest falls away. Second choice does not exist. Beware of those who talk about sacrifice.")[1]

The moment came when we should talk about compensation for my services, my fee. I hadn't the slightest idea what to ask for, since I realized by that point that I would work for her for anything, or for nothing at all. I said "I don't know." She smiled her smile—huge, marvelous, and sly all at the same time—and she said, "Well, we shall arrive at that by a combination of love and invention."

A combination of love and invention. That's the story I've told many times. But there's more. I came to Muriel Rukeyser's apartment twice a week. I read

---

[1] *The Life of Poetry*, 1949. See p. 176.

her mail to her, pulled roast chickens from the bottom shelf of the refrigerator where she couldn't reach, typed letters for her ("I am far behind my life . . . ," they would begin). I ran out for cartons of orange juice and Häagen-Dazs rum raisin ice cream, her favorite—which was definitely against doctor's orders, though it was a long time before I caught on to that.

These were the months during which her work was being rediscovered and celebrated, particularly among women poets, young and old. Her 573-page *Collected Poems* had just been published by McGraw-Hill ("A doorstopper," she called it). *Muriel.* Ninth-graders assigned compositions on her poems wrote letters to "Muriel." Those who had taken a single workshop with her a dozen years before sent notes that began, "Dear Muriel . . ." To everyone, it seemed, she was Muriel.

I, on the other hand, called her "Mrs. Rukeyser." This, I think now, was a gift we gave one another: the courtesy of distance. For as she grew more and more ill, I became her de-facto helper in difficult circumstances—trips to the hospital, or an emergency visit to her home when she'd taken a fall. That I called her "Mrs. Rukeyser" when I found her on her bedroom floor, hooked my arms under hers and lifted her back onto her bed was one way, I like to think, that I could say to her, "I recognize this intimacy as circumstantial, I do not presume." That she accepted the formality was her way, I like to believe, of saying to me: "I see what you are trying to offer."

Discretion, reserve, polite silences: these are the unquestioned modes of (non)communication hallowed by German Jews (which both of us were, or came from, anyway). These are also the civilized "No Trespassing" signs that her life's work stood in contrast to. I find it ironic that these were the tokens of affection we passed back and forth and between us for sixteen months. But, on another level, I don't find it strange at all.

"My contradictions set me tasks, errands," Rukeyser wrote in "Breaking Open," a poem about, among many other things, the constellation of forces—violent and joyful, public and private—that spin out the planet of an individual identity. Make no mistake about it: She was a woman of powerful contradictions. "No more masks! No more mythologies!" she called out in "The Poem as Mask." And: "What would happen if one woman told the truth about her life? / The world would split open," she wrote in "Käthe Kollwitz." (Two of those lines were to be taken up as the titles for groundbreaking anthologies of contemporary women's poetry published in the 1970s—Florence Howe's and Ellen Bass's *No More Masks!* and Louise Bernikow's *The World Split Open.*) Yet this was the same woman who never publicly revealed the identity of her son's father; this was the bisexual who never wrote in what we would deem explicit terms of her sexual relationships with women. "Take my hand.   What are you now? / I will tell you all.   I will conceal nothing," a voice promises in her "Effort at Speech Between Two People"; then, a few pages later, in the poem "Breathing Landscape," Rukeyser concedes how "even armored we hardly touch each other."

If Muriel Rukeyser doesn't "tell all" (though it could be argued that she does, like Emily Dickinson, "tell it slant"), what she does magnificently is offer a radical invitation: to journey alongside one woman as she goes searching and searching. All inventions, for Rukeyser, are discoveries; the forms and meanings of our own lives are there for us, her work tells us, if we are willing to "pay attention to what they tell you to forget." Imagine poetry and life as an interdependent, interconnected reality. Imagine poetry not as a *reflection* of life, but as life's voice, strong and sure, exploratory and faltering, hopeful, desperate, clear as the bell of an alarm clock, shrouded and urgent as the dream before the alarm clock rings.

A combination of love and invention. Muriel Rukeyser died on a Tuesday afternoon in February 1980, almost a year and a half after I walked through her door the first time. Years have passed. All but one of her books have gone out of print. That is a great loss. Everywhere I go, I hear people of intelligence, integrity, and imagination wrestling with the issues that Rukeyser braves in her work: our relationships to our nation's history and to our own histories, to our culture and how we define that culture, to our personal mysteries and public myths. Everywhere I hear women and men asking powerful questions for our future, questions that Rukeyser framed brilliantly a quarter of a century or more ago.

"I lived in the first century of world wars," she wrote,[2] and those wars come into her poems and prose. She was in Spain in 1936 when the Spanish Civil War broke out; she traveled to Hanoi in the 1970s, in the midst of the Vietnam War, to talk peace. "These are roads to take when you think of your country,[3]" she wrote, and she traveled these roads—to Scottsboro, Alabama, for the trial of nine young African-American men indicted and convicted for the alleged rape of two white women; to Gauley Bridge, West Virginia, where silicosis was turning the lungs of miners into suffocating crystal. "Surely it is time for the true grace of women / Emerging, in their lives' colors, from the rooms, from the harvests / From the delicate prisons . . . ,"[4] she wrote, and "Whatever can come to a woman can come to me,"[5] and when it all came—love, loss, passion, destruction, resurrection—she wrote out of its challenges. She knew the promise and betrayals of our history, and recognized our history as our living present, so that, echoing Lincoln, she could write: "Slave and slave-

[2] "Poem," *The Speed of Darkness,* 1968. See pp. 211–12.

[3] "The Road," *U. S. 1,* 1938. See pp. 31–32.

[4] "Letter to the Front," *Beast in View,* 1944. See pp. 102–6.

[5] "Waterlily Fire," *Waterlily Fire,* 1962. See pp. 201–6.

holder they are chained together / And one is ancestor and one is child. / Escape the birthplace: walk into the world / Refusing to be either slave or slaveholder."[6]

Fourteen years after Muriel Rukeyser's death, I come to the responsibility and joy of bringing some of that work back into print. I am deeply grateful to Adrienne Rich, who first proposed the idea of *A Muriel Rukeyser Reader* to her publishers at Norton. "Whatever help you need," she told me, "I'm here." She was. To Jane Cooper, who sent me to Muriel Rukeyser's door, I owe more than I can say. Over the last year, Jane was always on call. Her wisdom and sensitivity helped me to bring together words, facts, and feelings. My gratitude also to Julia Reidhead, senior editor at Norton, for her enthusiasm, support, and patience, and to William L. Rukeyser, Muriel Rukeyser's son and literary executor, who so generously made all his mother's writings available to me, and whose suggestions measurably enriched the book. For cheering me on when I was on the right track, and steering me back when I went astray, my thanks to Donna Masini, Micki Trager, and Kim Vaeth. And always, there has been Ken Sofer, who I thank for all the moonstone memories, and how they shine.

Finally, I am grateful to the person to whom this book is dedicated. "When I am dead, even then, / I will still love you, I will wait in these poems . . . ," she wrote.[7] How could it be otherwise? This book is dedicated to the memory, with love and invention, of Muriel Rukeyser.

JAN HELLER LEVI
New York City, 1993

---

[6] "Secrets of American Civilization," *Breaking Open,* 1973. See pp. 244–45.

[7] "Then," *The Gates,* 1976. See p. 285.

A NOTE TO THE READER

" 'All the poems' is a very curious idea," declared Rukeyser in her introduction to the 1978 publication of her *Collected Poems*. She went on to compare that hefty volume to "a film strip of a life in poetry," or to that image of the elongated body in Asian art where we can see the human being in all the stages of her life, from infancy to old age.

"*Some* of the poems, *some* of the prose" is an equally curious idea. Over the forty-five years of her writing life, Muriel Rukeyser published eleven full-length books of poetry, three biographies, the astonishing series of lectures that became *The Life of Poetry*, a novel, numerous translations, childrens' books, plays, and stories. There is also evidence in her papers, scattered in libraries across the country, of unpublished essays, short stories, novels, even screenplays. Obviously, *A Muriel Rukeyser Reader* can only include a portion of this body of work. But what portion? For hers is truly a *body* of work. A theme introduced in one poem reemerges in another, then another, in different but connected ways.

In thinking about how to organize this selection I was helped enormously by one idea: that when Rukeyser compared Whitman's work to an "ideal of water at the shore," she might have been describing her own: "[N]ot beginning nor ending," she wrote, "but endlessly drawing in, making forever its forms of massing and falling among the breakers, seething in the white recessions of its surf, never finishing, always making a meeting place."[1]

This is what I wanted to offer here: not a distillation of what might be called Rukeyser's greatest hits, (though lots of them are here, I think) but a feel for Rukeyser's journey ("not beginning nor ending") to some of those meeting places. When Rukeyser's work has appeared in anthologies, the poems included tend to be from her first book *Theory of Flight*, and then a great leap to the later ones, *Speed of Darkness, Breaking Open*, and *The Gates*. Ambitious and admittedly difficult works from the middle years have been unavailable for too long; this *Reader* corrects that omission. Some readers may bemoan the absence of one or more of their favorite Rukeyser poems. But knowing that some of these are available elsewhere gave me the freedom to reintroduce some lesser known works that deserve attention. I hope the *Reader* will speed us to the day when *all* of Rukeyser's work is back in print. I'll know I've done my job if this selection inspires readers to go looking for the work that I could not include.

[1] Muriel Rukeyser, *The Life of Poetry*, 1949. See p. 142.

I have included here poems from each of the eleven books Rukeyser drew from for her *Collected Poems*. In addition, there are excerpts here from three of her prose works, *The Life of Poetry, One Life,* and *Willard Gibbs,* and from her play *Houdini.* The books are arranged in chronological order, based on the years they were published. Within the books themselves, it's a different story. Those familiar with Rukeyser's work will immediately note a difference between her arrangement of poems in the original volumes and my ordering of poems here. It is my conviction that the poet, in shaping any volume, is, among other things, seeking to illuminate some relationship, or variety of relationships, among its parts (the individual poems in the volume). This, I think, would be nowhere more true than in the work of Muriel Rukeyser, who was drawn to a maxim of the American scientist Willard Gibbs: "The whole is simpler than its parts."

I take that as my maxim here too. I did not feel I could offer a real introduction to Rukeyser's work by merely presenting a collection of parts. I have tried to shape a new "whole" here for readers: a new book for readers of today that is, nevertheless, a book true to the spirit, vision, and proferred meanings of the original author.

The same holds true in my excerptings from some of the longer poems—specifically, "Theory of Flight," "Book of the Dead," and "Letter to the Front,"—and from what Kate Daniels has described as Rukeyser's "great prose meditation," *The Life of Poetry.* In each case, it was my goal to preserve the complexity of these ambitious works. At the same time, I felt compelled, for the purposes of this collection, to skip over some rather substantial passages. I'm tempted to call them "movements," as in music. (Readers should be aware that a series of three asterisks— *   *   * —indicates deleted material.) Again, I have hoped to give a new "whole." But I like to imagine new readers of Rukeyser searching out their local used bookstores for the 1978 *Collected Poems* and the 1974 paperback edition of *The Life of Poetry.* There is also, I am pleased to report, another selection of Muriel Rukeyser's poems now available. *Out of Silence,* edited by Kate Daniels, and published by Tri-Quarterly Press in 1992, includes some of these longer poems in their entirety.

Finally for readers new to Muriel Rukeyser, I have included brief editor's introductions to the individual works. (Thanks are due to Louise Kertesz, whose *The Poetic Vision of Muriel Rukeyser,* the only full-length critical study of Rukeyser, published by Louisiana State University Press in 1980, was an essential resource for biographical information as well as for critical responses to Rukeyser's books as they appeared over the years.) For readers who feel constrained by chronology, I urge you to choose your own path. Rukeyser's work, in its audacious music and imagery, its unorthodox mergings of past and present, its relentless quest for inclusiveness, urges us to travel beyond conventional signposts. Feel free to be audacious in your reading of her. For example, I have suggested to some friends intimidated by the density of her earlier work to "read her backward," to begin with the more accessible, plain-spoken, and often witty poems of the later years (poems like "Myth," "Paint-ers," "Ballad of Orange and Grape"); then to move to a longer, more intricate, multisectioned work like "Käthe Kollwitz" (after taking a look at Kollwitz's woodcuts and prints); then, with these as a foundation, to tackle the multi-layered, jump-cutting, seemingly "obscure" works of the middle and early years. They seem a whole lot less "obscure" then, my friends report.

Rukeyser was talking about poetry when she wrote:

If we have a resource that we are not using . . .

If this were a crop, . . . there would be a research project.

If it were a metal, the Un-American Activities committee, and several other communities, would concern themselves. Our scientists would claim their right of experiment and inquiry.[2]

We *do* have a resource that we are not using. My hope is that this *Reader* will serve as one, among many more research projects to come, into the resource that is Muriel Rukeyser.

JHL

[2] Ibid. See p. 125.

THEORY OF FLIGHT

Rukeyser was twenty-one when her first book, Theory of Flight, *won the prestigious Yale Younger Poets Award.*

"Breathe-in experience, breathe-out poetry," she declares in "Poem out of Childhood," and that is exactly what she does here. Rukeyser was six months old when a Serbian nationalist named Gavrila Prinzip assassinated Archduke Ferdinand in Sarajevo—the event that triggered the fighting of World War I. ("Prinzip's year bore us," she writes; imagine that line amended for the 1960s—"Oswald's year bore us"—to appreciate its power.)

In "Poem out of Childhood" sometimes contradictory, sometimes connected, images flow into one another, or jostle against one another with little or no explanation; this is the logic of the unfettered imagination. Though Rukeyser grew up far from the fighting, in a comfortable upper-middle-class home in New York City, she speaks as a representative but highly particularized young woman struggling to wrest meaning from the world she's inherited, and her moment in time. In a poem like "Sand-Quarry with Moving Figures," Rukeyser strikes no close to that quickening place of family love and conflict that the mingled cry and laughter in its final lines cuts to the nerve today. Similarly, "Effort at Speech Between Two People," even with its formal diction and modulated pacing, throbs with the effort implied in maintaining its surface restraint.

"Theory of Flight," the title poem of the volume, printed here in excerpts, is, in its original version, a twenty-six-page multipart exploration of human possibility in the machine age. (In fact, Rukeyser's own flying lessons served as an inspiration for the poem; the title itself comes from the first section of the flyer's and flight mechanics' manual from her course at the Roosevelt School of Aviation.) Rukeyser challenges us to see ourselves in the dynamo and the dynamo in us. In fierce, muscular imagery, she catapults us through time and place—from the jail cell of the "Scottsboro boys" in Alabama to the coal fields of West Virginia; from the contemporary bedroom of a pilot and his pregnant wife to the Renaissance studio of Leonardo da Vinci; from a hillside in Kitty Hawk and then into the engine of the plane itself.

"I contain multitudes" Whitman wrote, in Song of Myself. *At the age of twenty-one, Rukeyser burst onto the poetry scene of the 1930s to embrace and express the multitudes she recognized within herself, to chronicle the drama of what she was to call in* The Life of Poetry *the "moments at which one begins to see."*

.   .   .   .   .

EFFORT AT SPEECH BETWEEN TWO PEOPLE

: Speak to me.   Take my hand.   What are you now?
 I will tell you all.   I will conceal nothing.
 When I was three, a little child read a story about a rabbit
 who died, in the story, and I crawled under a chair   :
 a pink rabbit   :   it was my birthday, and a candle
 burnt a sore spot on my finger, and I was told to be happy.

: Oh, grow to know me.   I am not happy.   I will be open:
 Now I am thinking of white sails against a sky like music,
 like glad horns blowing, and birds tilting, and an arm about me.
 There was one I loved, who wanted to live, sailing.

: Speak to me.   Take my hand.   What are you now?
 When I was nine, I was fruitily sentimental,
 fluid   :   and my widowed aunt played Chopin,
 and I bent my head on the painted woodwork, and wept.
 I want now to be close to you.   I would
 link the minutes of my days close, somehow, to your days.

: I am not happy.   I will be open.
 I have liked lamps in evening corners, and quiet poems.
 There has been fear in my life.   Sometimes I speculate
 On what a tragedy his life was, really.

: Take my hand.   Fist my mind in your hand.   What are
       you now?
 When I was fourteen, I had dreams of suicide,
 and I stood at a steep window, at sunset, hoping toward
       death   :
 if the light had not melted clouds and plains to beauty,
 if light had not transformed that day, I would have leapt.
: I am unhappy.   I am lonely.   Speak to me.

3: I will be open.   I think he never loved me:
    he loved the bright beaches, the little lips of foam
    that ride small waves, he loved the veer of gulls:
    he said with a gay mouth: I love you.   Grow to know me.

3

: What are you now?   If we could touch one another,
  if these our separate entities could come to grips,
  clenched like a Chinese puzzle . . . yesterday
  I stood in a crowded street that was live with people,
  and no one spoke a word, and the morning shone.
  Everyone silent, moving. . . . Take my hand.   Speak to me.

SAND-QUARRY WITH MOVING FIGURES

Father and I drove to the sand-quarry across the ruined
        marshlands,
miles of black grass, burned for next summer's green.
I reached my hand to his beneath the lap-robe,
we looked at the stripe of fire, the blasted scene.

"It's all right," he said, "they can control the flames,
on one side men are standing, and on the other the sea;"
but I was terrified of stubble and waste of black
and his ugly villages he built and was showing me.

The countryside turned right and left about the car,
straight through October we drove to the pit's heart;
sand, and its yellow canyon and standing pools
and the wealth of the split country set us farther apart.
"Look," he said, "this quarry means rows of little houses,
stucco and a new bracelet for you are buried there;"
but I remembered the ruined patches, and I saw the land
        ruined,
exploded, burned away, and the fiery marshes bare.

"We'll own the countryside, you'll see how soon I will,
you'll have acres to play in"   :   I saw the written name
painted on stone in the face of the steep hill:
"That's your name, Father!   "And yours!" he shouted,
        laughing.

4

"No, Father, no!"   He caught my hand as I cried,
and smiling, entered the pit, ran laughing down its side.

POEM OUT OF CHILDHOOD

1

Breathe-in experience, breathe-out poetry   :
Not Angles, angels   :   and the magnificent past
shot deep illuminations into high-school.
I opened the door into the concert-hall
and a rush of triumphant violins answered me
while the syphilitic woman turned her mouldered face
intruding upon Brahms.   Suddenly, in an accident
the girl's brother was killed, but her father had just died   :
she stood against the wall, leaning her cheek,
dumbly her arms fell, "What will become of me?" and
I went into the corridor for a drink of water.
These bandages of image wrap my head
when I put my hand up I hardly feel the wounds.
We sat on the steps of the unrented house
raining blood down on Loeb and Leopold,
creating again how they removed his glasses
and philosophically slit his throat.

    They who manipulated and misused our youth,
    smearing those centuries upon our hands,
    trapping us in a welter of dead names,
    snuffing and shaking heads at patent truth. . . .

We were ready to go the long descent with Virgil
the bough's gold shade advancing forever with us,
entering the populated cold of drawing-rooms;
Sappho, with her drowned hair trailing along Greek waters,

weed binding it, a fillet of kelp enclosing
the temples' ardent fruit   :

                              Not Sappho, Sacco.
Rebellion pioneered among our lives,
viewing from far-off many-branching deltas,
innumerable seas.

2

In adolescence I knew travellers
speakers digressing from the ink-pocked rooms,
bearing the unequivocal sunny word.

        Prinzip's year bore us   see us turning at breast
        quietly while the air throbs over Sarajevo
        after the mechanic laugh of that bullet.
        How could they know what sinister knowledge finds
        its way among our brains' wet palpitance,
        what words would nudge and giggle at our spine,
        what murders dance?
        These horrors have approached the growing child;
        now that the factory is sealed-up brick
        the kids throw stones, smashing the windows,
        membranes of uselessness in desolation.

        We grew older quickly, watching the father shave
        and the splatter of lather hardening on the glass,
        playing in sandboxes to escape paralysis,
        being victimized by fataller sly things.
        "Oh, and you," he said, scraping his jaw, "what will you be?"
        "Maybe : something : like : Joan : of : Arc...."
        Allies Advance, we see,
        Six Miles South to Soissons.   And we beat the drums.
        Watchsprings snap in the mind, uncoil, relax,
        the leafy years all somber with foreign war.
        How could we know what exposed guts resembled?

        A wave, shocked to motion, babbles margins
        from Asia to Far Rockaway spiralling
        among clocks in its four-dimensional circles.

_____

Disturbed by war we pedalled bicycles
breakneck down the decline, until the treads
conquered our speed and pulled our feet behind them,
and pulled our heads.
We never knew the war, standing so small
looking at eye-level toward the puttees, searching
the picture-books for sceptres, pennants for truth;
see Galahad unaided by puberty.

Ratat a drum upon the armistice,
Kodak As You Go : photo : they danced late,
and we were a generation of grim children
leaning over the bedroom sills, watching
the music and the shoulders and how the war was over,
laughing until the blow on the mouth broke night
wide out from cover.
The child's curls blow in a forgotten wind,
immortal ivy trembles on the wall:
the sun has crystallized these scenes, and tall
shadows remember time cannot rescind.

3

Organize the full results of that rich past
open the windows : potent catalyst,
harsh theory of knowledge, running down the aisles
crying out in the classrooms, March ravening on the plain,
inexorable sun and wind and natural thought.
Dialectically our youth unfolds :
the pale child walking to the river, passional
in ignorance   in loneliness   demanding
its habitation for the leaping dream, kissing
quick air, the vibrations of transient light,
not knowing substance or reserve, walking
in valvular air, each person in the street
conceived surrounded by his life and pain,
fixed against time, subtly by these impaled :
death and that shapeless war.   Listening at dead doors,
our youth assumes a thousand differing flesh
summoning fact from abandoned machines of trade,
knocking on the wall of the nailed-up power-plant,

telephoning hello, the deserted factory, ready
for the affirmative clap of truth
ricochetting from thought to thought among
the childhood, the gestures, the rigid travellers.

THREE SIDES OF A COIN

1

Am I in your light?
                    No, go on reading
              (the hackneyed light of evening quarrelling with the bulbs;
              the book's bent rectangle solid on your knees)
only my fingers in your hair, only, my eyes
splitting the skull to tickle your brain with love
in a slow caress blurring the mind,
                              kissing your mouth awake
opening the body's mouth and stopping the words.
This light is thick with birds, and
evening warns us beautifully of death.
Slowly I bend over you, slowly your breath
runs rhythms through my blood
as if I said
                    I love you
and you should raise your head
listening, speaking into the covert night
    :   Did someone say something?
                         Love, am I in your light?
Am I?

Refrain   See how love alters the living face
            go spin the immortal coin through time
            watch the thing flip through space
                         tick   tick

2

We all had a good time
                              the throne was there and all
and there she was with that primitive unforgivable mouth
saying sophistications about nothing at all
as the young men cavorted up the room Darling
it's a swell party and those Martinis with
the olives so delicately soaked in alcohol
        and William Flesh, the inventor, being cute
about the revolution and the Negro Question
until Dick said "Lynch the Jews!" (his name was Fleischman
but the war brought about a number of changes)
and the Objectivist poet fresh from Butte
with his prePosterous suggestion. . . .
        After a while, of course, we left,
the room was getting so jammed with editors.
And William and Maurice and Del and I
went back and we took turns using the couch with them.
        We all had a good time
and Del had hysterics at about 3 A.M.
        we dashed water into her face
        I held her temples and Maurice said
        what could we hope to look for next:
        it's one thing to be faithful to the dead
        (he said) but for her to stick to an oversexed
old fool   :   but she only laughed and cried and beat the floor
until the neighbors rattled at the door.

Refrain   Runnels of wine ran down his chin and laughter
             softened his words until quite suddenly
             the walls fell and the night stood blank and after
                    tick   tick

3

He turned the lights on and walked to the window   :
Son of a bitch   :   he said   :   if it isn't the reds again
parading through the streets with those lousy posters.
The Village was never like this in the old days,
throw a brick down the street and you'd hit a female poet
and life went on like a string of roller coasters.

Workers of the world   :
we've worked the world for all the damn thing's worth
                    tick   tick
I was little and they promised me the hills of glory
a great life and a sounding name on the earth   :
                    tick   tick
            this is a different story.

Here's a list I've been making   :   reasons for living
on the right, reasons for my sudden death on the left.
Right now they balance so I could flip a coin
determine the imperative tonight
                    tick   tick
flip that amazing coin through time and space this night
and the Village   :   and the army with banners
                            and the hot girls
and the rotgut all gone
                            like a blown fuse   :
I'd get a paragraph or two of news
obituary as a shutting door
meaning no more
leaving the world to the sun and the workers
the straight beautiful children   the coins   the clocks
                    tick   tick

THEORY OF FLIGHT

from PREAMBLE

Earth, bind us close, and time   ;   nor, sky, deride
how violate we experiment again.
In many Januaries, many lips
have fastened on us while we deified
the waning flesh   :   now, fountain, spout for us,
mother, bear children   :   lover, yet once more   :
in final effort toward your mastery.
Many Decembers suffered their eclipse

death, and forgetfulness, and the year bore round   ;
now years, be summed in one access of power.
Fortresses, strengths, beauties, realities,
gather together, discover to us our wings
new special product of mortality.

      *   *   *

    Look! Be : leap ;
    paint trees in flame
    bushes burning
    roar in the broad sky
    know your color : be :
    produce that the widenesses
    be full and burst their wombs
    riot in redness, delirious with light,
    swim bluely through the mind
    shout green as the day breaks
    put up your face to the wind
    FLY

    chant as the tomtom hubbubs crash
    elephants in the flesh's jungle
    reck with vigor   sweat   pour your life
    in a libation to itself
    drink from the ripe ground
    make children over the world
    lust in a heat of tropic orange
    stamp and writhe   ;   stamp on a wet floor
    know earth   know water   know lovers
    know mastery
    FLY

    ·   ·   ·   ·   ·

    Walks down the street
    Kaleidoscope   a man
    where patterns meet
    his mind colored
    with mirage
    Leonardo's tomb
    not in Italian earth

but in a fuselage
designed
in the historic mind
time's instrument
blue-print of birth.

.   .   .   .   .

We know sky overhead, earth to be stepped
black under the toes, rubble between our fingers,
horizons are familiar   ;   we have been taught colors.
Rehearse these   ;   sky, earth, and their meeting-place,
confound them in a blur of distance, swallow
the blueness of guessed-at places, merge them now.
Sky being meeting of sky and no-sky
including our sources   the earth   water   air
fire to weld them   :   unity in knowing
all space in one unpunctuated flowing.
Flight, thus, is meeting of flight and non-flight.
We bear the seeds of our return forever,
the flowers of our leaving, fruit of flight,
perfect for present, fertile for its roots
in past   in future   in motility.

from THE GYROSCOPE

But this is our desire, and of its worth. . . .
Power electric-clean, gravitating outward at all points,
moving in savage fire, fusing all durable stuff
but never itself being fused with any force
homing in no hand nor breast nor sex
for buried in these lips we rise again,
bent over these plans, our faces raise to see.
Direct spears are shot outward from the conscience
fulfilling what far circuits?   Orbit of thought
what axis do you lean on, what strictnesses evade
impelled to the long curves of the will's ambition?
Centrifugal power, expanding universe
within expanding universe, what stillnesses

lie at your center resting among motion?
Study communications, looking inward, find what traffic
you may have with your silences   :   looking outward, survey
what you have seen of places   :
                           many times this week I seemed
        to hear you speak my name
                           how you turn the flatnesses
        of your cheek and will not hear my words
                           then reaching the given latitude
        and longitude, we searched for the ship and found nothing
                           and, gentlemen, shall we define desire
        including every impulse toward psychic progress?
Roads are cut into the earth leading away from our place
at the inevitable hub.   All directions are *out,*
all desire turns outward   :   we, introspective,
continuing to find in ourselves the microcosm
imaging continents, powers, relations, reflecting
all history in a bifurcated Engine.

        *   *   *

from *THE LYNCHINGS OF JESUS*

    from 2 / The Committee-Room

Let us be introduced to our superiors, the voting men.
They are tired   ;   they are hungry   ;   from deciding all day
around the committee-table.
            Is it foggy outside?   It must be very foggy
            The room is white with it.
The years slope into a series of flights, rocking sea-like,
shouting a black rush, enveloping time and kingdom
and the flab faces
            Those people engendered my blood swarming
            over the altar to clasp the scrolls and Menorah
            the black lips, bruised cheeks, eye-reproaches   :
            as the floor burns, singing Shema
Our little writers go about, hurrying the towns along,
running from mine to luncheon, they can't afford

to let one note escape their holy jottings:
today the mother died, festering   :   he shot himself   :   the
        bullet entered
the roof of the mouth, piercing the brain-pan
                How the spears went down in a flurry of blood;
                how they died howling
                                    how the triumph marched
                all day and all night past the beleaguered town
                blowing trumpets at the fallen towers;
                how they pulled their shoulders over the hill, crying
                for the whole regiment to hear   The Sea   The Sea
Our young men opening the eyes and mouths together,
facing the new world with their open mouths
                                    gibbering war
                                    gibbering conquest

Ha.   Will you lead us to discovery?

What did you do in school today, my darling?
                Tamburlaine rode over Genghis had a sword
                holding riot over Henry V Emperor of and
                the city of Elizabeth the tall sails
                crowding England into the world and Charles
                his head falling many times onto a dais
                how they have been monarchs and
                Calvin Coolidge who wouldn't say
                                    however, America

All day we have been seated around a table
                                    all these many days
One day we voted on whether he was Hamlet
or whether he was himself and yesterday
I cast the deciding vote to renounce our mouths.
Today we sentinel the avenue solemnly warning
the passers (who look the other way, and cough) that we
speak with the mouths of demons, perhaps the people's,
but not our own.
                    Tomorrow
the vote's to be cast on the eyes, and sex, and brain.
Perhaps we will vote to disavow all three.
We are powerful now : we vote
                death to Sacco a man's name
                and Vanzetti a blood-brother; death

to Tom Mooney, or a wall, no matter;
poverty to Piers Plowman, shrieking anger
to Shelley, a cough and Fanny to Keats;
thus to Blake in a garden; thus to Whitman;
thus to D. H. Lawrence.

                    And to all you women,
dead and unspoken-for, what sentences,
to you dead children, little in the ground
: all you sweet generous rebels, what sentences

This is the case of one Hilliard, a native of Texas,
in the year of our Lord 1897, a freeman.
Report . . . Hilliard's power of endurance seems to be
the most wonderful thing on record.   His lower limbs
burned off a while before he became unconscious;
and his body looked to be burned to the hollow.
Was it decreed (oh coyly coyly) by an avenging God
as well as an avenging people that he suffer so?

                                        We have

16 large views under magnifying glass.
8 views of the trial and the burning.
For place of exhibit watch the street bills.
                    Don't fail to see this.

Lie down dear, the day was long, the evening is smooth.
The day was long, and you were voting all day
                hammering down these heads
                tamping the mould about these diamond eyes
                filling the mouths with wax

                                lie down my dear
the bed is soft lie down to kindest dreams

        *   *   *

from 3 / The Trial

The South is green with coming spring   ;   revival
flourishes in the fields of Alabama.   Spongy with rain,
plantations breathe April   :   carwheels suck mud in the roads,

15

the town expands warm in the afternoons.   At night the
      black boy
teeters no-handed on a bicycle, whistling The St. Louis Blues,
blood beating, and hot South.   A red brick courthouse
is vicious with men inviting death.   Array your judges; call your
                                                    jurors; come,
here is your justice, come out of the crazy jail.
Grass is green now in Alabama; Birmingham dusks are quiet
relaxed and soft in the park, stern at the yards:
a hundred boxcars shunted off to sidings, and the hoboes
gathering grains of sleep in forbidden corners.
In all the yards   :   Atlanta, Chattanooga,
Memphis, and New Orleans, the cars, and no jobs.

Every night the mail-planes burrow the sky,
carrying postcards to laughing girls in Texas,
passionate letters to the Charleston virgins,
words through the South   :   and no reprieve,
no pardon, no release.

A blinded statue attends before the courthouse,
bronze and black men lie on the grass, waiting,
the khaki dapper National Guard leans on its bayonets.
But the air is populous beyond our vision:
all the people's anger finds its vortex here
as the mythic lips of justice open, and speak.

Hammers and sickles are carried in a wave of strength, fire-
      tipped,
swinging passionately ninefold to a shore.
Answer the back-thrown Negro face of the lynched, the flat
      forehead knotted,
the eyes showing a wild iris, the mouth a welter of blood,
answer the broken shoulders and these twisted arms.
John Brown, Nat Turner, Toussaint stand in this courtroom,
Dred Scott wrestles for freedom there in the dark corner,
all our celebrated shambles are repeated here   :   now again
Sacco and Vanzetti walk to a chair, to the straps and rivets
and the switch spitting death and Massachusetts' will.
Wreaths are brought out of history
      here are the well-nourished flowers of France, grown strong
            on blood,

Caesar twisting his thin throat toward conquest, turning
        north from the Roman laurels,
the Istrian galleys slide again to sea.
How they waded through bloody Godfrey's Jerusalem   !
How the fires broke through Europe, and the rich
and the tall jails battened on revolution   !
The fastidious Louis', cousins to the sun, stamping
those ribboned heels on Calas, on the people;
the lynched five thousand of America.
Tom Mooney from San Quentin, Herndon   :   here
is an army for audience
                        all resolved
to a gobbet of tobacco, spat, and the empanelled hundred,
a jury of vengeance, the cheap pressed lips, the narrow eyes like
                        hardware;
the judge, his eye-sockets and cheeks dark and immutably
        secret,
the twisting mouth of the prosecuting attorney.
Nine dark boys spread their breasts against Alabama,
schooled in the cells, fathered by want.
        Mother   :   one writes   :   they treat us bad.   If they
                send us
        back to Kilby jail, I think I shall kill myself.
        I think I must hang myself by my overalls.

Alabama and the South are soft with spring;
in the North, the seasons change, sweet April, December and
        the air
loaded with snow.   There is time for meetings
during the years, they remaining in prison.
                        In the Square.
a crowd listens, carrying banners.
Overhead, boring through the speaker's voice, a plane
circles with a snoring of motors revolving in the sky,
drowning the single voice.   It does not touch
the crowd's silence.   It circles.   The name stands   :
Scottsboro

        *   *   *

from THE TUNNEL

1

NO WORK is master of the mine today
tyrant that walks with the feet of murder here
under his cracked shoes a grass-blade dusted
dingy with coal's smear.
The father's hand is rubbed with dust, his body
is witness to coal, black glosses all his skin.
Around the pithead they stand and do not talk
looking at the obvious sign.

Behind his shoulder stands the black mountain
of unbought coal, green-topped with grass growing
rank in the shag, as if coal were native earth
and the top a green snowing

down on the countryside.   In the whole valley
eleven mines, and five of them are closed,
two are on strike, but in the others, workers
scramble down the shafts, disposed

to grub all day and all night, lording it
in the town because of their jobs and their bosses
at work with all the other mines graveyards.
These are the valley's losses

which even the company fails to itemize
in stubborn black and red in the company stores   :
the empty breasts like rinds, the father's hands,
the sign, the infected whores,

a puppy roasted for pregnant Mary's dinner . . .
On the cold evenings the jobless miners meet
wandering dully attracted to the poolroom,
walking down the grey street.

"Well," says the father, "nothing comes of this,
the strippings run to weeds, the roads all mucked.

A dead mine makes dead miners.   God, but I
was a fool not to have chucked

the whole damned ruin when I was a kid."
"And how'd you have a chance to throw it over?"
"Well," he said, "if I hadn't married   :   though then
the place had more in its favor.

Babies came quickly after summertimes.
You could work, and quit, and get a better job.
God knows if it'll ever be the same,
or if ever they'll think not to rob,

not to cut wages, not to weigh us short."
"All right," the other says, "maybe God does.
We'll be a long time dead, come that time, buried
under coal where our life was;

we were children and did not know our childhood,
we got infants, and never knew our wives,
year in and out, seeing no color but coal,
we were the living who could not have their lives."

            *   *   *

from 3

The cattle-trains edge along the river, bringing morning on a
      white vibration
breaking the darkness split with beast-cries   :   a milk-wagon
      proceeds
down the street leaving the cold bottles   :   the Mack truck
      pushes
around the corner, tires hissing on the washed asphalt.   A
      clear sky
growing candid and later bright.
            Ceiling unlimited.   Visibility unlimited.

They stir on the pillows, her leg moving, her face swung
      windowward
vacant with sleep still, modeled with light's coming   ;   his
      dark head

among the softness of her arm and breast, nuzzled in dreams,
mumbling the old words, hardly roused.   They return to
    silence.
            At the airport, the floodlights are snapped off.

Turning, he says, "Tell me how's the sky this morning?"
    "Fair," she answers,
"no clouds from where I lie; bluer and bluer."   "And later
    and later—
god, for some sleep into some noon, instead of all these
    mornings
with my mouth going stiff behind the cowling and wind
    brushing
away from me and my teeth freezing against the wind."
            Light gales from the northwest :   tomorrow, rain.

The street is long, with a sprinkling of ashcans   ;   panhandlers
begin to forage among banana-peels and cardboard boxes.
She moves to the window, tall and dark before a brightening sky,
full with her six-months' pregnancy molded in ripeness.
            Stands, watching the sky's blankness.

Very soon   :   "How I love to see you when I wake," he says,
"How the child's meaning in you is my life's growing."
She faces him, hands brought to her belly's level, offering,
wordless, looking upon him.   She carries his desire well.
            Sun rises   :   6:38 A.M.   Sun sets. . . .

"Flying is what makes you strange to me, dark as Asia,
almost removed from my world even in your closenesses   :
that you should be familiar with those intricacies
and a hero in mysteries which all the world has wanted."
            Wind velocity changing from 19 to 30.

"No, that's wrong," and he laughs, "no personal hero's left
to make a legend.   Those centuries have gone.   If I fly,
why, I know that countries are not map-colored, that seas
belong to no one, that war's a pock-marking on Europe"   :
            The Weather Bureau's forecast, effective until noon.

"Your friends sleep with strange women desperately,
drink liquor and sleep heavily to forget those skies.

20

You fly all day and come home truly returning
to me who know only land.   And we will have this child."
        New York to Boston   :   Scattered to broken clouds.

"The child will have a hard time to be an American,"
he says slowly, "fathered by a man whose country is air,
who believes there are no heroes to withstand
wind, or a loose bolt, or a tank empty of gas."
        To Washington   :   Broken clouds becoming overcast.

"It will be a brave child," she answers, smiling.
"We will show planes to it, and the bums in the street.
You will teach it to fly, and I will love it
very much."   He thinks of his job, dressing.
        Strong west northwest winds above 1000 feet.

He thinks how many men have wanted flight.
He ties his tie, looking into his face.
Finishes breakfast, hurrying to be gone,
crossing the river to the airport and his place.
        To Cleveland   :   Broken clouds to overcast.

She does not imagine how the propeller turns
in a blinding speed, swinging the plane through space;
she never sees the cowling rattle and slip
forward and forward against the grim blades' grinding.
        Cruising speed 1700 R.P.M.

Slipping, a failing desire   ;   slipping like death
insidious against the propeller, until the blades shake,
bitten by steel, jagged against steel, broken,
and his face angry and raked by death, staring
        Strong west northwest or west winds above 2000 feet.

She watches the clock as his return time hurries,
the schedule ticking off, eating the short minutes.
She watches evening advance   ;   she knows the child's stirring.
She knows night.   She knows he will not come.
        Ceiling unlimited.   Visibility unlimited.

        *   *   *

from THE STRUCTURE OF THE PLANE

1 / The Structure of the Plane

Kitty Hawk is a Caesar among monuments   ;
     the stiff bland soldiers predestined to their death
     the bombs piled neatly like children's marbles piled
     sperm to breed corpses eugenically by youth
     out of seductive death.
                  The hill outdoes our towers
     we might treasure a thistle grown from a cannon-mouth
     they have not permitted rust and scum and blossoms
     to dirty the steel,
              however we have the plane
the hill, flower among monuments.

"To work intelligently" (Orville and Wilbur Wright)
"one needs to know the effects of variations
incorporated in the surfaces. . . . The pressures on squares
are different from those on rectangles, circles, triangles, or
     ellipses . . .
The shape of the edge also makes a difference."

The plane is wheeled out of the hangar.   The sleeves shake
fixing the wind, the four o'clock blue sky
blinks in the goggles swinging over his wrist.
The plane rests, the mechanic in cream-colored overalls
encourages the engine into idling speed.
The instructor looks at his class
and begins the demonstration.

"We finally became discouraged, and returned to kite-flying.
But as we grew older we had to give up this sport,
it was unbecoming to boys of our ages."

On the first stroke of the piston the intake valve opens,
the piston moves slowly from the head of the cylinder,
drawing in its mixture of gas and air.   On the second stroke
the piston returns, the valve closes.   The mixture is
     compressed.
A spark occurs, igniting America, opening India,

finding the Northwest Passage, Cipango spice,
causing the mixture to burn, expanding the gases
which push the piston away on the power stroke.
The final exhaust stroke serves to release the gases,
allowing the piston to scavenge the cylinder.
        We burn space, we sever galaxies,
          solar systems whirl about Shelley's head,
          we give ourselves ease, gentlemen, art and these
             explosions
          and Peter Ronsard finger-deep in roses   ;
gentlemen, remember these incandescent points,
remember to check, remember to drain the oil,
remember Plato O remember me
          the college pathways rise
          the president's voice intoning sonnets
          the impress of hoofmarks on the bridle path
          the shining girls the lost virginities
          the plane over a skeletal water-tower
          our youth dissolving O remember
          romantically dissolving remember me.

    *   *   *

from 3 / The Lover

Answer with me these certainties
of glands swelling with sentiment
the loves embittered the salts and waters mixing
a chemic threatening destruction.

Answer the men walking toward death
leaping to death meeting death in a kiss
able to find of equilibrium none
except that last of hard stone kissing stone.

Answer the lover's questioning in the streets
the evenings domed with purple, the bones
easing, the flesh slipping perfume upon the air   :
all surfaces of flight are pared to planes

equal, equilibrated, solid in fulfilment.   No way
is wanted to escape, no explosions craved,
only this desire must be met, this motion
be balanced with passion   ;

        in the wreaths of time given to us what love
        may reach us in the streets   the books   the years
        what wreaths of love may touch our dreams,
        what skeins of fine response may clothe our flesh,
        robe us in valor brave as our dear wish

        lover haunting the ghosts of rivers, letting time
        slide a fluid runner into darkness
        give over the sad eyes the marble face of pain
        do not mourn   :   remember   :   do not forget
        but never let this treason play you mate,

        take to yourself the branches of green trees
        watch the clean sky signed by the flight of planes
        know rivers of love   be flooded thoroughly
        by love and the years and the past and know
        the green tree perishes and green trees grow.

     *   *   *

from NIGHT FLIGHT   :   NEW YORK

     *   *   *

Time is metric now with the regular advance   :   descend the skytrack
signal-red on the wingtips, defined by a glitter of bulbs   ;
we lean at the windows or roofrails, attentive
under inverted amphitheatre of sky.
The river is keen under blackness, weapon-malevolent,
crossed jagged marks mirrored against its steel.
Suddenly from a trance of speed are let fall bubbles slowly
blooming in pale light, but hardening to crystal
glows, into calcium brilliance, white bombs floating
      imperturbable
along the planes of the air, in chains of burning, destruction in
      the wake

of the beautiful transition.   City, shimmer in amusement,
spectators at the mocking of your bombardment.
City, cry out   :   the space is full of planes, you will be heard,
         the thin shark-bodies are concentrated to listen,
without a sound but the clean strength of the engines, dripping
         death-globes drifting down the wind
lifted by parachutes in a metaphor of death,
the symbol not the substance, merest detail of fact, going down
the wincing illuminated river, fading over the city.
Planes weave   :   the children laugh at the fireworks   :   "Oh,
         pretty stars!

                                        Oh, see the white!"

             *   *   *

Failure encompassed in success, the warplanes
dropping flares, as a historic sum of knowledge,
tallying Icarus loving the sun, and plunging,
Leonardo engraved on the Florentine pale evening
scheming toward wings, as toward an alchemy
transferring life to golden circumstance.
Following him, the warplanes travelling home,
flying over the cities, over the minds
of cities rising against imminent doom.
Icarus' passion, Da Vinci's skill, corrupt,
all rotted into war   :

Between murmur and murmur, birth and death,
is the earth's turning which follows the earth's turning,
a swift whisper of life, an ambiguous word spoken   ;
morning travelling quiet on mutinous fields,
muscles swollen tight in giant effort   ;   rain   ;   some stars
a propeller's glimpsing silver whirl, intensely upward,
intensely forward, bearing the plane   :   flying.

         •   •   •   •   •

Believe that we bloom upon this stalk of time   ;
and in this expansion, time too grows for us
richer and richer towards infinity.
They promised us the gold and harps and seraphs.
Our rising and going to sleep is better than future pinions.

We surrender that hope, drawing our own days in,
covering space and time draped in tornadoes,
lightning invention, speed crushing the stars upon us,
stretching the accordion of our lives, sounding the same chord
longer and savoring it until the echo fails.
Believe that your presences are strong,
O be convinced without formula or rhyme
or any dogma ;   use yourselves :   be :   fly.
Believe that we bloom upon this stalk of time.

THEORY OF FLIGHT

You dynamiting the structure of our loves
embrace your lovers solving antithesis,
open your flesh, people, to opposites
conclude the bold configuration, finish
the counterpoint :   sky, include earth now.
Flying, a long vole of descent
renders us land again.
Flight is intolerable contradiction.
We bear the bursting seeds of our return
we will not retreat   ;   never be moved.
Stretch us onward   include in us the past
sow in us history, make us remember triumph.
   O golden fructifying, O the sonorous calls
   to arms and embattled mottoes in one war
   brain versus brain for absolutes, ring harsh!
   Miners rest from blackness :   reapers, lay by the sheaves
   forgive us our tears   we go to victory
   in a commune of regenerated lives.
   The birds of flight return, crucified shapes
   old deaths restoring vigor through the sky
mergent with earth, no more horizons now
no more unvisioned capes, no death   ;   we fly.

       ·   ·   ·   ·   ·

Answer together the birds' flying
reconcile rest to rest
motion to motion's poise,

the guns are dying the past is born again
into these future minds the incarnate past
gleaming upon the present
                                    fliers, grave men,
lovers   :   do not stop to remember these,
think of them as you travel, the tall kind prophets,
the flamboyant leapers toward death,
the little painful children
                                    how the veins were slit
into the Roman basins to fill Europe with blood
how our world has run over bloody with love and blood
and the misuses of love and blood and veins.
Now we arrive to meet ourselves at last,
we cry beginnings
the criers in the midnight streets call dawn   ;
respond   respond
you workers   poets   men of science and love.

Now we can look at our subtle jointures, study our hands,
the tools are assembled, the maps unrolled, propellers spun,
do we say *all is in readiness   :*
the times approach, here is the signal shock   :   ?

Master in the plane shouts "Contact"   :
master on the ground   :   "Contact!"
        he looks up   :   "Now?" whispering   :   "Now."
        "Yes," she says.   "Do."
        Say yes, people.
        Say yes.
        YES

It may have been in the magazine New Masses *that Rukeyser first read about the tragic situation in Gauley Bridge, West Virginia, where, it was reported, miners were dying by the scores of silicosis, a painful and deadly lung disease. There was considerable evidence that officials of the New Kanawha Power Company knew of the danger to the workers, but had failed to provide adequate health protections. In fact, some sources said, when a high content of silica was discovered in the tunnel that was being dug, officials actually widened the scope of the project—silica was a valuable commodity in those days, they could sell the deadly byproduct at a handsome profit.*

In 1936, the twenty-two-year-old Rukeyser traveled to West Virginia. The result was one of the most original and harrowing documents of American literature, her 1938 multisectioned, multivoiced poem, "The Book of the Dead" (here printed in excerpts). It stands beside—and before—another classic in this vein, James Agee's and Walker Evans's Let Us Now Praise Famous Men, *published three years later. Rukeyser's "The Book of the Dead" brings together documentary evidence (including testimony from congressional hearings, letters, interviews, even financial printouts from the Stock Exchange) and complex, intertwined poetic explorations to, in effect, develop a new definition of what a poem might be. Taken as a whole, "The Book of the Dead" is an impassioned indictment of capitalist greed and a call for social justice. At the same time, it represents a struggle unprecedented on the part of any American poet to wrestle with the contradictions of power. Rukeyser had taken up this challenge in her "Theory of Flight." Here, like the miners she spoke with, she would dig even deeper: "What do you want?" she asks of those of us who may like our heroes and heroines nobler, our landscapes lovelier. "A foreland, sloped to sea and overgrown with roses? / These people live here."*

.   .   .   .   .

THE BOOK OF THE DEAD

THE ROAD

These are roads to take when you think of your country
and interested bring down the maps again,
phoning the statistician, asking the dear friend,

reading the papers with morning inquiry.
Or when you sit at the wheel and your small light
chooses gas gauge and clock; and the headlights

indicate future of road, your wish pursuing
past the junction, the fork, the suburban station,
well-travelled six-lane highway planned for safety.

Past your tall central city's influence,
outside its body: traffic, penumbral crowds,
are centers removed and strong, fighting for good reason.

These roads will take you into your own country.
Select the mountains, follow rivers back,
travel the passes. Touch West Virginia where

the Midland Trail leaves the Virginia furnace,
iron Clifton Forge, Covington iron, goes down
into the wealthy valley, resorts, the chalk hotel.

Pillars and fairway; spa; White Sulphur Springs.
Airport. Gay blank rich faces wishing to add
history to ballrooms, tradition to the first tee.

The simple mountains, sheer, dark-graded with pine
in the sudden weather, wet outbreak of spring,
crosscut by snow, wind at the hill's shoulder.

The land is fierce here, steep, braced against snow,
rivers and spring. KING COAL HOTEL, Lookout,
and swinging the vicious bend, New River Gorge.

Now the photographer unpacks camera and case,
surveying the deep country, follows discovery
viewing on groundglass an inverted image.

John Marshall named the rock (steep pines, a drop
he reckoned in 1812, called) Marshall's Pillar,
but later, Hawk's Nest. Here is your road, tying

you to its meanings: gorge, boulder, precipice.
Telescoped down, the hard and stone-green river
cutting fast and direct into the town.

STATEMENT: PHILIPPA ALLEN

—You like the State of West Virginia very much, do you not?
—I do very much, in the summertime.
—How much time have you spent in West Virginia?
—During the summer of 1934, when I was doing social work
    down there, I first heard of what we were pleased to call
    the Gauley tunnel tragedy, which involved about 2,000
    men.
—What was their salary?
—It started at 40¢ and dropped to 25¢ an hour.
—You have met these people personally?
—I have talked to people; yes.
    According to estimates of contractors
    2,000 men were
        employed there
        period, about 2 years
        drilling, 3.75 miles of tunnel.
        To divert water (from New River)
        to a hydroelectric plant (at Gauley Junction).
    The rock through which they were boring was of a high
        silica content.
    In tunnel No. 1 it ran 97–99% pure silica.
    The contractors
        knowing pure silica
        30 years' experience
        must have known danger for every man
    neglected to provide the workmen with any safety device. . . .

—As a matter of fact, they originally intended to dig that
        tunnel a certain size?
—Yes.
—And then enlarged the size of the tunnel, due to the fact
        that they discovered silica and wanted to get it out?
—That is true for tunnel No. 1.
    The tunnel is part of a huge water-power project
            begun, latter part of 1929
            direction: New Kanawha Power Co.
                    subsidiary of Union Carbide & Carbon Co.
            That company—licensed:
            to develop power for public sale.
            Ostensibly it was to do that; but
            (in reality) it was formed to sell all the power to
                    the Electro-Metallurgical Co.
                    subsidiary of Union Carbide & Carbon Co.
                        which by an act of the State legislature
                        was allowed to buy up
                    New Kanawha Power Co. in 1933.
—They were developing the power. What I am trying to
        get at, Miss Allen, is, did they use this silica from the
        tunnel; did they afterward sell it and use it in com-
        merce?
—They used it in the electro-processing of steel.
    SiO$_2$ SiO$_2$
    The richest deposit.
    Shipped on the C & O down to Alloy.
    It was so pure that
                    SiO$_2$
    they used it without refining.
—Where did you stay?
—I stayed at Cedar Grove. Some days I would have to hitch
        into Charleston, other days to Gauley Bridge.
—You found the people of West Virginia very happy to pick
        you up on the highway, did you not?
—Yes; they are delightfully obliging.
    (All were bewildered. Again at Vanetta they are asking,
        "What can be done about this?")

    I feel that this investigation may help in some manner.
    I do hope it may.
    I am now making a very general statement as a beginning.

There are many points that I should like to develop
later, but I shall try to give you a general history of
this condition first. . . .

GAULEY BRIDGE

Camera at the crossing sees the city
a street of wooden walls and empty windows,
the doors shut handless in the empty street,
and the deserted Negro standing on the corner.

The little boy runs with his dog
up the street to the bridge over the river where
nine men are mending road for the government.
He blurs the camera-glass fixed on the street.

Railway tracks here and many panes of glass
tin under light, the grey shine of towns and forests:
in the commercial hotel (Switzerland of America)
the owner is keeping his books behind the public glass.

Postoffice window, a hive of private boxes,
the hand of the man who withdraws, the woman who reaches
        her hand
and the tall coughing man stamping an envelope.

The bus station and the great pale buses stopping for food;
April-glass-tinted, the yellow-aproned waitress;
coast-to-coast schedule on the plateglass window.

The man on the street and the camera eye:
he leaves the doctor's office, slammed door, doom,
any town looks like this one-street town.

Glass, wood, and naked eye: the movie-house
closed for the afternoon frames posters streaked with rain,
advertise "Racing Luck" and "Hitch-Hike Lady."

Whistling, the train comes from a long way away,
slow, and the Negro watches it grow in the grey air,
the hotel man makes a note behind his potted palm.

34

Eyes of the tourist house, red-and-white filling station,
the eyes of the Negro, looking down the track,
hotel-man and hotel, cafeteria, camera.

And in the beerplace on the other sidewalk
always one's harsh night eyes over the beerglass
follow the waitress and the yellow apron.

The road flows over the bridge,
Gamoca pointer at the underpass,
opposite, Alloy, after a block of town.

What do you want—a cliff over a city?
A foreland, sloped to sea and overgrown with roses?
These people live here.

MEARL BLANKENSHIP

He stood against the stove
facing the fire—
Little warmth, no words,
loud machines.

Voted relief,
wished money mailed,
quietly under the crashing:

"I wake up choking, and my wife
"rolls me over on my left side;
"then I'm asleep in the dream I always see:
"the tunnel choked
"the dark wall coughing dust.

"I have written a letter.
"Send it to the city,
"maybe to a paper
"if it's all right."

    Dear Sir, my name is Mearl Blankenship.
    I have Worked for the rhinehart & Dennis Co

Many days & many nights
& it was so dusty you couldn't hardly see the lights.
I helped nip steel for the drills
& helped lay the track in the tunnel
& done lots of drilling near the mouth of the tunnell
& when the shots went off the boss said
If you are going to work Venture back
& the boss was Mr. Andrews
& now he is dead and gone
But I am still here
a lingering along

He stood against the rock
facing the river
grey river grey face
the rock mottled behind him
like X-ray plate enlarged
diffuse and stony
his face against the stone.

J C Dunbar said that I was the very picture of health
when I went to Work at that tunnel.
I have lost eighteen lbs on that Rheinhart ground
and expecting to loose my life
& no settlement yet & I have sued the Co. twice
But when the lawyers got a settlement
they didn't want to talk to me
But I didn't know whether they were sleepy or not.
I am a Married Man and have a family.   God
knows if they can do anything for me
it will be appreciated

if you can do anything for me
let me know soon

ABSALOM

I first discovered what was killing these men.
I had three sons who worked with their father in the tunnel:
Cecil, aged 23, Owen, aged 21, Shirley, aged 17.

They used to work in a coal mine, not steady work
for the mines were not going much of the time.
A power Co. foreman learned that we made home brew,
he formed a habit of dropping in evenings to drink,
persuading the boys and my husband—
give up their jobs and take this other work.
It would pay them better.
Shirley was my youngest son; the boy.
He went into the tunnel.

My heart   my mother   my heart   my mother
My heart   my coming into being.

My husband is not able to work.
He has it, according to the doctor.
We have been having a very hard time making a living since
        this trouble came to us.
I saw the dust in the bottom of the tub.
The boy worked there about eighteen months,
came home one evening with a shortness of breath.
He said, "Mother, I cannot get my breath."
Shirley was sick about three months.
I would carry him from his bed to the table,
from his bed to the porch, in my arms.

My heart is mine in the place of hearts,
They gave me back my heart, it lies in me.

When they took sick, right at the start, I saw a doctor.
I tried to get Dr. Harless to X-ray the boys.
He was the only man I had any confidence in,
the company doctor in the Kopper's mine,
but he would not see Shirley.
He did not know where his money was coming from.
I promised him half if he'd work to get compensation,
but even then he would not do anything.

I went on the road and begged the X-ray money,
the Charleston hospital made the lung pictures,
he took the case after the pictures were made.
And two or three doctors said the same thing.
The youngest boy did not get to go down there with me,

he lay and said, "Mother, when I die,
"I want you to have them open me up and
"see if that dust killed me.
"Try to get compensation,
"you will not have any way of making your living
"when we are gone,
"and the rest are going too."

I have gained mastery over my heart
I have gained mastery over my two hands
I have gained mastery over the waters
I have gained mastery over the river.

The case of my son was the first of the line of lawsuits.
They sent the lawyers down and the doctors down;
they closed the electric sockets in the camps.
There was Shirley, and Cecil, Jeffrey and Oren,
Raymond Johnson, Clev and Oscar Anders,
Frank Lynch, Henry Palf, Mr. Pitch, a foreman;
a slim fellow who carried steel with my boys,
his name was Darnell, I believe. There were many others,
the towns of Glen Ferris, Alloy, where the white rock lies,
six miles away; Vanetta, Gauley Bridge,
Gamoca, Lockwood, the gullies,
the whole valley is witness.
I hitchhike eighteen miles, they make checks out.
They asked me how I keep the cow on $2.
I said one week, feed for the cow, one week, the children's
        flour.
The oldest son was twenty-three.
The next son was twenty-one.
The youngest son was eighteen.
They called it pneumonia at first.
They would pronounce it fever.
Shirley asked that we try to find out.
That's how they learned what the trouble was.

I open out a way, they have covered my sky with crystal
I come forth by day; I am born a second time,
I force a way through, and I know the gate
I shall journey over the earth among the living.

38

He shall not be diminished, never;
I shall give a mouth to my son.

THE DISEASE

This is a lung disease. Silicate dust makes it.
The dust causing the growth of

This is the X-ray picture taken last April.
I would point out to you: these are the ribs;
this is the region of the breastbone;
this is the heart (a wide white shadow filled with blood).
In here of course is the swallowing tube, esophagus.
The windpipe. Spaces between the lungs.

          Between the ribs?

Between the ribs. These are the collar bones.
Now, this lung's mottled, beginning, in these areas.
You'd say a snowstorm had struck the fellow's lungs.
About alike, that side and this side, top and bottom.
The first stage in this period in this case.

          Let us have the second.

Come to the window again. Here is the heart.
More numerous nodules, thicker, see, in the upper lobes.
You will notice the increase   :   here, streaked fibrous tissue—

          Indicating?

That indicates the progress in ten months' time.
And now, this year—short breathing, solid scars
even over the ribs, thick on both sides.
Blood vessels shut. Model conglomeration.

          What stage?

Third stage. Each time I place my pencil point:
There and there and there, there, there.

"It is growing worse every day. At night
"I get up to catch my breath. If I remained
"flat on my back I believe I would die."

It gradually chokes off the air cells in the lungs?
I am trying to say it the best I can.
That is what happens, isn't it?
A choking-off in the air cells?

Yes.
There is difficulty in breathing.
Yes.
And a painful cough?
Yes.

Does silicosis cause death?

Yes, sir.

GEORGE ROBINSON: BLUES

Gauley Bridge is a good town for Negroes, they let us stand
    around, they let us stand
around on the sidewalks if we're black or brown.
Vanetta's over the trestle, and that's our town.

The hill makes breathing slow, slow breathing after you row
    the river,
and the graveyard's on the hill, cold in the springtime blow,
the graveyard's up on high, and the town is down below.

Did you ever bury thirty-five men in a place in back of your
    house,
thirty-five tunnel workers the doctors didn't attend,
died in the tunnel camps, under rocks, everywhere, world
    without end.

When a man said I feel poorly, for any reason, any weakness or
    such,
letting up when he couldn't keep going barely,
the Cap and company come and run him off the job surely.

40

I've put them
DOWN from the tunnel camps
to the graveyard on the hill,
tin-cans all about—it fixed them!—

TUNNELITIS
hold themselves up
at the side of a tree,
I can go right now
to that cemetery.

When the blast went off the boss would call out, Come, let's
    go back,
when that heavy loaded blast went white, Come, let's go back,
telling us hurry, hurry, into the falling rocks and muck.

The water they would bring had dust in it, our drinking water,
the camps and their groves were colored with the dust,
we cleaned our clothes in the groves, but we always had the dust.
Looked like somebody sprinkled flour all over the parks and
    groves,
it stayed and the rain couldn't wash it away and it twinkled
that white dust really looked pretty down around our ankles.

As dark as I am, when I came out at morning after the tunnel
    at night,
with a white man, nobody could have told which man was
    white.
The dust had covered us both, and the dust was white.

from THE DOCTORS

Dear Sir: Due to illness of my wife and urgent professional duties,
I am unable to appear as per your telegram.
    Situation exaggerated. Here are facts:
    We examined. 13 dead. 139 had some lung damage.
    2 have died since, making 15 deaths.
    Press says 476 dead, 2,000 affected and doomed.
    I am at a loss to know where those figures were obtained.
    At this time, only a few cases here,
    and these only moderately affected.
    Last death occurred November, 1934.

It has been said that none of the men knew of the hazard connected with the work. This is not correct. Shortly after the work began many of these workers came to me complaining of chest conditions and I warned many of them of the dust hazard and advised them that continued work under these conditions would result in serious lung disease. Disregarding this warning many of the men continued at this work and later brought suit against their employer for damages.

While I am sure that many of these suits were based on meritorious grounds, I am also convinced that many others took advantage of this situation and made out of it nothing less than a racket.

* * *

ALLOY

This is the most audacious landscape. The gangster's
stance with his gun smoking and out is not so
vicious as this commercial field, its hill of glass.

Sloping as gracefully as thighs, the foothills
narrow to this, clouds over every town
finally indicate the stored destruction.

Crystalline hill: a blinded field of white
murdering snow, seamed by convergent tracks;
the travelling cranes reach for the silica.

And down the track, the overhead conveyor
slides on its cable to the feet of chimneys.
Smoke rises, not white enough, not so barbaric.

Here the severe flame speaks from the brick throat,
electric furnaces produce this precious, this clean,
annealing the crystals, fusing at last alloys.

Hottest for silicon, blast furnaces raise flames,
spill fire, spill steel, quench the new shape to freeze,
tempering it to perfected metal.

42

Forced through this crucible, a million men.
Above this pasture, the highway passes those
who curse the air, breathing their fear again.

The roaring flowers of the chimney-stacks
less poison, at their lips in fire, than this
dust that is blown from off the field of glass;

blows and will blow, rising over the mills,
crystallized and beyond the fierce corrosion
disintegrated angel on these hills.

from THE DAM

All power is saved, having no end. Rises
in the green season, in the sudden season
the white the budded
                        and the lost.
Water celebrates, yielding continually
sheeted and fast in its overfall
slips down the rock, evades the pillars
building its colonnades, repairs
in stream and standing wave
retains its seaward green
broken by obstacle rock; falling, the water sheet
spouts, and the mind dances, excess of white.
White brilliant function of the land's disease.

      *   *   *

Mr. Griswold. "A corporation is a body without a soul."
Mr. Dunn. When they were caught at it they resorted to the methods employed
    by gunmen, ordinary machine gun racketeers. They cowardly tried to buy
    out the people who had the information on them.
Mr. Marcantonio. I agree that a racket has been practised, but the most damn-
    able racketeering that I have ever known is the paying of a fee to the very
    attorney who represented these victims. That is the most outrageous racket
    that has ever come within my knowledge.
Miss Allen. Mr. Jesse J. Ricks, the president of the Union Carbide & Carbon

Corporation, suggested that the stockholder had better take this question
up in a private conference.
The dam is safe. A scene of power.
The dam is the father of the tunnel.
This is the valley's work, the white, the shining.

High	Low	Stock and Dividend in Dollars	Open	High	Low	Last	Net Chge.	Bid	Closing Ask	Sales
111	61¼	Union Carbide (3.20)...	67¼	69½	67¼	69½	+3	69¼	69½	3,400

The dam is used when the tunnel is used.
The men and the water are never idle,
have definitions.

                    *   *   *

THE DISEASE : AFTER-EFFECTS

This is the life of a Congressman.
Now he is standing on the floor of the House,
the galleries full; raises his voice; presents the bill.
Legislative, the fanfare, greeting its heroes with
ringing of telephone bells preceding entrances,
snapshots (Grenz rays, recording structure) newsreels.
This is silent, and he proposes:
                              embargo on munitions
to Germany and Italy
as states at war with Spain.
He proposes
                Congress memorialize
the governor of California : free Tom Mooney.
A bill for a TVA at Fort Peck Dam.
A bill to prevent industrial silicosis.

This is the gentleman from Montana.
—I'm a child, I'm leaning from a bedroom window,
clipping the rose that climbs upon the wall,
the tea roses, and the red roses,

one for a wound, another for disease,
remembrance for strikers. I was five, going on six,
my father on strike at the Anaconda mine;
they broke the Socialist mayor we had in Butte,
the sheriff (friendly), found their judge. Strike-broke.
Shot father. He died : wounds and his disease.
My father had silicosis.

Copper contains it, we find it in limestone,
sand quarries, sandstone, potteries, foundries,
granite, abrasives, blasting; many kinds of grinding,
plate, mining, and glass.

Widespread in trade, widespread in space!
Butte, Montana; Joplin, Missouri; the New York tunnels,
the Catskill Aqueduct. In over thirty States.
A disease worse than consumption.

Only eleven States have laws.
There are today one million potential victims.
500,000 Americans have silicosis now.
These are the proportions of a war.

      Pictures rise, foreign parades, the living faces,
      Asturian miners with my father's face,
      wounded and fighting, the men at Gauley Bridge,
      my father's face enlarged; since now our house

      and all our meaning lies in this
      signature: power on a hill
      centered in its committee and its armies
      sources of anger, the mine of emphasis.

      No plane can ever lift us high enough
      to see forgetful countries underneath,
      but always now the map and X-ray seem
      resemblent pictures of one living breath
      one country marked by error
      and one air.

It sets up a gradual scar formation;
this increases, blocking all drainage from the lung,

eventually scars, blocking the blood supply,
and then they block the air passageways.
Shortness of breath,
pains around the chest,
he notices lack of vigor.

Bill blocked; investigation blocked.

These galleries produce their generations.
The Congressmen are restless, stare at the triple tier,
the flags, the ranks, the walnut foliage wall;
a row of empty seats, mask over a dead voice.
But over the country, a million look from work,
five hundred thousand stand.

from THE BOOK OF THE DEAD

These roads will take you into your own country.
Seasons and maps coming where this road comes
into a landscape mirrored in these men.

Past all your influences, your home river,
constellations of cities, mottoes of childhood,
parents and easy cures, war, all evasion's wishes.

What one word must never be said?
Dead, and these men fight off our dying,
cough in the theatres of the war.

What two things shall never be seen?
They : what we did.   Enemy : what we mean.
This is a nation's scene and halfway house.

What three things can never be done?
Forget.   Keep silent.   Stand alone.
The hills of glass, the fatal brilliant plain.

The facts of war forced into actual grace.
Seasons and modern glory.   Told in the histories,
        how first ships came

seeing on the Atlantic thirteen clouds
lining the west horizon with their white
        shining halations;

they conquered, throwing off impossible Europe—
could not be used to transform; created coast—
        breathed-in America.

See how they took the land, made after-life
fresh out of exile, planted the pioneer
        base and blockade,

pushed forests down in an implacable walk
west where new'clouds lay at the desirable
        body of sunset;

taking the seaboard. Replaced the isolation,
dropped cities where they stood, drew a tidewater
        frontier of Europe,

a moment, and another frontier held,
this land was planted home-land that we know.
        Ridge of discovery,

until we walk to windows, seeing America
lie in a photograph of power, widened
        before our forehead,

and still behind us falls another glory,
London unshaken, the long French road to Spain,
        the old Mediterranean

flashing new signals from the hero hills
near Barcelona, monuments and powers,
        parent defenses.

Before our face the broad and concrete west,
green ripened field, frontier pushed back like river
        controlled and dammed;

the flashing wheatfields, cities, lunar plains
grey in Nevada, the same fantastic country
        sharp in the south,

liveoak, the hanging moss, a world of desert,
the dead, the lava, and the extreme arisen
                    fountains of life,

the flourished land, peopled with watercourses
to California and the colored sea;
                    sums of frontiers

and unmade boundaries of acts and poems,
the brilliant scene between the seas, and standing,
                    this fact and this disease.

            *   *   *

PANACEA

Make me well, I said.—And the delighted touch.
You put dead sweet hand on my dead brain.
The window cleared and the night-street stood black.
As soon as I left your house others besieged me
forcing my motion, saying, Make me well.

Took sickness into the immense street,
but nothing was thriving   I saw blank light   the crazy
blink of torture   the lack   and there is no
personal sickness strong to intrude there.
Returned. Stood at the window. Make me well.

Cannot? The white sea, which is inviolable,
is no greater, the disallied world's unable,
daylight horizons of lakes cannot caress me well.
The hypocrite leper in the parable,
did he believe would be kissed whole by kisses?

I'll try beyond you now. I'll try all flame.
Some force must be whole, some eye inviolable—

———————

48

look, here I am returned! No help. Gone high again;
legend's no precedent. This perseveres.
The sun, I say, sincere, the sun, the sun.

MORE OF A CORPSE THAN A WOMAN

Give them my regards when you go to the school reunion;
and at the marriage-supper, say that I'm thinking about them.
They'll remember my name; I went to the movies with that one,
feeling the weight of their death where she sat at my elbow;
              she never said a word,
              but all of them were heard.

all of them alike, expensive girls, the leaden friends:
one used to play the piano, one of them once wrote a sonnet,
one even seemed awakened enough to photograph wheat-
       fields—
the dull girls with the educated minds and technical passions—
              pure love was their employment,
              they tried it for enjoyment.

Meet them at the boat : they've brought the souvenirs of
       boredom,
a seashell from the faltering monarchy;
the nose of a marble saint; and from the battlefield,
an empty shell divulged from a flower-bed.
              The lady's wealthy breath
              perfumes the air with death.

The leaden lady faces the fine, voluptuous woman,
faces a rising world bearing its gifts in its hands.
Kisses her casual dreams upon the lips she kisses,
risen, she moves away; takes others; moves away.
              Inadequate to love,
              supposes she's enough.

Give my regards to the well-protected woman,
I knew the ice-cream girl, we went to school together.
There's something to bury, people, when you begin to bury.
When your women are ready and rich in their wish for the
    world,
                destroy the leaden heart,
                we've a new race to start.

HOMAGE TO LITERATURE

When you imagine trumpet-faced musicians
blowing again inimitable jazz
no art can accuse nor cannonadings hurt,

or coming out of your dreams of dirigibles
again see the unreasonable cripple
throwing his crutch headlong as the headlights

streak down the torn street, as the three hammerers
go One, Two, Three on the stake, triphammer poundings
and not a sign of new worlds to still the heart;

then stare into the lake of sunset as it runs
boiling, over the west past all control
rolling and swamps the heartbeat and repeats
sea beyond sea after unbearable suns;
think: poems fixed this landscape: Blake, Donne, Keats.

FROM
A TURNING WIND
(1 9 3 9)

Rukeyser arrived in Spain on the day the Spanish Civil War broke out. She had traveled there as a journalist to cover the opening of the Popular, or Anti-Fascist Olympics in Barcelona, the alternative to the official Olympics scheduled in Berlin. When the fighting broke out, she and other visitors to the country were quickly gathered aboard a ship bound for France. They were traveling toward safety, but for Rukeyser, they were also traveling toward responsibility; the responsibility of communicating what they had witnessed.

A Turning Wind *was completed on September 1, 1939, on the eve, as the critic Louise Kertesz points out, of Hitler's invasion of Poland. The turning winds of world war, and the horror of the civil war in Spain (where Rukeyser lost a lover to the fighting), swirl through the poems in the book. Even some of the lighter, more whimsical lyrics—like "Nuns in the Wind" or "From the Duck Pond to the Carousel"—can be read as determined assaults of joy and possibility against "the long smoky madness / a broken century cannot reconcile."*

For a suite of five long poems entitled "Lives," Rukeyser chose her five American subjects—the scientist Willard Gibbs, the painter Albert Pinkham Ryder, the poet and essayist John Jay Chapman, the labor organizer Ann Burlak, and the composer Charles Ives—because they were, for her, individuals whose "value to our generation is very great and partly unacknowledged." (Three years later, she would publish a full-length biography of Willard Gibbs, calling it "a footnote to the poem.")

Rukeyser's "biographical" poems—there would be many more to come—are like no one else's. Just as they seem to require that the reader be familiar with events and individuals the poems refer to, they are predicated on the knowledge that the reader has no such understanding. In the "Lives," jump-cut images pass before our eyes like frames from a movie. We're pulled in for close-ups; just as we begin to focus, we're tugged away for a long shot, or a wide pan. Those looking for a straightforward narrative will not find that here.

Always, for Rukeyser, it is relationships that make meaning, and, as she writes in her preamble poem to the suite: "there are more in the scheme : the many born charging our latest moment with their wave, a shaking sphere whose center names us all as core." No life, for Rukeyser, exists in isolation. Hence, these living, leaping poems, that seem to refuse boundaries, that seem to go on beneath, above, beyond the page.

•   •   •   •   •

FOR FUN

It was long before the national performance,
preparing for heroes,
carnival-time, time of
political decorations and the tearing of treaties.
Long before the prophecies came true.
For cities also play their brilliant lives.
They have their nightmares.   They have their nights of peace.
Senility, wisecracks, tomb, tomb.

Bunting, plaster of Paris whores, electrified unicorns.
Pyramids of mirrors and the winking sphinx,
flower mosaics on the floors of stores,
ballets of massacres.   Cut-glass sewers,
red velvet hangings stained the walls of jails,
white lacquer chairs in the abortionists',
boxers, mummies for policemen, wigs
on the meat at the butchers', murderers
eating their last meal under the Arch of Peace.

The unemployed brought all the orange trees,
cypress trees, tubbed rubber-plants, and limes,
conifers, loblolly and the tamaracks,
incongruous flowers to a grove wherein
they sat, making oranges. For in that cold season
fruit was golden could not be guaranteed.

It was long before the riderless horse came streaming
hot to the Square.   I walked at noon and saw
that face run screaming through the crowd saying Help
but its mouth would not open and they could not hear.

It was long before the troops entered the city
that I looked up and saw the Floating Man.
Explain yourself I cried at the last. I am
the angel waste, your need which is your guilt,
answered, affliction and a fascist death.

It was long before the city was bombed I saw
fireworks, mirrors, gilt, consumed in flame,
we show this you said the flames, speak it speak it
but I was employed then making straw oranges.
Everything spoke : flames, city, glass, but I
had heavy mystery thrown against the heart.

It was long before the fall of the city.
Ten days before the appearance of the skull.
Five days until the skull showed clean,
and now the entry is prepared.
Carnival's ready.
Let's dance a little before we go home to hell.

NUNS IN THE WIND

As I came out of the New York Public Library
you said your influence on my style would be noticed
and from now on there would be happy poems.
                    It was at that moment
the street was assaulted by a covey of nuns
going directly toward the physics textbooks.
Tragic fiascos shadowed that whole spring.
The children sang streetfuls, and I thought:
O to be the King in the carol
kissed and at peace; but recalling Costa Brava
the little blossoms in the mimosa tree
and later, the orange cliff, after they sent me out,
I knew there was no peace.
                    You smiled, saying : Take it easy.

That was the year of the five-day fall of cities.
          First day, no writers. Second, no telephones. Third
          no venereal diseases. Fourth, no income tax. And on
          the fifth, at noon.
The nuns blocked the intersections, reading.

I used to go walking in the triangle of park,
seeing thát locked face, the coarse enemy skin,
the eyes with all the virtues of a good child,
but no child was there, even when I thought, Child!
The 4 A.M. cop could never understand.
You said, not smiling, You are the future for me,
but you were the present and immediate moment
and I am empty-armed without, until to me is given
two lights to carry : my life and the light of my death.

If the wind would rise, those black throbbing umbrellas
fly downstreet, the flapping robes unfolding,
my dream would be over, poisons cannot linger
when the wind rises. . . .

All that year, the classical declaration of war was lacking.
There was a lot of lechery and disorder.
And I am queen on that island.

Well, I said suddenly in the tall and abstract room,
time to wake up.
Now make believe you can help yourself alone.
And there it was, the busy crosstown noontime
crossing, peopled with nuns.
                    Now, bragging now,
that flatfoot slambang victory,
                    thanks to a trick of wind
will you see faces blow, and though their bodies
by God's grace will never blow,
cities shake in the wind, the year's over,
calendars tear, and their clothes blow. O yes!

FROM THE DUCK-POND TO THE CAROUSEL

Playing a phonograph record of a windy morning
you gay   you imitation summer

                    let's see you slice up the Park
in green from the lake drawn bright in silver salt
while the little girl playing   (in iodine and pink)
tosses her crumbs and they all rise to catch
lifting up their white and saying Quack.

O you pastoral lighting what are you getting away with?
Wound-up lovers   fidgeting balloons   and a popsicle man
running up the road on the first day of spring.
And the baby carriages whose nurses with flat heels
(for sufferance is the badge of all their tribe)
mark turning sunlight on far avenues
etch beacons on the grass.   You strenuous baby
rushing up to the wooden horses
with their stiff necks, their eyes,
and all their music!

Fountains!   sheepfolds!   merry-go-round!
The seal that barking slips Pacifics dark-
diving into his well until up! with a fish!
The tiglon resembling his Siberian sire,
ice-cream and terraces and twelve o'clock.
O mister with the attractive moustache,
        How does it happen to be you?
Mademoiselle   in   cinnamon   zoo,
        Hello,   hello.

READING TIME : 1 MINUTE 26 SECONDS

The fear of poetry is the
fear : mystery and fury of a midnight street
of windows whose low voluptuous voice
issues, and after that there is no peace.

56

That round waiting moment in the
theatre : curtain rises, dies into the ceiling
and here is played the scene with the mother
bandaging a revealed son's head.   The bandage is torn off.
Curtain goes down.   And here is the moment of proof.

That climax when the brain acknowledges the world,
all values extended into the blood awake.
Moment of proof.   And as they say Brancusi did,
building his bird to extend through soaring air,
as Kafka planned stories that draw to eternity
through time extended.   And the climax strikes.

Love touches so, that months after the look of
blue stare of love, the footbeat on the heart
is translated into the pure cry of birds
following air-cries, or poems, the new scene.
Moment of proof.   That strikes long after act.

They fear it.   They turn away, hand up palm out
fending off moment of proof, the straight look, poem.
The prolonged wound-consciousness after the bullet's shot.
The prolonged love after the look is dead,
the yellow joy after the song of the sun.

M-DAY'S CHILD IS FAIR OF FACE

M-Day's child is fair of face,
Drill-day's child is full of grace,
Gun-day's child is breastless and blind,
Shell-day's child is out of its mind,
Bomb-day's child will always be dumb,
Cannon-day's child can never quite come,

But the child that's born on the Battle-day
is blithe and bonny and rotted away.

GIBBS

It was much later in his life he rose
in the professors' room, the frail bones rising
among that fume of mathematical meaning,
symbols, the language of symbols, literature ... threw
air, simple life, in the dead lungs of their meeting,
said, "Mathematics *is* a language."

Withdrew.   Into a silent world beyond New Haven,
the street-fights gone, the long youth of undergraduate
riots down Church Street, initiation violence,
secret societies gone : a broken-glass isolation,
bottles smashed flat, windows out, street-fronts broken :

                              to quiet,
the little portico, wrought-iron and shutters' house.
A usable town, a usable tradition.
                              In war or politics.
Not science.
                Withdrew.
                          Civil War generates, but
Not here. Tutors Latin after his doctorate
when all of Yale is disappearing south.
There is no disorganization, for there is no passion.
Condense, he is thinking.   Concentrate, restrict.
This is the state permits the whole to stand,
the whole which is simpler than any of its parts.
And the mortars fired, the tent-lines, lines of trains,
earthworks, breastworks of war, field-hospitals,

For background on Willard Gibbs, see page 70.—Ed.

———————

Whitman forever saying, "Identify."
Gibbs saying
          "I wish to know systems."

To be in this work.   Prepare an apocryphal
cool life in which nothing is not discovery
and all is given, levelly, after clearest
most disciplined research.
                    The German years
of voyage, calmer than Kant in Koenigsberg, to states
where laws are passed and truth's a daylight gift.

Return to a house inheriting Julia's keys,
sister receiving all the gifts of the world,
white papers on your desk.
                    Spiritual gift
she never took.
              Books of discovery,
haunted by steam, ghost of the disembodied engine,
industrialists in their imperious designs
made flower an age to be driven far by this
serene impartial acumen.
                    Years of driving
his sister's coach in the city, knowing the
rose of direction loosing its petals down
atoms and galaxies.   Diffusion's absolute.
Phases of matter! The shouldering horses pass
turnings (snow, water, steam) echoing plotted curves,
statues of diagrams, the forms of schemes
to stand white on a table, real as phase,
or as the mountainous summer curves when he
under New Hampshire lay while shouldering night
came down upon him then with all its stars.
Gearing that power-spire to the wide air.
Exacting symbols of rediscovered worlds.

Through evening New Haven drove.   The yellow window
of Sloane Lab all night shone.

Shining an image whole, as a streak of brightness
bland on the quartz, light-blade on Iceland spar
doubled! and the refraction carrying fresh clews.

Withdrew.
It will be an age of experiment,
or mysticism, anyway vastest assumption.
He makes no experiments. Impregnable retires.
Anyone having these desires will make these researches.
Laws are the gifts of their systems, and the man
in constant tension of experience drives
moments of coexistence into light.
It is the constitution of matter I must touch.

Deduction from deduction : entropy,
heat flowing down a gradient of nature,
perpetual glacier driving down the side
of the known world in an equilibrium tending
to uniformity, the single dream.
He binds
himself to know the public life of systems.
Look through the wounds of law
at the composite face of the world.

If Scott had known,
he would not die at the Pole, he would have been
saved, and again saved—here, gifts from overseas,
and grapes in January past Faustus' grasp.
Austerity, continence, veracity, the full truth flowing
not out from the beginning and the base,
but from accords of components whose end is truth.
Thought resting on these laws enough becomes
an image of the world, restraint among
breaks manacles, breaks the known life before
Gibbs' pale and steady eyes.
He knew the composite
many-dimensioned spirit, the phases of its face,
found the tremendous level of the world,
Energy : Constant, but entropy, the spending,
tends toward a maximum—a "mixed-up-ness,"
and in this end of levels to which we drive
in isolation, to which all systems tend,
Withdraw, he said clearly.

The soul says to the self : I will withdraw,
the self saying to the soul : I will withdraw,

---

and soon they are asleep together
spiralling through one dream

                              Withdrew, but in
his eager imperfect timidities, rose and dared
sever waterspouts, bring the great changing world
time makes more random, into its unity.

ANN BURLAK

Let her be seen, a voice on a platform, heard
as a city is heard in its prophetic sleep when
one shadow hangs over one side of a total wall
of houses, factories, stacks, and on the faces
around her tallies, shadow from one form.

An open square shields the voice, reflecting it
to faces who receive its reflections of light as
change on their features. She stands alone, sending
her voice out to the edges, seeing approach people
to make the ring ragged, to fill in blacker
answers.
               This is an open square of the lit world
whose dark sky over hills rimmed white with evening
squares lofts where sunset lies in dirty patterns
and rivers of mill-towns beating their broken bridges
as under another country full of air.
Dark offices evening reaches where letters take the light

As a leader in the National Textile Workers' Union, Anne Burlak (b. 1911) was an active labor organizer during the textile workers strikes in the 1930s. Journalists of the time regularly referred to her as the "Red Flame." She has continued her commitment, throughout her life, to "organizing the unorganized." For these facts—not the least of which is the correct spelling of Burlak's first name—I am grateful to Anne Herzog, author of a forthcoming dissertation on Rukeyser's poetry and politics, who, in the course of her research, tracked down Burlak and interviewed her in the spring of 1993.—Ed.

even from palest faces over script.
Many abandon machines, shut off the looms,
hurry on glooming cobbles to the square. And many
are absent, as in the sky about her face, the birds
retreat from charcoal rivers and fly far.

The words cluster about the superstition mountains.
The sky breaks back over the torn and timid
her early city whose stacks along the river
flourished darkness over all, whose mottled sky
shielded the faces of those asleep in doorways
spread dark on narrow fields through which the father
comes home without meat, the forest in the ground
whose trees are coal, the lurching roads of autumn
where the flesh of the eager hangs, heavier by
its thirty bullets, barbed on wire.   Truckdrivers
swing ungrazed trailers past, the woman in the fog
can never speak her poems of unemployment,
the brakeman slows the last freight round the curve.
And riveters in their hardshell fling short fiery
steel, and the servant groans in his narrow room,
and the girl limps away from the door of the shady doctor.
Or the child new-born into a company town
whose life can be seen at birth as child, woman, widow.
The neighbor called in to nurse the baby of a spy,
the schoolboy washing off the painted word
"scab" on the front stoop, his mother watering flowers
pouring the milk-bottle of water from the ledge,
who stops in horror, seeing.   The grandmother going
down to her cellar with a full clothes-basket,
turns at the shot, sees men running past brick,
smoke-spurt and fallen face.
                            She speaks of these:
the chase down through the canal, the filling-station,
stones through the windshield. The woman in the bank
who topples, the premature birth brought on by tear-gas,
the charge leaving its gun slow-motion, finding those
who sit at windows knowing what they see;
who look up at the door, the brutalized face appraising
strangers with holsters; little blackened boys
with their animal grins, quick hands salvaging coal
among the slag of patriotic hills.

She knows the field of faces at her feet,
remembrances of childhood, likenesses of parents,
a system of looms in constellation whirled,
disasters dancing.
                    And behind her head
the world of the unpossessed, steel mills in snow flaming,
nine o'clock towns whose deputies' overnight power
hurls waste into killed eyes, whose guns predict
mirages of order, an empty coat before the blind.
Doorways within which nobody is at home.
The spies who wait for the spy at the deserted crossing,
a little dead since they are going to kill.
Those women who stitch their lives to their machines
and daughters at the symmetry of looms.

She speaks to the ten greatest American women:
The anonymous farmer's wife, the anonymous clubbed picket,
the anonymous Negro woman who held off the guns,
the anonymous prisoner, anonymous cotton-picker
trailing her robe of sack in a proud train,
anonymous writer of these and mill-hand, anonymous city walker,
anonymous organizer, anonymous binder of the illegally
        wounded,
anonymous feeder and speaker to anonymous squares.
She knows their faces, their impatient songs
of passionate grief risen, the desperate music
poverty makes, she knows women cut down
by poverty, by stupid obscure days,
their moments over the dishes, speaks them now,
wrecks with the whole necessity of the past
behind the debris, behind the ordinary
smell of coffee, the ravelling clean wash,
the turning to bed, undone among savage night
planning and unplanning seasons of happiness
broken in dreams or in the jaundiced morning
over a tub or over a loom or over
the tired face of death.
                    She knows
the songs : *Hope to die, Mo I try, I comes out,*
Owin boss mo, I comes out, Lawd, Owin boss mo
food, money and life.

                    Praise breakers,
praise the unpraised who cannot speak their name.
Their asking what they need as unbelieved
as a statue talking to a skeleton.
They are the animals who devour their mother
from need, and they know in their bodies other places,
their minds are cities whose avenues are named
each after a foreign city.   They fall when cities fall.

They have the cruelty and sympathy of those
whose texture is the stress of existence woven
into revenge, the crime we all must claim.
They hold the old world in their new world's arms.
And they are the victims, all the splinters of war
run through their eyes, their black escaping face
and runaway eyes are the Negro in the subway
whose shadowy detective brings his stick
down on the naked head as the express pulls in,
swinging in locomotive roars on skull.
They are the question to the ambassador
long-jawed and grim, they stand on marble, waiting
to ask how the terms of the strike have affected him.
Answer: "I've never seen snow before. It's marvellous."
They stand with Ann Burlak in the rotunda, knowing
her insistent promise of life, remembering
the letter of the tear-gas salesman : "I hope
"this strike develops and a damn bad one too.
"We need the money."
                    This is the boundary
behind a speaker : Main Street and railroad tracks,
post office, furniture store.   The soft moment before storm.
Since there are many years.
And the first years were the years of need,
the bleeding, the dragged foot, the wilderness,
and the second years were the years of bread
fat cow, square house, favorite work,
and the third years are the years of death.
The glittering eye all golden. Full of tears.
Years when the enemy is in our street,
and liberty, safe in the people's hands,
is never safe and peace is never safe.

Insults of attack arrive, insults
of mutilation.   She knows the prophetic past,
many have marched behind her, and she knows
Rosa whose face drifts in the black canal,
the superstitions of a tragic winter
when children, their heads together, put on tears.
The tears fall at their throats, their chains are made
of tears, and as bullets melted and as bombs let down
upon the ominous cities where she stands
fluid and conscious.   Suddenly perceives
the world will never daily prove her words,
but her words live, they issue from this life.
She scatters clews.   She speaks from all these faces
and from the center of a system of lives
who speak the desire of worlds moving unmade
saying, "Who owns the world?" and waiting for the cry.

F R O M
CHARLES IVES

*   *   *

This is Charles Ives.
Gold-lettered insurance windows frame his day.
He is eclectic, he sorts tunes like potatoes
for better next-year crops, catching the variable
wildest improvisations, his clusters of meaning;
railing against the fake sonorities, "sadness
"of a bathtub when the water is being let out,"
knowing the local hope knocking in any blood.
"Today we do not choose To die or to dance,

Charles Ives (1874–1954) was an American composer whose innovative works (most composed before 1915) incorporated popular tunes and hymns, and explored dissonance and atonality. Virtually ignored in his time, Ives was later championed by later twentieth-century composers like John Cage and Elliott Carter.—Ed.

"but to live and walk."

Inventor, beginner of strong
coherent substance of music, knowing all
apple-reflecting streams, loons across echoing lake,
cities and men, as liners aloof in voyage,
and their dead eyes, so much blue in the ground
as water, as running song he loves and pours
at water into water, music in music.

Walks
a starfall or under the yellow dragons of sunset
among the ritual answers and the secular wish,
among spruce, and maroon of fallen needles, walks
the pauper light of dawn imagining truth,
turning from recommended madness, from Europe
who must be forced to eat what she kills, from cities
where all the throats are playing the same tune
mechanically.

He was young.   He did not climb
four flights on hands and knees to the piano.   Heard
the band in the square,   Jerusalem the Golden
from all the rooftops, blare of foreground horns,
violins past the common; in the street
the oral dissonance, the drum's array.
Far breaking music indistinct with wheels'
irregular talk, the moving world, the real
personal disagreement of many voices;
clusters of meaning break in fantastic flame,
silver of instruments rising behind the eye.

He gathers the known world total into music,
passion of sense, perspective's mask of light
into suggestion's inarticulate
gesture, invention.   Knowing the voices, knowing
these faces and music and this breeding landscape
balanced between the crisis and the cold
which bears the many-born,   he parcels silence
into a music which submerges prayer,
rising as rivers of faces overhead,
naming the instruments we all must hold.

FOURTH ELEGY. THE REFUGEES

*   *   *

A line of birds, a line of gods.   Of bells.
And all the birds have settled on their shadows.
And down the shadowed street a line of children.
You can make out the child ahead of you.
It turns with a gesture that asks for a soft answer.
It sees the smaller child ahead of it.
The child ahead of it turns.   Now, in the close-up
faces throw shadow off.   It is yourself
walks down this street at five-year intervals,
seeing yourself diminishing ahead,
five years younger, and five years younger, and young,
until the farthest infant has a face
ready to grow into any child in the world.

*   *   *

F R O M

WILLARD GIBBS

(1 9 4 2)

Some people resist the idea that a poet would write a biography of a scientist, and particularly a scientist whose highly theoretical work is formidable even to those trained in the field. Willard Gibbs (1839–1903) is considered the father of thermodynamics, the branch of physics concerned with the relations of heat and energy, and the states of physical systems. He was the discoverer of the Phase Rule, what Rukeyser calls "one of the most celebrated and beautiful laws of theoretical physics." Scientists and engineers in the fields of manufacturing, medicine, and telecommunications acknowledge their debt to Willard Gibbs. Yet his name is still unknown to many of us.

This might have been enough to draw Muriel Rukeyser to Gibbs. She had always been interested in the unacknowledged similarities between the poet and the scientist—those two "hunters of the improbable." Moreover, in Gibbs's work she found something she felt our culture desperately needed: "the language of process, . . . language of the kind of life that is not a point-to-point movement, but a real flow in which everything is seen as deeply related to everything else."

Willard Gibbs, *in its dazzling synthesis of material, is more than a biography of an isolated genius in New Haven. It is a biography of our axiom-bound and axiom-breaking nation. It's hard to imagine any other writer who would begin her biography of a sheltered and privileged white scholar at Yale University with the story of fifty-three African men, women, and children, bound and brutalized beneath the decks of a Spanish slaveship. But Rukeyser sees the connections, and in the course of this brilliant book, she makes us see them, too.*

"One of the reasons that I wrote this book," Rukeyser said about Willard Gibbs, *"was that I needed to read it."*

.   .   .   .   .

THE *AMISTAD* MUTINY

In the spring of 1839 a long, low, black schooner set sail from Havana with a cargo of assorted merchandise and fifty-three kidnapped Africans, its crew, and the two Spanish owners who had bought the slaves, against all the treaties then in existence.

The slave trade on the west coast of Africa was a thriving and universal business in February 1839, the most profitable business of the country. Everybody who could be was engaged in it. Extensive wars were being fought, and the captives taken in these tribal wars could be shipped down the streams and river to the slave-ports, or herded from the slopes through the low-lying rice fields. They would find their way to the slave factories on the Atlantic coast at last, whose depots were on islands in the rivers and lagoons. Towns made war for no other reason than to obtain slaves; in the peaceable villages, many Africans were sold for their crimes, and many for their debts. Black men captured other black men from these villages, and brought them to the coast; no white man had yet been into the interior, and none dared be the first. But the slave-traders on this coast were the educated men of Sierra Leone; they were trained at the slave-depots, made their periodic trips inland, and became the principal dealers.

There was an island in the Gallinas River, the place called by the Spaniards Lomboko. A hundred years ago, a large number of these natives were brought here, and put on a boat sailing for Havana under the Portuguese flag.

They were confined on board the slaver according to the customs. Seated in a space three feet three inches high, they had scarcely room to sit or to lie down. There were a good many men in this chamber, but far more women and children. All the slaves were fastened in couples, chained tightly by the wrists and ankles with irons that left deep scars of laceration. They were kept like this day and night, sleeping twisted on the floor, and crouching by day between those decks, crowded to overflowing. They suffered every hour. They were given rice to eat, more than they could swallow, plenty of rice, but hardly anything to drink. They were ill; they wanted water; many men, women, and children died on that passage.

They were spared the last sudden horror of many of these slave-ships, running the long journey from Africa to the New World—the horror of being dragged above decks and flung all in irons overboard, at the sight of another

Willard Gibbs is the one book of Muriel Rukeyser's that is still in print. The 1988 reprint is available from Ox Bow Press in Woodbridge, Connecticut. For keeping this work available, and for permission to reprint this chapter, I am grateful to Ox Bow.—Ed.

ship, the dark chained bodies twirling down through the middle ocean. They were not hidden as many had been behind the coils of rope and under piles of cargo, as on one boat 240 people had been hidden, so that only the sight of a black leg gave away the presence of a villageful of Africans to the boarding party, come to search the ship.

For all of this suffering was illegal; it all ran counter to the laws and decrees and treaties among the countries of Europe and America. The robber-chiefs of Africa, the Atlantic pirates, and the representatives of three continents were going against the decree of Spain of 1817. All slaves imported from Africa after 1820, according to that decree, were automatically declared free. In May 1818 the minister in Washington of the Spanish government, Don Onis, communicated to the government of the United States the treaty between Great Britain and Spain to that effect, and the agreement between Spain and the United States was revised in February 1819, after long negotiations between Don Onis and John Quincy Adams, then Secretary of State.

But the slave-markets of Havana did a tremendous business. That pale extensive city waited at the end of the long crossing for more slaves, its width sectioned off like a slaughterhouse into the teeming barracoons, fitted up exclusively for the housing and sale of lately landed Africans. And this new shipload, after their kidnapping and waiting in Sierra Leone, and the two-month crossing of the Middle Passage, landed by night at a small village near Havana. Their wounds were deep, they had been beaten and flogged, and some of them had had vinegar and gunpowder rubbed into their open flesh.

Cuba was beautiful. The aromatic island, with its rush of green, its rapid plants, the stone-works of the harbor, after the long sea. But its coveted harbors were crowded with this traffic, and the masonry of the Morro Castle hid behind them, according to a letter written to Adams in 1836, advocating Atlantic and Caribbean naval bases, "a mean and degraded people." But the brooks and the fields and the fortifications! "They were the most numerous fortifications in the Caribbean, and their people had the least energy for defending them." It was easy to see what value this "American Britain" had, this chain of islands : Summer Island, or Bermuda, was another, and naval officers were talking also to General Jackson about the misunderstood bars and shoals and islands of the sea, all the way from here to Charleston.

Africans did not see this land. It was like what they had left : the slave-cages in the marshy, vivid-green fields. Their village was like what they had left : huts like their huts in the glare of day, and the strong angular shadows of sub-tropical night. They stayed here for about ten days, until several white men arrived. Among these men was Ruiz, whom they learned to call by his Spanish nickname, Pipi. He looked them over, selected the ones he liked, and lined them up in the fierce sun. And then he went down the line making the traditional tests, feeling of them in every part, opening their mouths to see if their teeth were sound; the examination was carried to a degree of minuteness.

It was time to separate these terrible companions. Forty-nine of them had been bought by Señor Don José Ruiz, and four by Señor Don Pedro Montez, and these were taken from the others. When it was time to part at Havana, there was weeping among the women and children, and some of the men wept. Cinquez, a powerful young rice planter, a natural leader even on that journey, wept. He had been kidnapped from his home, where he left a wife and three children, and now this remnant, all taken from his country, were to be parted again. Another young planter, a short active man named Grabeau, did not weep—he felt it was not manly—but sat aside from the others, with Kimbo, older than most of the others, who had been a king's slave. They talked to each other for the last time of their friends and their country. At night, the fifty-three were led through the narrow streets of Havana. The white walls stood out plain, slashed and sectioned by the deep black shadows : a thick crowded city, bigger than anything they had ever seen, far and lost from the thatch and fields of their country, where they had worshipped the spirits living in the cotton tree, the stream, and on the mountain.

They were put on board a long, low, black schooner when they reached Havana Harbor—a schooner already loaded and ready, swinging at anchor there, with the letters AMISTAD painted large on her. During that night, they were kept in irons again—heavier irons than before, locked on their hands and feet and necks. During the day they were more mildly treated : some of them were freed of their chains, although the Spaniards took care never to free them all at once. They communicated with their new owner by signs, or through Antonio, the cabin-boy, who was the only one on the ship who spoke both Spanish and the dialect they all had in common.

The *Amistad* was bound for Guanaja, the intermediate port for Principe, and the Spaniards held papers certifying that these were their slaves. But, down in the hold, the Africans did not understand why they should be on this new boat, nor where they were being taken. When the mulatto cook, Selestino Ferrer, who was the slave of Captain Ramón Ferrer, came down with the cabin-boy to feed them, they asked him their questions, through Antonio; they knew they were completely lost, they were very hungry, and the hot nights and days were made longer by thirst. There was much whipping, and their questions were not answered. On the fourth day out, the cook and the cabin-boy looked at each other when the questions were again repeated; then the cabin-boy, Antonio, laughed and said that they were just sailing at the pleasure of the Spaniards, and, as for the Africans, *they* were to be cooked and eaten whenever the Spaniards got ready for them.

During the three days out from Havana, the wind had been ahead. On this fourth day and night, it rained; a storm came up, and all hands were on deck, hard at work. Late in the evening, mattresses were thrown down for them. Clouds covered the sky; the moon had not yet risen; it was very dark. All of the crew but the man at the helm were asleep by eleven o'clock. But the Africans, below deck, were not asleep; they were up and working at their chains and whispering in short tense phrases, passing on the information about the knives they had seen, the long knives used to cut sugar cane.

At three in the morning, there was a noise in the forecastle.

None of the Spaniards ever knew how the thing began; but the freed Africans were among them, swinging their machetes. Ruiz picked up an oar and clubbed at the four men who had seized him, and then, up the deck, he heard his yell of "No! No!" followed by a boy's cry of murder. He heard the captain scream to Antonio to go below and get some bread. In the black and cloudy night, it was very late to think of pacifying these men by throwing them scraps. Antonio rushed up, in time to see the captain struck across the face two or three times; the cook was struck oftener. Neither of them groaned before he died.

By now the rest of the Africans were unchained and pouring onto the deck, armed with machetes; and when the man at the wheel and the other hand saw this, they ran for the small canoe, lowered it, and escaped into the clouded sea. Montez ran up on deck, and they met him with knives; he defended himself with his own knife and a stick until he was slashed twice, on the head and on the arm. Then he ran for it, scurrying below and wrapping himself in a sail in his panic, trying to hide between two barrels. They came after him, as he burrowed farther in, trying frantically to work himself into a crevice of safety. They would have killed him, but another black man followed and ordered the first not to kill Montez, but to bring him back on deck.

The decks were covered with blood. Ruiz was begging as he stood there, yelling not to be killed, calling that they spare the life of the old man, Montez. The Africans tied the two Spaniards together by the hands until they had had time to go down to the passengers' cabin and go through the trunks. Then they set to work. They had accomplished their purpose; they had their freedom, and they had killed the two great threats to their lives, the captain and the cook. They threw the bodies overboard and washed down the slippery deck. There were some who wanted the cabin-boy killed. He was African by birth, but he had lived a long time in Cuba as the slave of the captain, whose name he used. The fact of his years in Cuba saved his life, for he was the only link of communication between the Africans and the Spaniards. Cinquez assumed responsibility here; he stopped in his inventory of the cargo, and gave order that Antonio Ferrer was not to be killed, as he was needed for the rest of the voyage.

All night long the Africans washed the decks and went through the schooner they had captured. She was a fairly new ship, clipper-built in Baltimore only six years before, of 120 tons burden. The vessel and cargo were worth $40,000 when they left Havana. The Africans had been bought at a price between twenty and thirty thousand dollars; and vessel and cargo had been insured in Havana, as under the captaincy of Ramón Ferrer.

With favorable winds, the *Amistad* should have made Principe in two days. The distance was only about one hundred leagues. But, when the winds are adverse, the short voyage sometimes takes as much as fifteen days.

The *Amistad* was not going on to Principe. All that the Africans knew was that they lived two moons due east. They gave the Spaniards their orders accordingly. Through Antonio, they ordered Ruiz and Montez to hold the course due east by the sun. Montez had been a sea captain before he went into business for himself at Principe. He was now about fifty years old, and although he had been given wounds in the night whose scars he would always carry, from this time on the Africans were friendly to him, and promised that once they had reached the coast of Africa, he would be permitted to find his way home.

After the floggings and starvation, the vinegar, chains, and terribly cramped quarters, it was sweet to have the freedom of the ship, the clothing that was among the cargo in place of the slave rags, and to know that the sea stretching so far and blue before them led home, to the African village with its palm trees, its round huts and cone-shaped thatch, the beads and blankets, pointed teeth and peace. But the Spaniards were trying to work out a very different plan.

Ruiz, who had been unconscious for most of the day after the uprising, began to recover from his head-wound, and he and Montez plotted together at the wheel. A heavy gale was coming on, and in the clouds over the high seas, the sun was covered. The Africans relied completely on the Spaniards for their knowledge of navigation; they were inland people, all of them, knowing the mountains of the interior, the fenced towns and rice fields, and now they faced an unknown sea; they steered by the sun, and the sun was hidden. The Spaniards had an idea.

They had started out six or seven leagues from land. Now they headed for open sea. During the next four days, they boxed about in the Bahama Channel, and then the *Amistad* was steered for the island of St. Andrew, near New Providence. From here she went on to the Green Key, where they cast anchor. And again she headed out. During the day the Africans sailed eastward, eastward, toward home and full freedom, and threatened the lives of the Spaniards when the wind changed, they were so suspicious and dreaded so to be captured a second time. But at night, steering by the stars, Pedro Montez and José Ruiz headed north and west. And so the fabulous voyage continued, until ominous stories began to appear in Eastern newspapers, advising of the "long, low, black schooner," seen first at one point, and then at another on an altogether different course, following no possible route that any observer could discover. By day east, by night northwest, the *Amistad* zigzagged up the Atlantic, within hail of other ships from time to time, casting anchor when water and supplies were needed, losing their anchor at New Providence. For sixty-three days they sailed, while ten of their number died, while the Spaniards hoped continually that they would fall in with some warship, or be able to run into some port, and while the Africans looked continually for the coasts of home. Several times vessels drew up alongside, and they were boarded; once even an American schooner sent a party on board. That was on the 18th of August, 1839, and the stories of this phantom ship were already in the papers; but the American boat was friendly; it sold the *Amistad* a demijohn of water for a doubloon, and the Spaniards, locked up below, could not even shout until the American boat was out of sight. Two days later, they were twenty-five miles from New York, and Pilot Boat No. 3 came alongside and gave them some apples. Now it was clear what the Spaniards' trick had done. It had taken them almost due north, to a strange country and a strange civilization, from Africa and the Spanish depots and the Spanish bright town of Havana up the Atlantic to Long Island.

The Africans knew they were not anywhere near home. When Pilot Boat No. 4 came up, it found them armed, refusing to allow anyone on board. The *Amistad* headed along the coast, and on the 24th it was off Montauk Point, the tip of Long Island, with its wiry sharp grasses, its sand dunes—the end of America. Here Cinquez ordered the ship steered for Montauk Light, whose tall freestone tower stood 250 feet above the beach, flashing its two lights—one blinking white, one shining steady and red over Shagwong Reef. Cinquez hoped he could go ashore here, but the tide drifted the boat up the bay, and it finally was anchored just off Culloden Point.

On the morning of the 26th, Cinquez and ten other men went ashore for water. The little houses on the Point looked strange to them, thick and thick-colored after the thatch and stucco. They were the little trim places of the lighthouse-keeper and a few fishermen. The white dunes were brilliant in the late summer sunlight, and out on the bright water, their ship was very black. The still beach was hot, but windy—and quite still until a dog barked, and then, from a second house, another dog barked. From around the cove a straggling line of white men came to meet the Africans. The black men plowed through the soft sand. They were spots of brilliant and impressive color. The first man, Cinquez, the leader, was naked to the waist. He was about twenty-six years old, dark and powerful, erect and handsome, the symmetrical lines of his fine face curving in toward the eyes and mouth. He stood five feet eight, and that was tall for his race; he had already proved himself a match for any two men on the schooner; he had kept order during the long voyage; and now, as he stood on the beach in his white trousers, his white planter's hat, and with a brilliant and many-colored necklace against his naked chest, he commanded the respect of any man. Behind him were the wild colors of Spanish shawls, used as trousers; gauze and Canton crepe wound around the dark throats. One man had an ornate and beautiful bridle in his hand; one wore a linen cambric shirt with complicated embroidery worked across the bosom. They jingled doubloons in their hands. They were the strangest boatload that had ever landed at Montauk Point.

Cinquez pointed toward the dogs that ran beside the white men, held out some money, and the first sale was made : a couple of dogs bought at the rate of three doubloons each. But what they had come for was water. Cinquez sent three men up to one of the houses with the white patrol.

News travelled rapidly from house to house on the Point. Captain Green, who lived near the tip of the island, had read about the "long, low, black schooner" in the newspapers, and knew at once that the end of the riddle was here. Ever since early in August, orders had been given, to the U.S.S. *Fulton* and to several revenue cutters, to chase the ship along its crazy manoeuvering. Captain Green called together four or five of his friends and went down to the beach. There she was, the schooner, swinging at anchor just offshore, and eight or ten black men were now waiting on the beach for the rest of their party to return with water. As they saw this new group come toward them ominously over the dunes, marching through the stiff pale grass, they massed together in alarm, and Cinquez whistled sharply—the prearranged signal for the others to run back to the beach. Down from the house they came running, the red and pink silks flying behind them. Captain Green's men turned and fled. These blacks were unarmed, but the neighbors with the Captain had thought to leave guns in the wagon standing on the shore road. When they came back, stepping gingerly, they held their rifles ready. The Africans waited together; and, seeing that the whites bore arms, the Africans sat down on the beach, and Cinquez waved his arm in a sign of peace and an invitation to talk. Captain Green sat on the sand, and his men gathered behind him, and there they held their parley, drawing crude pictures in the sand and making the hand-signs by which men understand each other's simple basic fears and wishes, even when they have no words.

There were two questions the Africans first must have indicated. These were their two deepest dreads : Are there any slaves in this country? Are there any Spaniards? And when these two were answered, they were reassured, and sat smiling and talking to one another in tones that anyone might have known were those of congratulation. They were safe; they were free; they were in a good country. But Captain Green destroyed their moment. He drew the clumsy, thick-lined drawing of a ship with his finger in the sand. Next to it he drew the heavy guns of a vessel of war. They knew by these signs that they were being pursued.

The parley on the beach lasted until late afternoon, four hours of slow exchange, by signal and drawing, until the Africans had turned over to Captain Green two guns, a knife, and a hat. Besides these tokens of peace and friendship, they had given their agreement to turn the schooner over to the Captain, who was to take them to another part of the island, and from there to sail with them to Sierra Leone.

And then another vessel came in sight, slowly, from the straits between Montauk and Gardner's Point. It was the U.S. brig *Washington,* Lieutenant Gedney in command, which was making soundings. It had sighted the strange ship lying inshore, and, as it watched, the small boat was seen crossing from the shore to the ship, and then back. Lieutenant Gedney had his career ahead of him, and he saw a prize in this black ship, riding so close to the beach. She looked like a pirate, he thought, as he squinted through the glass ... and those people on the beach, with their carts and horses, and that boat crossing back and forth from land. He barked out his orders, and a boat was armed and dispatched with an officer.

As they rocked alongside the *Amistad,* riding in almost four fathoms of water, about three-quarters of a mile off free New York State, she seemed to them like some Flying Dutchman of dream, a derelict, impossible ship. Her rigging and her sails were torn and hung in shrouds and bandages down to the deck. The sides of the hull were bright green below the water-line, green and in motion, with the long, waving sea-grass that covered them and covered the crusting of barnacles on the wood. The sailors from the *Washington* swarmed up the green sides of the *Amistad* and for the first time saw the deck.

Stacked and coiled across the ship were the piles of goods they had captured : rice, silk, firearms, raisins, vermicelli, cotton goods. Everything seemed to be heaped here : bread and thin, sick Africans, emaciated almost to the skeleton, books and mirrors, hardware, olives, saddles and holsters, luxuries and fruit and jars of olive oil. The twenty men left to guard the ship waited for the first hostile move of the boarding-party; and over against the windlass, three little girls between eight and thirteen laughed at the strangers, who were prying into the cabin and the hold, uncovering still more fruits and silk, the calico heaped high, the crepe, the pictures, the entire rich cargo of the *Amistad.*

They came to a long bundle wrapped in black bombazine, lying on the forward hatch, and pulled back the black. There was a naked corpse, the last of the ten who had died on the passage. Kon-no-ma, who was watching over the body, pulled back the shroud, frowning at the intruders; he was the most ferocious-looking of the Africans, short, with a large, round head, a diamond-shaped tattoo mark on his forehead, and filed teeth that projected past his lips. The men from the *Washington* stepped back, and one said to another, "Cannibal!" But there was no reason for fear. The Africans had given up their guns—and, besides, they were in a free country. They offered no resistance.

Cinquez's boatload rowed up and boarded, and the Africans crowded around him, talking and pointing. There was still no reason for anxiety. But in that minute the entire situation changed forever : a breathless sailor climbed up from the cabin, yelling something about two white men, and in a moment Ruiz and Montez were brought up from below. Ruiz, who spoke English, demanded protection and the arrest of everyone on board. Cinquez could see what was coming, even before the officer started his quick and formal statement of possession. He rushed to the rail, stood balanced for a second, and then cut a swift arc in the air. Once in the water, while everyone on deck rushed to the side, the down-turned faces full of alarm and grief, he made a twisting motion, unbuckling the money belt around his waist. The doubloons—he had three hundred—sank, turning and seeming to darken and melt in the water. The faces watched, horrified; but he was already swimming back to the green side of the *Amistad.* They raised him, dripping, to the deck, and he gave himself up to the government of the United States.

The boat from the *Washington* rowed back with Ruiz, Montez, and Cinquez on it, leaving a guard mounted on the *Amistad.* Once on the *Washington,* however, Cinquez showed such distress that Lieutenant Gedney allowed him to return; the Africans clustered around him as he reached them, laughing, and wildly happy. He spoke to them in words the Americans had never heard, but the Africans seemed so roused by what he said that the officer in command saw to it that Cinquez was led away by force. On the following day, Cinquez signified by motions that if the sailors would take him aboard the *Amistad,* he would show them a handkerchief full of doubloons. They rowed him over once again; the irons, in which he had been manacled while he was on the *Washington,* were removed; he went below, and made another speech to his own people. They were even more wildly excited than they had been the day before; when Cinquez looked at the white sailors who were with him, the Africans shouted, and talked to each other with the same determination his voice carried. The sailors found this terrifying : the strange tongue, the looks, the Africans leaping in the crowded cabin—these black men who had already killed and gone through a fearful voyage for their freedom! There was no further indication concerning doubloons. They locked the irons on Cinquez again and took him back to the *Washington.* This time he said nothing, but he kept his eye steadily fixed on the long, low, black schooner.

Lieutenant Gedney had sent an express to the U.S. Marshal at New Haven, and he in turn had given information to His Honor A. T. Judson, U.S. District

Judge. He set sail that night for New London, and the *Amistad* followed. In the morning the two ships lay off the fort, and the gentlemen arrived to hold court on the deck of the *Washington,* a musket-shot away from the schooner. The cutter *Experiment* took the newspapermen, who had arrived, on board the *Washington* for the judicial investigation, and the New London *Gazette* published a complete report at once, which was reprinted immediately up and down the East. It began :

> We have just returned from a visit to the *Washington* and her prize, which are riding at anchor in the bay, near the fort. On board the former we saw and conversed with the two Spanish gentlemen, who were passengers on board the schooner, as well as owners of the negroes and most of the cargo. One of them, Jose Ruiz, is a very gentlemanly and intelligent young man, and speaks English fluently. He was the owner of most of the slaves and cargo, which he was convey-ing to his estate on the Island of Cuba. The other, Pedro Montez, is about fifty years of age, and is the owner of four of the slaves. He was formerly a ship master, and has navigated the vessel since her seizure by the blacks. Both of them, as may be naturally supposed, are most unfeignedly thankful for their deliverance. Jose Pedro is the most striking instance of complacency and unalloyed delight we have ever witnessed, and it is not strange, since only yesterday his sentence was pro-nounced by the chief of the bucaniers, and his death song chanted by the grim crew, who gathered with uplifted sabres around his devoted head, which, as well as his arms, bear the scars of several wounds inflicted at the time of the murder of the ill-fated captain and crew. He sat smoking his Havana on the deck, and to judge from the martyr-like serenity of his countenance, his emotions are such as rarely stir the heart of man. When Mr. Porter, the prize master, assured him of his safety, he threw his arms around his neck, while gushing tears coursing down his furrowed cheek, bespoke the overflowing transport of his soul. Every now and then he clasped his hands, and with uplifted eyes, gave thanks to "the Holy Virgin" who had led him out of his troubles. Senor Ruiz has given us two letters for his agents, Messrs. Shelton, Brothers & Co. of Boston, and Peter A. Harmony & Co. of New York. It appears that the slaves, the greater portion of whom were his, were very much attached to him, and had determined after reaching the coast of Africa, to allow him to seek his home what way he could, while his poor companion was to be sacrificed.

After a description of the Africans on the *Amistad,* the reporter goes on :

> We were glad to leave this vessel, as the exhalations from her hold and deck, were like any thing but "gales wafted over the gardens of Gul."

And then to the point of the entire incident :

> There is a question for the laws of Admiralty to decide, whether captain Ged-ney and his fellow officers are entitled to prize or salvage money. To one or the

other they are most surely entitled, and we hope they will get their just dues. Captain Gedney, when he first espied the Amistad, was running a line of sounding towards Montauk Point. He had heard nothing of this vessel being on the coast till after his arrival in this port.

The judicial investigation took place on the *Washington* on August 29, 1839. Complaints were lodged by Montez and Ruiz against Cinquez and the thirty-eight other Africans who were left alive, and the depositions of the two Spaniards were taken through interpreters. After they had gone to their cabins, the investigation adjourned to the schooner to inspect it and to allow Antonio, the cabin-boy, to identify the Africans according to their roles in the mutiny. The examination proceeded exactly as if Ruiz and Montez had owned the *Amistad,* and as if Connecticut and New York had been passionate slave states. At the end of the investigation, Ruiz and Montez caused a notice to be printed in all the city papers as a token of their thankfulness, and all the male Africans stood committed for trial before the next Circuit Court at Hartford. The three little girls and Antonio were held in $100 bond apiece, and being unable to produce the money, were sent along with the rest on board a sloop.

In charge of Lieutenant Holcomb, of the *Washington,* and Colonel Pendleton, keeper of the prison to which they were being taken, they sailed up the Sound, and arrived in New Haven on Sunday morning, September 1, 1839.

Living in the county jail was not too different from living on the *Amistad.* The great wooden room in which most of them lived together was not unlike the hold of the ship. It was larger, lighter, cleaner. Here thirty-six of them were kept, and the rest were in three smaller chambers, the three little girls in one, the sick in another. They could be together, could talk together in their own tongue, which none of these strangers seemed to understand. And once a day they were taken out of their confinement for exercise.

There was nothing in the lives of the Africans to prepare them for that scene. The glare of Sierra Leone, the sharp glimpse of angled Havana, was what they knew; and this was intensely different, this New England autumn of a century ago.

This color that they saw, these flickering delicate elms, the wide sweep of the Green, the profound sky—nothing in the tropics, nothing on the sea, could have predicted this! But there was more; for past the avenues of feathers gleamed a whiteness never seen before, in soft round pillars rising as marble never seen before, a new and enchanting whiteness, fluted intricately, and rising to support great shapes that floated like white reefs over these pale and columned porches, whose steps rose up to them in the whiteness of astounding sand; and beyond this, a warm red never seen before, warm walls taller than they had dreamed, with shining squares, the gleaming windows in the warm brick. More feathers, feathery trees in double and triple arches, fell into green shadows, green brilliance, wherever they looked. And under these walked tall, pale men in black; and through all these crowds women passed, swathed at the shoulders and thighs, bound tight at the waist, in the most voluptuous bindings and cascade and swirl of clothes they yet had seen. This field, these temples, these ox-carts moving among such fantastically dressed white men and women, these deep wild bells sounding from the pinnacles of the white steeples—this was the softest, most luxurious, most surrealist scene possible to dream. Even the grass was softer here, the leaves cut and curled into softness. The smells of farm-wagons, the fruit, the early fall vegetables, the oyster-booths at the corner of the Green, mixed with the grass-smells; and the rich shadows fell among this light more softly, more graciously, than shadows ever fell.

But, as far as the Africans were concerned, this was their prison-yard and their time of day for exercise—these minutes when they were brought out on the Green, while a crowd of these swathed women and men in clothes like tubes, and children in little clothes like the men's, came and watched their acrobatics.

Some of the white men even came into the jail. Many were beginning to visit the prison-rooms to stare, paying the admission price of twelve and a half cents; but some others arrived, making sounds at them, saying words not quite so strange as all the other words they had heard since the *Amistad* was boarded off Montauk. And then these gentlemen would turn to each other and talk for a long time.

In New York City, at a meeting of "a few friends of freedom," a committee was appointed to defend the Africans, and Lewis Tappan, Simeon S. Jocelyn, and Joshua Leavitt were now ready to receive donations, employ counsel, and act in any other ways as they saw fit for the conduct of the trial. The counsel that was engaged was Seth P. Staples and Theodore Sedgwick of New York, and, in New Haven, the rising and liberal lawyer, Roger S. Baldwin.

The main problem now was one of communication. The Africans spoke a language that was completely incomprehensible to anyone who had yet seen them; they were being tried, according to some, for a crime that included the worst, most anarchic list of separate crimes : mutiny, murder, theft of a ship on the high seas, abduction, piracy . . . but others, even while recognizing that the lack of speech might cover any sort of villainy, here saw these captives as people involved in a fight for their own freedom, against the strongest force possible : international business. For it was plain that, even at this early date, the Spanish government was going to make claims; the owners were demanding their rights; and Washington was rather ready to listen. By September 14th, the papers were noting that the Spanish Minister had asked for the ship, the cargo, and the slaves, and would probably get them. Most of the press sneered at the abolitionists, saying that if they were really friendly to the blacks, they would leave them alone. The abolitionists gave them clothes, but the prisoners would not keep them on, said the mocking articles. In the election campaign, the hostile newspapers poured out laughter, calling for Cinquez for President. But other newspapers answered, comparing democracy to the man's jack-knife—he had had it for years, though it had had nine new blades and thirteen new handles. And now the Spanish Minister, the Chevalier de Argaiz, was making new claims. He was asking for a trial at Havana, where the slave trade was wide open and the whole thing could be railroaded through. One thing was on the side of a speedy trial, however. It was going to be held in Connecticut. Mr. Holabird, the U.S. District Attorney, and Ralph I. Ingersoll, already prominent in New Haven law, were counsel for the prosecution.

Abolitionist feeling was high in New England. Case after case in Connecticut alone had laid open the structure of the country, the structure, indeed, of the country's will and feeling and economic existence. Sixty years before, Lafayette had been horrified at the spectacle of black and white Revolutionary soldiers eating together at the same mess; and during these years, the shape of the country was making itself plain. The South was farm country, breeding country, and it had become a breeding-farm for slaves; annually Virginia was exporting forty thousand Negroes southward; and New England, which stood by, watching with a certain horror and making steady profits out of the end-products of the cotton fields, had a shaky and equivocal position to maintain. The symptoms cropped up, in the small towns of New York and Massachusetts and Connecticut. All of the legalists involved in this new trial had been arguing one side of the slavery question in the courts for years, and the judge, Andrew Judson, had been prosecutor in the Prudence Crandall case, in 1833, which ended the persecution—her life had been threatened, her house attacked, her reputation smeared endlessly—of Prudence Crandall, a young schoolteacher who had admitted Negro children into her school at Canterbury.

The first trial, at Hartford, held on the habeas-corpus writ, served only to indicate how far-reaching the pressures were. A man named John Ferry, a native African, had been found in New York, who was able to speak freely with one or two of the prisoners, and imperfectly with the others, being a member of the Gissi tribe. Communication had become the most important objective for the defense. The Africans had at first been committed for murder, but the Circuit Court decided that it could take no legal cognizance of an act on board a Spanish vessel. Gedney, as master of the ship that took the *Amistad,* then filed a libel on the vessel and cargo. This cargo included the prisoners, whom he claimed as salvage. Montez claimed the three little girls,

Teme, Kagne, and Margru, who were listed in the passports which had been whipped up at Havana as Joana, Josepha, and Francisca. But District Attorney Holabird, in filing two claims for the United States, spoke for the split country. The first claim and libel was on behalf of the United States at the instance of the Spanish Minister, and called for the restoration of the Africans to the Spaniards. The second, also on behalf of the United States, claimed that the Africans were free persons, wrongfully brought into the country, and to be returned to their native land. The court was adjourned after the session on Saturday afternoon, September 21st, and the Africans were sent back to the County house at New Haven.

The crowd gathering to watch them on the Green—the men in the long, black, tubed clothes, the swathed women—did not include one who could speak to them. In the courthouse, John Ferry had shown the long papers under which they had marked their signs. But they had not yet been heard once. People had stared at them, pointing and laughing, strange, busy men had come into the jail and drawn pictures of them; plaster casts had been made for Mr. Fowler; and Mr. Fletcher, the phrenologist, was measuring their heads and jotting down notes on the number of inches from the root of the nose to the occipital protuberance over the top of the head, to determine their temperaments. It was not until the day after they returned from Hartford that a tall, thin man all in black, with strikingly deepset eyes under a smooth bland forehead, its brown hair brushed in a wide swathe across—with lined and knotted cheeks, whose muscles of control tightened the jaw and mouth sternly together—came into the jail, walking in that day with his head down, in that stride they were to know well, brooding, remote, and careless. He came in, sat down among them, and with nods and thrustings of his fingers one after the other soon made them understand. He put out one finger, and nodded and smiled at them. *"E-ta,"* said one of the Africans, in recognition, and one of the little girls repeated it like a lesson—*"e-ta,"* she said, and held up one finger. The tall clerical man wrote down the letters for it. And held up two fingers this time. Now several of them were answering, caught up in the game. *"Fe-le,"* they said; and for three fingers, *"sau-wa,"* and four, *"na-ni,"* and so on, *"do-lu, we-ta, waw-fe-la, wai-ya-gba, ta-u,"* up to ten, *"pu."* The white man took his page of notes and smiled at them, another smile with the beginning of knowledge and promise in it.

He strode off, filled with this new possibility, striding across the Green that they had seen as soft and voluptuous, that he saw scarcely at all, lost in his plans.

"Good day, Professor Gibbs," said a bonneted, mittened woman as he passed without seeing her. He turned and spoke, courteously, but with a distance in his voice.

Josiah Willard Gibbs*, professor of theology and sacred literature at Yale, had devoted his forty-nine years to religion, to the language of religion, and to the new comparative study of languages which German scholarship, in the early years of the century, was illuminating as a study of the nature of man expressed in his words, the sounds and the structure of their various grammars. Born in Salem, he was the third son of Henry Gibbs, a merchant who had been in the class of 1766 at Harvard, and had then taught school at Rowley, at New Castle, N.H., and at Lynn, before he married Mercy Prescott of Salem and settled there. His father had died when he was four, and his mother had brought up the children, sending young Josiah to his uncle at New Haven— sending him to Yale rather than to Harvard, where the Gibbs family had always gone, and the Willards as well, as far back as Samuel Willard, acting president of the College from 1701 to 1707. Scholars and librarians, the family had handed down its qualities, unselfish scholarship, modesty, constitutional frailty, a single-minded pursuit of truth in son after son. And the women they married were the rare intellectual women of early New England whose spirits reach out still from the old portraits—fine, tempered, and thin. A merchant like Henry Gibbs in this family was almost an aberration. It was possible, perhaps, after many years of teaching. The tradition was one of withdrawal, of a canalized passion given mainly to scholarship, of a remoteness among which this visit to the jail was a thunderclap.

But this was a combining occasion, one of those events that bring a life into focus, summoning qualities that until such a moment seem remote from each other, alien and useless. It was the first and only moment in Josiah Gibbs's career that could call into play his religious belief in the value of the human being, his skill in language and the reconstruction, as from fossils, of a grammar from the broken phrases set down in travel books, in the letters of missionaries, or on such a visit as he had just made—and the wish to affirm truth as he saw it that motivated a good section of the small faculty of Yale.

Walking home with his head down, almost looking behind him in the posture familiar to New Haven, he went from the College to Crown Street, where he lived in President Day's house, rented some time ago, with his wife—he had married when he was forty—the three small daughters, and the baby, his son and namesake who had just been born. He could be glad of his wife's understanding. For it was quite clear what he was to do. Communication— that was the problem here; and he held the key. Now he must find an interpreter. The abolitionists were eager for an adequate defense; his cousin, Roger Baldwin, would go to any length to give this trial its due, for it was now obvious that the deepest rights of the individual were concerned—and more,

*Father of (Josiah) Willard Gibbs, the scientist. The younger Gibbs had just been born that year.—Ed.

the deep rights of the inarticulate individual, the rights that must be fought for without the persuasion and argument that would move the Yankee mind. Tappan and Staples could be counted on to raise the money, at any sacrifice. But money and conviction were not enough without him. He, Gibbs, was the link. Communication was the link here.

Two days later he was on his way to New York. The port was the most likely place to find someone who could speak both Mendi, the dialect of the Africans, and English. The union stages left New Haven on Mondays at 3 A.M. and 11 A.M. and the early stage would take him through the morning darkness of Milford and Stratford to Bridgeport, from where the *Nimrod* and the *Fairfield* sailed for New York. For $1.75, the whole trip could be made, the hills rocking past the curtains of the stagecoach as the blackness lightened, and then the marvellous colored dawn over the farm-land of the valley, just beginning to turn metal and red in mid-September; then the clang and hurry at the dock, as the bales and casks were loaded on the packet, with its decks like the floors of a warehouse, its machinery showing as the connecting-rod and two tall black chimneys rose high above the wheelhouse, the whole thing standing high out of the water; and now the last-comers rustling up the gangway; and the still blue hours on the Sound. The orchard-lands and the drowned valleys slid by, and the turns of the river arrived—Hell's Gate, the Hog's Back, the Frying Pan; and at last the fenced-in island, behind its miles of masts and wooden piers, after the channels with their villas on the shore, the turf and trees, the lighthouse, the cheering inmates of the madhouse, and the jail. One could see from the deck as clear as water-color the Dutch houses, almost brick by brick, see the gables and the little steps to the roofs and the shining weathercocks that gleamed in the bright air. The crowded streets, with their carts and omnibuses. The buildings and the flags and the bells. A sunny, vivid city under an Italian sky, moving slowly as the boat pushed among the river-traffic, among all the red-and-black smokestacks of the ferries. And the New York sounds began, the puffing and churning of these boats, with their paddles, the clipped notes of the horses' hoofs as a carriage went by at the trot; until the last turn was made, and the slanting sails of the great packets at Sandy Hook began to fill the harbor. As he landed, he could hear the street-cries, "Ice," "Hot corn, *hot* corn," and he had the city before him, with a fantastic clue in his hand, the letters spelling out how the Africans had counted up to ten.

He made his way from ship to ship in the harbor, pausing to introduce himself and ask for a Negro boy who could understand his *"E-ta, fe-le, sau-wa,"* to be disappointed again and again. From the Battery, with the crickets chirping in the trees, he went farther uptown, to the elegant section of Waverley and Lafayette Places, with their cream-painted brick houses, white lines in the seams, the section of parasols and coaches, as against the bowling-saloons and oyster-cellars and general wretchedness of the Five Points. Offal was thrown into the streets, wherever one turned pigs ran wild, great brown, black-blotched hogs shunting their snouts along the curbs, nudging the walkers, feasting in the gutters at City Hall.

From boat to boat he went, until at last, on the *Buzzard,* a British armed brig under Captain Fitzgerald, he found, among the Africans employed there, two who he thought would do, Charles Pratt and James Covey. The brig was lying in the harbor with a number of vessels seized by her on the coast of Africa for being engaged in the slave trade, and when Captain Fitzgerald was shown the request of the committee, he gave his permission that the two interpreters be brought to New Haven. James Covey was about twenty years old; he was born in the Mendi country, and his mother was Gissi. Covey had been kidnapped when he was very young, and sold as a slave to the king of a neighboring tribe. He was used to plant the queen's rice-fields for three years, at the end of which he was sold to a Portuguese and taken to Lomboko. He and about three hundred others were put on a slave-ship to be sent to America; but, about four days out from Lomboko, the ship was captured by a British vessel, and Covey obtained his freedom in Sierra Leone, where he learned English at the Church Missionary Society. At the end of 1838, he enlisted as a sailor on the *Buzzard.* Pratt was a native Mendi, and had been rescued from a slave-ship about seven years before.

Gibbs and the two sailors started for New Haven at once.

There was "unspeakable joy" when they got to the jail. Professor Gibbs wrote to the committee about this meeting : "It would have done your heart good to witness the joy of the Africans at finding themselves able to converse with the men." And another witness added :

> We called with the interpreters at the prison this morning, just as the African captives were at breakfast. The Marshal objected to the entrance of the interpreters until the breakfast was over, but one of the captives coming to the door and finding a fellow-countryman who could talk in their own language, took hold of him, and literally dragged him in. Such a scene ensued as you may better conceive than describe. Breakfast was forgotten, all crowded round the two men, and all talking as fast as possible. The children hugged one another with transport.

And now the trials began : a series of court sessions and newspaper debates, of international duplicity and intrigue on overlapping intrigue. The five sets of claims crossed a dozen ways : the Africans claimed freedom, charging Ruiz and Montez with assault, battery, and false imprisonment; Gedney (who had already earned prominence for supervising the dredging of the deep channel in New York Harbor which bears his name) claimed salvage on the vessel, the cargo, and the slaves; Captain Green and the Long Islanders who had met Cinquez at Montauk had filed a claim identical with Gedney's; the Spanish Minister, Calderón, and the new Minister, De Argaiz, claimed the boat and the Africans under the treaty of 1795, held that the trials should take place in Cuba, and objected that the effect of a "trial and execution" in Connecticut was not as good, and these Spanish demands were supported by a strong American pro-slavery press; and, finally, District Attorney Holabird claimed that the Africans should be held, according to the 1819 act, subject to the pleasure of the President. Acting according to the slavery interests, Holabird wrote to John Forsyth, the Secretary of State, asking whether the Federal government could deliver the Africans up to Spain *before* the court had actually sat. He inquired about possible treaty stipulations covering such an act. The Secretary of State knew there were no such stipulations, but he instructed Holabird to see that the court proceedings did not put the Africans out of the Federal jurisdiction; and he turned the letter over to the pro-slavery Attorney General, Felix Grundy, who could see no reason to investigate the possibilities, and declared that they should be surrendered, together with the cargo, to persons designated by Calderón.

But President Van Buren, with all the sympathy in the world for the Spanish Minister, was unable to do this. There was no extradition treaty with Spain.

When the Circuit Court ruled that the *Amistad* had been found on the high seas, and the Africans were not to be held for such a murder, De Argaiz wrote another letter, denying the rights of the United States courts, and asked the President to send the Africans back to Cuba in a government boat. Van Buren, far from resenting this, sent an order to Lieutenants Gedney and Meade to stand ready to convey the Africans from New Haven. This order was sent *before* the court assembled at New Haven, on January 7, 1840.

At this trial the matter of the passports took on even greater weight. There was a distinction made in the terms for Africans newly landed in the New World, who were called *bozales,* and Africans landed before the prohibition of the slave trade in 1820, who were called *ladinos.* The mass passports made out for these "slaves" were by owner—one passport for forty-nine slaves belonging to J. Ruiz, and one for three slaves belonging to P. Montez (the three little girls; for the little boy, Kale, whom Montez later demanded, there was no passport at all), and in these documents, the Africans are called *"cuerenta y nueva negros ladinos"* and *"tres negras ladinas."* Now, through the interpreters, it became possible to prove that the Africans had not been in Cuba and knew not a single word of Spanish. The stories of their kidnapping and sale became known, as they told their history, living and dying in the New Haven jail. Six more had died since the beginning of their captivity, and had been buried. Local clergymen, including Leonard Bacon, had spoken at the funerals. At the funeral of Kaperi, prayers were offered in the room, and the substance of his friends' remarks was, "Kaperi is dead. His body is still, and will be laid in the ground. The soul of Kaperi is alive. It will never die. Our souls will never die. They will live after our bodies are dead and cold. The Bible tells us how our souls may go to the good place. You must learn to read the Bible. Pray to God, become good, and then when your bodies die, God will take your souls to the good place, and make you happy forever." And then, with a great number of the New Haven people, they walked in procession to the grave. A hymn was sung and read there, and Mr. Bacon offered a prayer.

The Africans were learning to read and write. They could say "Merica," when asked where they were. They could make simple conversation. But the shadow over their religious and linguistic education was their anxiety, according to their teachers, Professor Gibbs and the "young gentlemen connected with Yale College." They had uncertainty in respect to the future. They dreaded going back to Havana, and would interrupt their prayers, in the middle of "*O ga-wa-wa* [O great God], *bi-a-bi yan-din-go* [Thou art good], *bi-a-bi ha-ni gbe-le ba-te-ni* [Thou hast made all things]," to speak of this. When the nature of an oath was explained to them, and it was added that God would visit the man who violated an oath with His displeasure, they asked, "What will be done to the people of the United States if they send us back to Havana?"

In a contemporary account, there is a description of the scene when they received the news of the decision of the District Court.

They were assembled and seated in a commodious room—they knew that their case was pending—some of them had been called to testify in court—they were of course deeply anxious for the event. All being present and quiet, they were informed that the judge had decreed their return, not to Havana, but to their native land. They leaped from their seats, rushed across the room, threw themselves prostrate at the feet of those who brought them the glad tidings, while "thank you, thank you" was the expression of every tongue.

The succeeding day Mr. Baldwin, one of their counsel, entered the jail. Cinquez was seated behind a table, and members of his class on either side of him. As Mr. B. approached, Cinquez was told that he pleaded his cause; said it would be wrong to send him to Havana. He dropped his book, rose from his seat, seeming for a moment deliberating whether he should leap the table. Seeing this to be attended with difficulty, he reached forward, and seizing the extended hand of Mr. B. with a firm grasp, and looking him in the face, his own countenance beaming with the most grateful emotion, exclaimed, "We thank you, we bless you, this is all we can do for you."

During this icy winter, the *Grampus* lay in New Haven Harbor. It had been sent up from the Brooklyn Navy Yard early in January, to the open dismay of most of New Haven, and a little later the anti-slavery group had stationed another schooner offshore, in the hope of running the Africans to Canada if any open attempt were made to ship them to Cuba or Spain. It was obvious that the verdict that they were freemen, not property—men who had fought to regain their lost freedom, not criminals—acquitted men, and not condemned slaves—it was obvious that any such verdict would not be allowed to stand. The case was appealed by order of the Secretary of State the moment the verdict was announced. The District Attorney rushed a special messenger through the icy mud of the road to Washington, so that the President might correct a clerical error in his order to hold the Africans. Van Buren sent a flagrant message to the Marshal—a message pandering at every point to the Spanish government, pandering in a manner so impossible for the Chief Executive of the United States that he was later forced to deny that it was his. But, with Justice Thompson on the bench, the decision of the District Court was affirmed pro forma, and the whole matter was left to the United States Supreme Court on appeal.

This was the end of April 1840. And now, with the addition of other members to the legal staff of the defense, the committee was prepared to go ahead without stint of time or money to the last appeal, before the Supreme Court. They needed a counsel whose argument would be brilliant and unquestioned in its honesty; they needed a defense that would set this case before history as a pivotal point in the climb towards freedom. They needed, not a lawyer, but an idealistic philosopher. The man they went to was John Quincy Adams.

He was ex-President, seventy-three years old, ill, tired, long ago defeated in a great and personal defeat. He was the "old man eloquent"; he was the President who had committed political suicide for the sake of science; and he had not been in a court for thirty-two years. He was one of the great peaks in democratic civilization, standing for law and human dignity, for science and faith. His standard was George Washington, and, as Brooks Adams says, "to him it was from the very outset clear that, if the democratic social system were capable of progression upward to a level at which it could hope to ameliorate the lot of men on earth, it must tend, at least, to produce an average which, if it did not attain to the eminent ability of the first President, might at least be capable of understanding and appreciating his moral altitude." He was at home in Quincy on October 27, 1840, when Ellis Loring and Lewis Tappan came to call, to enlist his sympathy in the case and to leave the two great scrapbooks of the *Amistad* captives—letters, press clippings, reports. As for his sympathy, that had been long ago enlisted. There was a sympathy in John Quincy Adams that must include these Africans. A year before, when he had had Loring's first letter about the case, just after the Hartford trial, he had begun to watch the developments; by that October he had been absorbed in their meaning; and only a few months ago, he had offered a resolution in the House, calling on the President for papers concerning the *Amistad.*

He pushed back the two huge scrapbooks. He could not possibly take this case. He was old, he was infirm, he had been away from these lists too long. They argued with him; this was a matter of life and death, but that was the least argument; the case was critical, it touched his interests, causes in which he had spent a lifetime. He alone was equal to this. And after long demurring, he pulled the scrapbooks across the table toward him. He would take the case. And he wrote in the diary which is only one of his monuments: "I implore the mercy of Almighty God so as to control my temper, to enlighten my soul, and to give me utterance, that I may prove myself in every respect equal to the task." And again, writing at night: "Oh, how shall I do justice to this case and to these men?"

Three weeks later, at five-thirty in the morning, he took the cars from Hartford to New Haven. At eight o'clock he arrived and went straight to the Tontine Hotel, the best in town, although the Quinnipiac was trying hard to equal it. He had a quiet breakfast there, and during breakfast Roger Baldwin called on him, talked for a while about the case, and invited him to his office to inspect the papers on the *Amistad* trials. They talked there for about two hours, and then Mr. Adams, with Baldwin, Marshal Wilcox, Deputy Pendleton, and a keeper, went through the rooms at the jail and met the Africans. He did not see the three little girls, who were in a separate chamber, but he met the men—of whom there were now thirty-two. They were sleeping double in crib beds, in a room thirty feet by twenty—"negro face, fleece, and form," he writes, "but varying in color from ebon black to dingy brown. 1 or 2 of them almost mulatto bright. Cinquez & Grabow, the 2 chief conspirators, have very remarkable countenances." They were put through their paces for him; while he listened politely, three of them took turns at reading part of a chapter in the English New Testament, "very indifferently." One boy writes, he noted. Mr. Ludlow was teaching them, but they learned slowly, huddled together as they were, with no one to talk to.

In lesser natures, there is always the danger in an issue of this sort that a lack of impressiveness in the prisoners themselves may make a possible champion lose faith. The public expects its martyrs to be saints, and it is only the defender who puts the cause above the man, the fight for life above the individual life, who can be reconciled to the fact that he is a martyr and part of a cause, and not too much more. Adams was not only passionately devoted to the cause under which the *Amistad* Africans were defended, he was committed to a future in which its justification would be taken for granted. He was concerned with the future—a future living in one's own time, whose origins are to be seen in the flowing present, a future that must daily be found and helped clear. "Besides anticipating by nearly a hundred years some of

the most enlightened measures of conservation," say the Beards, "Adams fore-
saw in a livid flash the doom of slavery in a social war." Repudiated by his
country, conscious of failure at every step of his effort toward the country's
enlightenment, he knew the depth of the contemporary antagonism—the cleft
in the republic, the great split in which he acted a firm and frightful role,
prophetic, integrated, and hostile to a planted majority.

By the 30th he was in Washington, where he spoke to Attorney General
Gilpin about the case, urging him to submit to the President to have the case
dismissed by consent, without argument. The Africans were obviously *bozales,* newly imported; that fact destroyed the last Spanish claim, which rested
upon their passports. In the documents, the term *ladino* had been wilfully
mistranslated as "sound." Early December was spent in going over the translations, particularly of Document No. 185—and on December 11th, Gilpin's
report came through. The President would not dismiss the case because of
the Spanish Minister's claim. Adams records that he quarreled with Gilpin on
the spot, and he writes on December 12, 1840, that he is preparing the case—

> with deep anguish of heart, and a painful search of means to defeat and expose
> the abominable conspiracy, Executive and Judicial, of this Government against
> the lives of those wretched men. How shall the facts be brought out? How shall
> it be possible to comment upon them with becoming temper—with calmness,
> with moderation, with firmness, with address, to avoid being silenced, and to
> escape the imminent danger of giving the adversary the advantage in the argu-
> ment by overheated zeal? Of all the dangers before me, that of losing my self-
> possession is the most formidable. I am yet unable to prepare the outline of the
> argument, which I must be ready to offer the second week in January. Let me not
> forget my duty.

December in Washington brought its bright sky and snow-chilled air, and
the slush and mud for which the unfinished capital was notorious abroad.
There were continual admissions and exasperations : the proofreader con-
fessed that the mistranslation was his fault; Adams, in going over the records,
fumes against Gedney, raging for the Lieutenant's having taken the men on
the shore, without right, and the ship on the high seas, without right. He
wished the whole thing were over; talking to the President, complaining about
the difficulty and importance of correct printing, putting through the new
license for the *Amistad.* In January, Gedney's sister-in-law arrived, pleading
for the newly made Captain. He was ill, she said, and not very sound in mind.
Adams answered her stream of appeal with the assurance that he would have
all due consideration for the condition of Captain Gedney. And when Baldwin
came in three days later, Adams signed the brief, and sighed over his diary,
"I know not yet how to order my speech aright."

Francis Scott Key, the United States District Attorney who wrote "The Star-Spangled Banner," came up to him, talking pessimistically about the case—this case for which Mr. Adams' heart was ready, while his unpreparedness more and more rankled in him. Key had argued the *Antelope* case, which was similar enough, and which Adams knew he would have to review in his defense. Now document after document turned up—the Chief Clerk's letter saying he had been sorry to see "the rascally blacks fall into the hands of the abolitionists with whom Hartford is filled." The day after this came out into the open, a postponement was granted. Mr. Adams knew a momentary relief, but his suspense was too real. He was immediately involved with the British Minister, Henry Stephen Fox, who wished advice as to what he might do in case of a judgment against the *Amistad* captives. Adams advised him to write to the Secretary of State; and with the new date pushed ahead to February 16th, and Baldwin's return to Connecticut until then, he plunged deep into the House debate, which was furious at the moment. These were desperate days for John Quincy Adams. Opposed by what were to him the most malignant forces of evil in the country, the reactionaries—the *popular* reactionaries—and by the slave oligarchy, he was fighting an isolated fight in the House, for free speech, for scientific innovations, for the civilized application of that education whose uncivilized use was creating the conflict now gathering its storm. The furious, brainless, heartless debate in the House could only be abandoned—he went back to read the old cases—he rose and went back to the House, to plunge into his savage feud with General Wise, attacking in this death-struggle. In the meantime, Fox had still had no answer to his letter. Time was growing short. Mr. Adams was deep in the demonic struggle in the House. He prayed. Praying for control, always more control, for he was swung from hell to hell in his passion, an immortal passion for America, for the mind of God in America, he raged against his "eccentric, wild, extravagant freaks of passion." Seeing this mind, this country, split, he remembered tragic Coriolanus and the Voices. He remembered the red and white roses in the Temple gardens.

And soon the trial itself was on him, among all the reading, the books of the *Antelope* record piled high, the pathetic death of the servant Jeremy Leary and his funeral, the last postponement to the 22nd ("I have yet to prepare a frame for my argument")—and now Baldwin begins, "sound and eloquent but exceedingly mild," carrying the legalistic burden in answer to Attorney General Gilpin. And on the 23rd, with the hour rushing on him, he is still writing, "The very skeleton of my argument is not yet put together." But that night it breaks; he begins to come through; he finds his form; and on the morning of the 24th, the scene.

The great hall of the Court, and on the bench, under the carvings and panellings, the nine among whom Adams might have taken his place. He saw other faces, the judges of his day, dead, all dead—he was standing, as he knew and said, for the last time, before this court, with its new judges, scanning the double image of the Declaration hanging on the wall opposite. He began, with his inflamed left eye still giving him pain, old, shaken with his palsy—his hand off the eagle rest on which it lay in the House—ill with the rheumy affection from which he suffered. He was old, he was old, and his eyes watery, his voice shrill, and he trembled with emotion as he gathered himself together for one of the greatest denunciations offered against the entire government of the United States. For he laid open the craft and hypocrisy he saw leading up to "the death-struggle now in continual operation between the spirit of liberty and the spirit of bondage on this continent of North America." In this great blast—"Justice!" he cried, "I stand before a Court of Justice. . . . I am obliged to take this ground, because, as I shall show, another Department of the Government of the United States has taken, with reference to this case, the ground of utter injustice, and these individuals for whom I appear, stand before this Court, awaiting their fate from its decision, under the array of the whole Executive power of this nation against them, in addition to that of a foreign nation."

He spoke of Shakespeare's Wolsey, and his virtue; of the Code Noir, the slave system, of the national sympathy with the slave-traders of the barracoons, officially declared to be the prime motive of action of the government. He spoke of the demands of the Spanish Ambassador on the President, marking how the Secretary of State should have called on the Ambassador to name another instance where such a demand had been made by any other government on an independent government. "He should have told him, that such a demand was treating the President of the United States, not as the head of a nation, but as a constable, a catchpole. . . ." He breaks down the charge that the two Spaniards, Ruiz and Montez, were "victims of an intrigue." After their cruelty, he says, that killed men on their boat, men in New York advised with the lawyers—"fanatics, perhaps, I must call them, according to the general application of language, but if I were to speak my own language in my own estimate of their character, so far as concerns this case, and confining my remarks exclusively to this present case, I should pronounce them the FRIENDS OF HUMAN NATURE. . . ." This was to be done: human beings were to be saved from slavery and death. In a careful analysis of the legal factors, with an interruption caused by the death of Judge Barbour in the middle of the trial, Adams goes ahead with his passionate insistence on personal liberty. "Is it possible that a President of the United States should be ignorant that the right of personal liberty is individual? That the right to it of every one, is *his own*—JUS SUUM . . ." He rages in praise of the Africans, in the face of "such a scene of Liliputian trickery enacted by the rulers of a great, magnanimous, and Christian nation." As for Cinquez and Grabeau, they "are not slaves. Let them bear in future history the names of Harmodius and Aristogiton." He swings around, trembling, the old man, the eagle voice, pointing to the Declaration on the wall, speaking of the Official Journal which gives the war-right of slavery—"Is that the principle on which these United States stand before the world?"

On March 8th the verdict was handed down. He wrote to Tappan and Baldwin that they had been confirmed. But he knew, he knew; and he wrote this in the diary, after the Africans went free:

> I am yet to revise for publication my argument in the case of the Amistad Africans; and, in merely glancing over the slave-trade papers lent me by Mr. Fox, I find impulses of duty upon my own conscience which I cannot resist, while on the other hand are the magnitude, the danger, the insurmountable burden of labor to be encountered in the undertaking to touch upon the slave-trade. No one else will undertake it; no one but a spirit unconquerable by man, woman, or fiend can undertake it but with the heart of martyrdom. The world, the flesh, and all the devils in hell are arrayed against any man who now in this North American Union shall dare to join the standard of Almighty God to put down the African slave-trade; and what can I, upon the verge of my seventy-fourth birthday, with a shaking hand, a darkening eye, a drowsy brain, and with all my faculties dropping from me one by one, as the teeth are dropping from my head—what can I do for the cause of God and man, for the progress of human emancipation, for the suppression of the African slave-trade? Yet my conscience presses me on; let me but die upon the breach.

And after the prison, the plaster casts, the phrenologists, the tales of their African homes, the trials and appeals and final acquittal, the green fields of Westville, the Bible and the promise of return to Sierra Leone with the missionary society, Kinna—the young, the bright-countenanced, the good scholar—wrote to Professor Gibbs:

> dear friend
> I wish to write you a letter because you have been so kind to me and because you love Mendi people I think of you very often I shall pray for you Dear friend would you must pray for me If you love Jesus Christ and Christ will bless you and would you must come sometime to see Mendi people we must want to see you and I see you I am very Glad and Dear friend I pray for you My good love to your wife and all your family I love them very much I pray for them. . . .

BEAST IN VIEW

"Nothing was true in the sense / I wanted it to be true," Rukeyser writes in "Love and Its Doors and Windows." Many of the poems in Rukeyser's Beast in View are dark. More often than not, their settings are places of darkness—woods, caves, the midnight sky, an empty letter box, a house with blackened windows. "It is all much worse than I dreamed," she writes.

But the beast in view in these poems is the poet herself. These poems are documents of the struggle to acknowledge the wars that rage around her, and those that rage within her. "I want to grow up," Rukeyser declares in "Eighth Elegy. Children's Elegy." It is a sentiment so rarely heard in American poetry that it can almost slip past us. "I want to grow up," she writes. "To come back to love."

.   .   .   .   .

WHO IN ONE LIFETIME

Who in one lifetime sees all causes lost,
Herself dismayed and helpless, cities down,
Love made monotonous fear and the sad-faced
Inexorable armies and the falling plane,
Has sickness, sickness.   Introspective and whole,
She knows how several madnesses are born,
Seeing the integrated never fighting well,
The flesh too vulnerable, the eyes tear-torn.

She finds a pre-surrender on all sides:
Treaty before the war, ritual impatience turn
The camps of ambush to chambers of imagery.
She holds belief in the world, she stays and hides
Life in her own defeat, stands, though her whole world burn,
A childless goddess of fertility.

June 1941

CHILD IN THE   GREAT WOOD

It is all much worse than I dreamed.
The trees are all here,
Trunk, limb, and leaf,
Nothing beyond belief
In danger's atmosphere
And the underbrush is cursed.
But the animals,
Some are as I have dreamed,
Appear and do their worst
Until more animals
With recognizable faces

Arrive and take their places
And do their worst.

It is all a little like dreaming,
But this forest is silent,
This acts out anxiety
In a midnight stillness.
My blood that sparkles in me
Cannot endure this voiceless
Forest, this is not sleep
Not peace but a lack of words.
And the mechanical birds
Wing, claw, and sharpened eye.
I cannot see their sky.

Even this war is not unlike the dream,
But in the dream-war there were armies,
Armies and armor and death's etiquette,
Here there are no troops and no protection,
Only this wrestling of the heart
And a demon-song that goes
For sensual friction
Is largely fiction
And partly fact
And so is tact
And so is love,
And so is love.

The thin leaves chatter. There is a sound at last
Begun at last by the demon-song.
Behind the wildest trees I see the men together
Confessing their lives and the women together.
But really I cannot hear the words.   I cannot hear the song.
This may still be my dream
But the night seems very long.

LOVE AND ITS DOORS AND WINDOWS

History melts my houses,
But they were all one house
Where in the dark beginning
A tall and maniac nurse
Hid tortures behind the door
And afterwards kissed me
Promising all as before.

The second house was music;
The childish hands of fear
Lying on a piano
That was blackness and light,
Opened my life with sound—
Extorting promises
Loud in the ringing air.

After that, broken houses,
The wealthy halls of cloud
Haunted by living parents
And the possessive face.
Power and outrage looking
At the great river
Marvellous filthy and gold.

When love lay in my arms
I all night kissed that mouth,
And the incredible body
Slept warm at my side;
But the walls fell apart
Among my lifetime dream—
O, a voice said crying,
My mother's broken heart.

Nothing was true in the sense
I wanted it to be true.
Victory came late,
Excitement returned too soon.

If my love were for the dead,
Desire would restore
Me to my life again.

My love is for the living;
They point me down to death,
And death I will not take.
My promises have grown,
My kiss was never false,
The faint clear-colored walls
Are not forever down.

SONG

The world is full of loss; bring, wind, my love,
    My home is where we make our meeting-place,
    And love whatever I shall touch and read
    Within that face.

Lift, wind, my exile from my eyes;
    Peace to look, life to listen and confess,
    Freedom to find to find to find
    That nakedness.

FROM
LETTER TO THE FRONT

1

Women and poets see the truth arrive.
Then it is acted out,
The lives are lost, and all the newsboys shout.

Horror of cities follows, and the maze
Of compromise and grief.
The feeble cry Defeat be my belief.

All the strong agonized men
Wear the hard clothes of war,
Try to remember what they are fighting for.

But in dark weeping helpless moments of peace
Women and poets believe and resist forever:
The blind inventor finds the underground river.

2

Even during war, moments of delicate peace
Arrive; ceaseless the water ripples, love
Speaks through the river in its human voices.
Through every power to affirm and heal
The unknown world suggests the air and golden
Familiar flowers, and the brief glitter of waves,
And dreams, and leads me always to the real.
Even among these calendars of fire.

Sings: There is much to fear, but not our power.
The stars turn over us; let us not fear the many.
All mortal intricacies tremble upon this flower.
Let us not fear the hidden.   Or each other.
We are alive in an hour whose burning face
Looks into our death, death of our dear wish.
And time that will be eating away our flesh
Gives us this moment when blue settles on rose
And evening suddenly seems limitless silver.
The cold wind streaming over the cold hill-grasses
Remembers and remembers.   Mountains lift into night.
And I am remembering the face of peace.

I have seen a ship lying upon the water
Rise like a great bird, like a lifted promise.

        *   *   *

7

To be a Jew in the twentieth century
Is to be offered a gift. If you refuse,
Wishing to be invisible, you choose
Death of the spirit, the stone insanity.
Accepting, take full life.   Full agonies:
Your evening deep in labyrinthine blood
Of those who resist, fail, and resist; and God
Reduced to a hostage among hostages.

The gift is torment.   Not alone the still
Torture, isolation; or torture of the flesh.
That may come also.   But the accepting wish,
The whole and fertile spirit as guarantee
For every human freedom, suffering to be free,
Daring to live for the impossible.

                    *   *   *

9

Among all the waste there are the intense stories
And tellers of stories.   One saw a peasant die.
One guarded a soldier through disease.   And one
Saw all the women look at each other in hope.
And came back, saying, "All things must be known."

They come home to the rat-faced investigator
Who sneers and asks, "Who is your favorite poet?"
Voices of scissors and grinders asking their questions:
"How did you ever happen to be against fascism?"
And they remember the general's white hair,
The food-administrator, alone and full of tears.

They come home to the powder-plant at twilight,
The girls emerging like discolored shadows.
But this is a land where there is time, and time;
This is the country where there is time for thinking.
"Is he a 'fellow-traveler'?— No. —Are you sure? —No."
The fear.   Voices of clawhammers and spikes clinking.

_____

If they bomb the cities, they must offer the choice.
Taking away the sons, they must create a reason.
The cities and women cry in a frightful voice,
"I care not who makes the laws, let me make the sons."
But look at their eyes, like drinking animals'
Full of assurance and flowing with reward.
The seeds of answering are in their voice.
The spirit lives, against the time's disease.
You little children, come down out of your mothers
And tell us about peace.

I hear the singing of the lives of women,
The clear mystery, the offering and pride.
But here also the orange lights of a bar, and an
Old biddy singing inside:

　　Rain and tomorrow more
　　They say there will be rain
　　They lean together and tell
　　The sorrow of the loin.

　　Telling each other, saying
　　"But can you understand?"
　　They recount separate sorrows.
　　Throat.　Forehead.　Hand.

　　On the bars and walls of buildings
　　They passed when they were young
　　They vomit out their pain,
　　The sorrow of the lung.

　　Who would suspect it of women?
　　They have not any rest.
　　Sad dreams of the belly, of the lip,
　　Of the deep warm breast.

　　All sorrows have their place in flesh,
　　All flesh will with its sorrow die—
　　All but the patch of sunlight over,
　　Over the sorrowful sunlit eye.

10

Surely it is time for the true grace of women
Emerging, in their lives' colors, from the rooms, from the harvests,
From the delicate prisons, to speak their promises.
The spirit's dreaming delight and the fluid senses'
Involvement in the world.   Surely the day's beginning
In midnight, in time of war, flickers upon the wind.

*   *   *

DARKNESS MUSIC

The days grow and the stars cross over
      And my wild bed turns slowly among the stars.

F R O M

EIGHTH ELEGY. CHILDREN'S ELEGY

*   *   *

This is what they say, who were broken off from love:
However long we were loved, it was not long enough.

We were afraid of the broad big policeman,
of lions and tigers, the dark hall and the moon.

After our father went, nothing was ever the same,
when mother did not come back, we made up a war game.

My cat was sitting in the doorway when the planes
went over, and my cat saw mother cry;
furry tears, fire fell, wall went down;
did my cat see mother die?

Mother is gone away, my cat sits here coughing.
I cough and sit.   I am nobody's nothing.

However long they loved us, it was not long enough.
For we have to be strong, to know what they did, and then
our people are saved in time, our houses built again.

You will not know, you have a sister and brother;
my doll is not my child, my doll is my mother.

However strong we are, it is not strong enough.
I want to grow up. To come back to love.

      *   *   *

SUICIDE BLUES

I want to speak in my voice!
I want to speak in my real voice!

This street leads into the white wind
I am not yet ready to go there.
Not in my real voice.

The river.   Do you know where the river springs?
The river issues from a tall man,
From his real voice.

Do you know where the river is flowing?
The river flows into a singing woman,
In her real voice.

Are you able to imagine truth?
Evil has conspired a world of death,
An unreal voice.

The death-world killed me when the flowers shine,
In spring, in front of the little children,
It threw me burning out of the window
And all my enemies phoned my friends,
But my legs went running around that building
Dancing to the suicide blues.

They flung me into the sea
The sunlight ran all over my face,
The water was blue the water was dark brown
And my severed head swam around that ship
Three times around and it wouldn't go down.

Too much life, my darling, embraces and strong veins,
Every sense speaking in my real voice,
Too many flowers, a too-knowing sun,
Too much life to kill.

THE GREEN WAVE

By the mid-1940s Rukeyser was living in California. In 1945, she entered into a brief and what she called "disastrous" marriage with a young painter. (The marriage was annulled after just twelve weeks.) By 1947, she was single, living in San Francisco, teaching at the California Labor School, and pregnant. On September 25, 1947, her son Bill was born.

But there is no simple cause and effect to explain how the dark paths of Beast in View *have now become the "dark and marvelous ways" of* The Green Wave— *except the poems themselves. Everywhere in* The Green Wave, *darkness is chronicled as the place where a new kind of vision is possible. Like Orpheus, Rukeyser seems to have traveled through hell, a necessary journey ("past all loss," she writes in "Clouds, Airs, Carried Me Away") to come "into my clear being" as she wrote in "Then I Saw What the Calling Was." The language of these poems is clear, calm, steady, never lazy or complacent. At their most polished, these poems have the sheen of sea glass tumbled and swept into beauty by long contact with a pounding surf.*

"Trust in the rhythms of experience," she wrote. More and more, Rukeyser's poems speak of a trust in the rhythms and textures of a woman's experience: a woman's dreams, a woman's wakings.

.   .   .   .   .

THE MOTIVE OF ALL OF IT

The motive of all of it was loneliness,
All the panic encounters and despair
Were bred in fear of the lost night, apart,
Outlined by pain, alone.   Promiscuous
As mercy.   Fear-led and led again to fear
At evening toward the cave where part fire, part
Pity lived in that voluptuousness
To end one and begin another loneliness.

This is the most intolerable motive :   this
Must be given back to life again,
Made superhuman, made human, out of pain
Turned to the personal, the pure release:
The rings of Plato and Homer's golden chain
Or Lenin with his cry of Dare We Win.

EYES OF NIGHT-TIME

On the roads at night I saw the glitter of eyes:
my dark around me let shine one ray;   that black
allowed their eyes :   spangles in the cat's, air in the moth's
    eye shine,
mosaic of the fly, ruby-eyed beetle, the eyes that never weep,
the horned toad sitting and its tear of blood,
fighters and prisoners in the forest, people
aware in this almost total dark, with the difference,
the one broad fact of light.

Eyes on the road at night, sides of a road like rhyme;
the floor of the illumined shadow sea

and shallows with their assembling flash and show
of sight, root, holdfast, eyes of the brittle stars.
And your eyes in the shadowy red room,
scent of the forest entering, various time
calling and the light of wood along the ceiling
and over us birds calling and their circuit eyes.
And in our bodies the eyes of the dead and the living
giving us gifts at hand, the glitter of all their eyes.

THEN I SAW WHAT THE CALLING WAS

All the voices of the wood called "Muriel!"
but it was soon solved;   it was nothing, it was not for me.
The words were a little like Mortal and More and Endure
and a word like Real, a sound like Health or Hell.
Then I saw what the calling was   :   it was the road I traveled,
    the clear
time and these colors of orchards, gold behind gold and the full
shadow behind each tree and behind each slope.   Not to me
the calling, but to anyone, and at last I saw   :   where
the road lay through sunlight and many voices and the marvel
orchards, not for me, not for me, not for me.
I came into my clear being;   uncalled, alive, and sure.
Nothing was speaking to me, but I offered and all was well.

And then I arrived at the powerful green hill.

THIS PLACE IN THE WAYS

Having come to this place
I set out once again
on the dark and marvelous way
from where I began:
belief in the love of the world,
woman, spirit, and man.

Having failed in all things
I enter a new age
seeing the old ways as toys,
the houses of a stage
painted and long forgot;
and I find love and rage.

Rage for the world as it is
but for what it may be
more love now than last year
and always less self-pity
since I know in a clearer light
the strength of the mystery.

And at this place in the ways
I wait for song.
My poem-hand still, on the paper,
all night long.
Poems in throat and hand, asleep,
and my storm beating strong!

A CERTAIN MUSIC

Never to hear, I know in myself complete
that naked integrated music;   now
it has become me, now it is nerve, song, gut,
and my gross hand writes only through Mozart;   see
even in withholding what you have brought to me.

Renewed, foolish, reconciled to myself, I walk
this winter-country, I fly over its still-flock'd clouds,
always in my isolated flesh I take
that theme's light certainty of absolute purpose
to make quick spirit when spirit most might break.

Naked you walked through my body and I turned
to you with this far music you now withhold.
O my destroyed hope!   Though I never again
hear developing heaven, the growing grave-bearing earth,
my poem, my promise, my love, my sleep after love;
my hours, listening, along that music move,
and have been saved and hardly know the cold.

THE CHILDREN'S ORCHARD

In the full sun.   In the fruitfall season.
Against my knees the earth and the bucket, and the soft blue prunes
echoing red   echoing purple   echoing in the silver bucket
sun, and over the flames of earth the sun flies down.

Over my head the little trees tremble alive in their black branches
and bare-ribbed boys golden and shouting stoop here to gather the blue,

the wild-red, the dark.   Colors of ripeness in the fruitfall season.
I will remember the last light on the lowest branch.

Will see these trees as they were in spring, wild black rooted in light,
root-deep in noon, the piercing yellow noon of mustard-blossom.
Sun breathing on us the scent of heat, richness of air where my hands know
blue, full summer, strong sun.   I tell you harvest.

FOGHORN IN HORROR

I know that behind these walls is the city, over these rooftops is the sun.
But I see black clothes only and white clothes with the fog running in
and all their shadows.
Every minute the sound of the harbor
intruding on horror with a bellow of horror:
blu-a!   blu-aa!   Ao. . . .

I try to write to you, but here too I meet failure.
It has a face like mine.
Silence and in me and over the water
only the bellowing,
Niobe howling for her life and her children.
Did you think this sorrow of women was a graceful thing?
Horrible Niobe down on her knees:
Blu-a!   Blu-aa!   Ao. . . .

Thirty years, and my full strength, and all I touch has failed.
I sit and see
the black clothes on the line are beautiful, the sky drifting away.
The white clothes of the fog beyond me, beautiful, and the shadows.
Blu-aa!   Blu-aa!   AO.

NINE POEMS
(for the unborn child)

5

Eating sleep, eating sunlight, eating meat,
Lying in the sun to stare
At deliverance, the rapid cloud,
Gull-wing opposing sun-bright wind,
I see the born who dare
Walk on green, walk against blue,
Move in the nightlong flare
Of love on darkness, traveling
Among the rings of light to simple light,
From nowhere to nowhere.
And in my body feel the seasons grow.
Who is it in the dim room?   Who is there?

THE LIFE OF POETRY

Of all the works of Rukeyser that have slipped out of print, perhaps the greatest loss to us has been The Life of Poetry *(1949).*

The subject is, ostensibly, the role of poetry in our lives. But it is Rukeyser's goal to show us that our relationship to poetry is an index of our deepest fears and greatest possibilities as a culture.

Forty years before the debates about ethnocentrism in our classrooms, Rukeyser draws us to the dream songs of Native Americans, the blues of W. C. Handy, Ma Rainey, and Jelly Roll Morton. A quarter-century before French feminist theorists are deconstructing the binary oppositions that grip Western culture, and questioning the authority of the single, white male "universal" voice, Rukeyser speaks for the multiplicity of experience, and reminds us that "there is not meaning, but meanings; not liberty, but liberties."

Even if The Life of Poetry *had ended with the first section, "The Resistances," Rukeyser would have already produced a work of lasting merit. Taking on all the objections to poetry that our culture throws at us—I don't have the time, it isn't relevant to my life, it's boring, it doesn't make sense, it's intentionally obscure, it's just for women and "sissies"—Rukeyser examines each in turn. No one who reads her analysis of these resistances can think of poetry in quite the same way again.*

But she goes on. Again, the subject is ostensibly poetry. Herman Melville is here. But so is Margeret Mead. Emily Dickinson is here. But so is Charles Darwin. Soon, we're hearing about Albert Einstein and Sergei Eisenstein, Woodrow Wilson and Walt Whitman, Sigmund Freud and Ernest Fenollosa. Berenice Abbott, Li Chu, Alfred Hitchcock, John Brown, Gene Kelly, Karen Horney, Clerk Maxwell, Beethoven, Buddha, and Bessie Smith—all are part of her story. So are movies and music, dance and drama. War and peace are here. Birth and death are here. The streets of New York City and the caves at Ajanta are here. The panorama demands new ways of seeing.

The triumph of The Life of Poetry *is not that Rukeyser succeeds in bringing together all these seemingly disparate elements. As she said in an interview in 1976, "It isn't that one brings life together—it's that one will not allow it to be torn apart."*

Here, in excerpts, is a glimpse of a lost treasure. May it be reprinted in its entirety very soon.

.   .   .   .   .

INTRODUCTION

In time of crisis, we summon up our strength.

Then, if we are lucky, we are able to call every resource, every forgotten image that can leap to our quickening, every memory that can make us know our power. And this luck is more than it seems to be: it depends on the long preparation of the self to be used.

In time of the crises of the spirit, we are aware of all our need, our need for each other and our need for our selves. We call up, with all the strength of summoning we have, our fullness. And then we turn; for it is a turning that we have prepared; and act. The time of the turning may be very long. It may hardly exist.

I think now of a boat on which I sailed away from the beginning of a war. It was night-time, and over the deep fertile sea of night the voices of people talking quietly; some lights of the seacoast, faraway; some stars.

This was the first moment of stillness in days of fighting. We had seen the primitive beginnings of the open warfare of this period: men running through the silvery groves, the sniper whose gun would speak, as the bullet broke the wall beside you; a child staring upward at a single plane. More would come; in the city, the cars burned and blood streamed over the walls of houses and the horse shrieked; armies formed and marched out; the gypsies, the priests, in their purity and violence fought. Word from abroad was coming in as they asked us to meet in the summer leafy Square, and told us that they knew. They had seen how, as foreigners, we were deprived; how we were kept from, and wanted, above all things one: our responsibility.

This was a stroke of insight: it was true. "Now you have your responsibility," the voice said, deep, prophetic, direct, "go home: tell your peoples what you have seen."

We had seen a beginning. Much more would come.

I remember how the boys climbed into those trucks, with their ill-matched rifles, as the radio played Beethoven and Bing Crosby and the dances of the country. The machine-guns clattered like a loud enormous palm-tree, and a baby cried to its mother to come. On the floor of the train were strewn the foreign papers with their pictures printed dark: the possessed man, Nijinsky, giving his first interview from the sanatorium in all those years—the pictures of him, standing as he stood against the great black cross he years before had unrolled on the floor, dancing the insane dance, War and Death.

No darker than this night.

Yes, darker. For the night was living, all of us alive, the living breeze a flaw of coolness over the distant warmth of vineyards, over this central sea. The refugees on the boat were talking. There were people from many countries, thrown abruptly together in time of crisis, and speaking, somehow, the opinions which, later, their countries held.

I did not know this then. But we spoke as if we were shadows on that deck, shadows cast backward by some future fire of explosion.

We were on a small ship, five times past our capacity in refugees, sailing for the first port at peace. On the deck that night, people talked quietly about what they had just seen and what it might mean to the world. The acute scenes were still on our eyes, immediate and clear in their passion; and there were moments, too, in which we were outsiders and could draw away, as if we were in a plane and rose far, to a high focus above that coast, those cities and this sea, with sight and feelings sharper than before. Everything we had heard, some of all we loved and feared, had begun to be acted out. Our realization was fresh and young, we had seen the parts of our lives in a new arrangement. There were long pauses between those broken images of life, spoken in language after language.

Suddenly, throwing his question into talk not at all leading up to it—not seeming to—

a man—a printer, several times a refugee— asked, "And poetry—among all this—where is there a place for poetry?"

Then I began to say what I believe.

PART ONE
THE RESISTANCES

CHAPTER 1

In this moment when we face horizons and conflicts wider than ever before, we want our resources, the ways of strength. We look again to the human wish, its faiths, the means by which the imagination leads us to surpass ourselves.

If there is a feeling that something has been lost, it may be because much has not yet been used, much is still to be found and begun.

Everywhere we are told that our human resources are all *to be used*, that our civilization itself means the uses of everything it has—the inventions, the histories, every scrap of fact. But there is one *kind* of knowledge—infinitely precious, time-resistant more than monuments, here to be passed between the generations in any way it may be: never to be used. And that is poetry.

It seems to me that we cut ourselves off, that we impoverish ourselves, just here. I think that we are ruling out one source of power, one that is precisely what we need. Now, when it is hard to hold for a moment the giant clusters of event and meaning that every day appear, it is time to remember this other kind of knowledge and love, which has forever been a way of reaching complexes of emotion and relationship, the attitude that is like the attitude of science and the other arts today, but with significant and beautiful distinctness from these—the attitude that perhaps might equip our imaginations to deal with our lives—the attitude of poetry.

What help is there here?

Poetry is, above all, an approach to the truth of feeling, and what is the use of truth?

How do we use feeling?

How do we use truth?

*   *   *

Do you remember the poems of your early childhood—the far rhymes and games of the beginning to which you called the rhythms, the little songs to which you woke and went to sleep?

Yes, we remember them.

But since childhood, to many of us poetry has become a matter of distaste. The speaking of poetry is one thing: one of the qualifications listed for an announcer on a great network, among "good voice" and "correct pronunciation," is the "ability to read and interpret poetry." The other side is told conclusively in a letter sent ninety years ago by the wife of the author of *Moby-Dick*. Mrs. Melville said to her mother—"Herman has taken to writing poetry. You need not tell anyone, for you know how such things get around."

What is the nature of this distaste?

If you ask your friends about it, you will find that there are a few answers, repeated by everyone. One is that the friend has not the *time* for poetry. This is a curious choice, since poetry, of all the arts that live in time—music, theatre, film, writing—is the briefest, the most compact. Or your friends may speak of their boredom with poetry. If you hear this, ask further. You will find that "boredom" is a masking answer, concealing different meanings. One person will confess that he has been frightened off forever by the dry dissection of lines in school, and that now he thinks with disappointment of a poem as simply a set of constructions. He expects much more. One will say that he returned from the scenes of war to a highschool classroom reading

"Bobolink, bobolink / Spink, spank, spink." A first-rate scientist will search for the formal framework of the older poetry in despair, and finally stop. One will confess that, try as he will, he cannot understand poetry, and more particularly, modern writing. It is intellectual, confused, unmusical. One will say it is willfully obscure. One that it is inapplicable to the situation in which he finds himself. And almost any man will say that it is effeminate: it is true that poetry as an art is sexually suspect.

In all of these answers, we meet a slipping-away which is the clue to the responses, and which is strong enough to be called more than direct resistance.

This resistance has the quality of fear, it expresses the fear of poetry.

I have found in working with people and with poems, that this fear presents the symptoms of a psychic problem. A poem does invite, it does require. What does it invite? A poem invites you to feel. More than that: it invites you to respond. And better than that: a poem invites a total response.

This response is total, but it is reached through the emotions. A fine poem will seize your imagination intellectually—that is, when you reach it, you will reach it intellectually too—but the way is through emotion, through what we call feeling.

The angry things that have been said about our poetry have also been said about our time. They are both "confused," "chaotic," "violent," "obscure."

There is a clue here, and it is more than a reflection. It is not that an art "reflects," as the schoolbooks say, an age. But in the relationship may be a possible answer, a possible direction.

The illumination will lie in the relationship itself.

One way to look at scientific material, or the data of human life, is fact by fact, deriving the connections.

Another way, more fruitful I believe, is to look at the relationships themselves, learning the facts as they feed or destroy each other. When we see that, we will see whether they tend toward an equilibrium, or strain spent on war away, or be poised at the rare moment of balance.

I think of the work of Willard Gibbs in science.

Or of Karen Horney in psychoanalysis, here: defining action in terms of relationship, so that the individual is seen not only as an individual, but as a person moving toward other persons, or a person moving away from other persons, or a person moving against other persons.

And I think of a scene at the Rockefeller Institute I saw: the rabbit, its great thrust and kick of muscular pride, as it was carried under the fluorescent lights, where against the colored unbroken skin glowed the induced cancers, fluorescing violet. A research doctor had come up from Johns Hopkins to talk to a biophysicist working in ways resembling his own. And in the basement lab, with its tubes, its beakers, its electrophoresis setup, he told how the work he was doing in cancer had changed in its nature, in its meaning. His colleagues and himself were no longer looking at cancer as a fact, an isolated fact.

They were taking another approach: they were dealing with cancer and the body on which it fed as one thing—an equilibrium which had been set up, in which the cancer fed on the host. One could not exist in this state without the other in that state. It was the relationship which was the illness. And he felt that these terms led to the right questions.

When we talk about relationships in art, we can see at once how all kinds of activity have taken this direction. The work of Freud and Picasso and Einstein are familiar to us as the masterwork in relative values, in the search for individual maturity, in visual imagination, in physical science; Joyce we recognize as working in the relationships of language, Marx in social relationship from which the fact could be derived—and these are the key-names alone, in a few fields.

In our own time, we have become used to an idea of history in which process and relationship are stressed. The science of ecology is only one example of an elaboration of the idea, so that the life of land may be seen in terms of its tides of growth, the feeding of one group on another, the equilibrium reached, broken, and the drive toward another balance and renewal.

We think of the weather now as a dance of airs, predictable in relationship, with its parades of clouds, the appetites of pressure areas, and aftermath of foreseen storms.

But in the areas dealing with emotion and belief, there is hesitation. The terms have not been invented; and although that does not impede expressive writing—a poem, a novel, or a play *act emotions out* in terms of words, they do not describe—the lack does impede analytical work. We have no terms, for example, for "emotional meaning," or "emotional information." We have not even the English for Claude Bernard's "milieu intérieur," that internal condition of a body, the *in*vironment where live the inner relationships.

That obstacle is nothing.

We are poets; we can make the words.

The emotional obstacle is the real one.

For the question is asked in a thousand ways each day: Is poetry alive? Is there a place for poetry? What is that place?

In our schools, we are told that our education is pragmatic, that the body of knowledge is divided into various "subjects," that all of these subjects on which we pour our youth are valuable and useful to us in later life. We are told that our civilization depends on further and new uses for everything it has, the development and exploitation of these. We may go ahead and specialize in any of these usable fields.

Except for one.

There is one *kind* of knowledge that will be given us all through school and high school which we are told is precious, it defies time, it strikes deep into memory, it must go on being taught. No matter what cities fall, what languages are mis-heard and "corrupted" and reborn. This is here, to be passed on. But not to be used. Among all this pragmatic training, never to come into the real and active life.

That is what we learn about poetry.

I remember a psychologist with whom I talked in New Haven. That is a good town to produce an image of the split life: it is a split town, part fierce industrial city, part college, very little reconciled—and in the center of the town, on the Green, is a symbol which is as good as any for this meaning. On the New Haven Green, itself a hub of tradition, there is a church which is old, respected, well-proportioned and serene. Down to its cornerstones: but these stones, these stones are set up as monuments to two of the English regicides who escaped to America after the Restoration. Two of the men who killed King Charles. A church founded on the stones of king-killers, men who broke the most extreme of tabus! But that is the gesture, the violent axiom-breaking gesture of the imagination that takes its side, chooses its tradition and sets to work.

In such a town, I spoke to a psychologist, a man who has made his work and his theme the study of fear, and the talk went well enough until poetry was mentioned. Then, with extreme violence, a violence out of any keeping with what had gone before, the psychologist began to raise his voice and cut the air with his hand flat. He said, his voice shaking, that he had cut poetry out of his life, that that was something he had not time for, that was something out of his concern.

I have thought of him often.

His attitude is the attitude of the schools. It is widespread now; but the symbol of the church is, I think, closer to our people. I choose it and I speak for it.

*   *   *

The fear that cuts off poetry is profound: it plunges us deep, far back to the edge of childhood. Beyond that it does not go.

Little children do not have this fear, they trust their emotions. But on the threshold of adolescence the walls are built.

124

Against the assaults of puberty, and in those silvery delicate seasons when all feeling casts about for confirmation. Then, for the first time, you wonder "What should I be feeling?" instead of the true "What do you feel?" "What do I feel?" Now the easily talented and the easily skillful are loved in classrooms and the field.

It takes a great pressure behind an adolescent wish to make it persist through all the change of growth.

The first stoppage of expression becomes final here, a malignant process may now begin. If you visit these rooms, you will see it happen, the wonder dried out of a passage read and reread aloud for emphasis; the stories undercut by parsings and explanations, often for language alone, the shell of language, seldom for meaning.

Grammar and criticism need not destroy; but they will, if words are raised above language, if criticism is projected by the critic's lack, if a dry perfectionism is substituted for the creative life.

You will remember the times: were you the highschool junior in the streetcar who shook his head—No—when you were asked, half in contempt, half in the hope of another answer—"Do you read poetry?"

In adults, you know those who put poetry far behind them; not naturally, like children outgrowing toys who forget them (or beat them to pieces), but with a painful shocked awareness that here was something outside their reach. It would be all right, because society likes that attitude; however, neurotically, they call attention to it still. More than one editor, introducing his anthology, will confess that poetry is something he "knows nothing about"; there are reviewers who will go glibly on about any kind of novel or first biography, but who write uneasily, in language as clumsy as the first page of a diary, whenever they face a book of poems.

If we have a resource that we are not using . . .

If this were a crop, about which these things were said, there would be a research project.

If it were a metal, the Un-American Activities Committee, and several other committees, would concern themselves. Our scientists would claim their right of experiment and inquiry.

There are many causes for waste in our life. We are very sure of ourselves in some powers and wildly insecure in others: the imbalance leads to random action, waste, hostilities out of reason. Margaret Mead describes us as a "third-generation" society. She does not mean, of course, that we are all the grandchildren of pioneers and immigrants; but she does mean that our parents shared the attitudes of the children of foreigners, who because of their strange families, with their old-country ways, their effusive gestures, the flavor of their speech, leaned over backward to rule out any foreignness, any color at all.

We suffer from that background, with its hunger for uniformity, the shared norm of ambition and habit and living standard. The repressive codes are everywhere. Our movies are censored before they are plotted; our radio comedy is forbidden its list of themes; have you noticed how our best-selling books are written in reaction to the dominating woman?

This code strikes deep at our emotional life.

Its action means that our emotions are supposed to be uniform. Since that is impossible, our weaknesses send us to meet any divergence from the expected with dread or conflict.

This leads on the one hand to the immense incidence of "mental" disease which we find in America now; and, on the other, I believe we may say that it leads to a fear of poetry.

Our education is one of specialization. We become experts in some narrow "field." That expertness allows us to deal with the limited problems presented to us; it allows us to face emotional reality, symbolic reality, very little. That can be seen very clearly in our movies, which now will use clever methods to imitate reality—in one battle film, the cameraman shook his camera at the moment of explosion, so that an entire scene would shake—Hollywood movies have absorbed documentary methods, and have then stopped just short of reality, or of creating an arrangement by which a movie can give us a sense of reality. A first-rate scientist, or a fine prose writer, is able to say "How can I know a good poem? I can tell an honest piece of work in my own field from a phony piece of work, but how can I tell a fine poem from a phony poem?" And what has to be said to such a question is that these are people who cannot trust their emotional reactions, their total reactions.

They are people who are insecure enough not to trust themselves when images are related to images and emotions to emotions.

One characteristic of modern poetry is that arrangement of parts which strikes many people as being violent or obscure. It is a method which is familiar enough on the screen; when you see the picture of a night-club, and then see the heroine's face thrown back as she sings, you make the unity without any effort, without even being conscious of your process. * * *

Much of modern poetry moves in terms of quick, rhythmic juxtapositions. Our contemporary journalism still uses even more linkage. Each method prepares you for the climaxes of the poem. If you can be flexible of mind, remembering movies you have liked, and being aware of their richness and suspense and the dense texture of their realities, you are approaching what may have seemed to you the most broken of modern poetry.

*   *   *

During the war, we felt the silence in the policy of the governments of English-speaking countries. That policy was to win the war first, and work out the meanings afterward. The result was, of course, that the meanings were lost. You cannot put these things off.

One of the invitations of poetry is to come to the emotional meanings at every moment. That is one reason for the high concentration of music, in poetry.

The putting-off of meaning has already been reflected in the fashionable writing of the last years. Our most popular novels and poems have been works of easy mysticism or easy wit, with very little between. One entire range is represented, for us, in the literature of aversion. There has been much silence.

The silence of fear. Of the impoverished imagination, which avoids, and makes a twittering, and is still.

Communication comes, to make this place fertile, to make it possible to meet the world with all the resources we have, the fund of faith, the generous instruments of imagination and knowledge.

Poetry may be seen as one sum of such equipment, as an image of the kind of fullness that can best meet the evening, the hostile imagination—which restricts, denies, and proclaims death—and the inner clouds which mask our fears.

Now we turn to memory, we search all the days we had forgotten for a tradition that can support our arms in such a moment. If we are free people, we are also in a sense free to choose our past, at every moment to choose the tradition we will bring to the future. We invoke a rigorous positive, that will enable us to imagine our choices, and to make them.

*   *   *

CHAPTER 3

It used to be agreed that painting was a visual, music an auditory art. R. G. Collingwood, in his brilliant *The Principles of Art,* goes on to tell how Cézanne came then, and began to paint like a blind man. His rooms are full of volumes: these tables, the people in these chairs are bulks which have been felt with the hands. These trees are not what trees look like, they are what trees feel like. And Mont Saint-Victoire is over one's head, rearing in voluntary power like Wordsworth's mountain.

Impossible it was to reach poetry according to the old aesthetic. A break was made between spoken poetry and written poetry. The function of the poet—whether he was heard, read, or for that matter, forgotten—entered the argument and complicated its error. For the fact is that painting is not a visual art. A painting is made by the hands of the painter, setting up the imaginative experience taken through his eyes. Music is written by the hand of the composer, giving us the imaginative experience through the ears. Poetry is made by the hand of the poet, and if we read the poem, we take the imaginative experience through the eyes with a *shadow* of sound; if we hear it, we take it through the ears with a *shadow* of sight.

Limits may be set on this by work with the illiterate, the blind and the deaf, who can help us to know the ways of sense.

But the reality of all the arts is that of the imagination.

The fear of poetry is an indication that we are cut off from our own reality.

*　　*　　*

The even pitch of life and culture is not our scene. The moment of great height, of infinite depth, is here. There is a famous passage in the works of the great imaginative scientist, Clerk Maxwell, in which he draws attention to the implications of what are called in mathematics "singular points." A stone poised on another stone, a ball rolling in perfect motion on a perfect wedge, a supersaturated solution, are examples, and the equations for their systems break down at these extraordinary moments in their history. Maxwell believed that the science of the future would be deeply concerned with these crises in "systems of high rank." We may be said to be living in a system which has reached such a point.

Unless you share such conception, you will be likely to see what is happening as "confusion"; to say with one that culture is dying in a shift of powers, or with another that we have lost the way and must live as well as we can.

The way is before us, and culture is the future as well as the past.

*　　*　　*

The poetic image is not a static thing. It lives in time, as does the poem. Unless it is the first image of the poem, it has already been prepared for by other images; and it prepares us for further images and rhythms to come. Even if it is the first image of the poem, the establishment of the rhythm prepares us—musically—for the music of the image. And if its first word begins the poem, it has the role of putting into motion all the course of images and music of the entire work, with nothing to refer to, except perhaps a title.

If we look at a few images that open their poems, these descriptions will at once be plain:

Give me my scallop-shell of quiet,

sets the song-rhythm, the scene of a palmer's journey, and the tone of spiritual necessity, which Raleigh's *His Pilgrimage* carries through the lyric.

They flee from me that sometime did me seek,
With naked foot stalking within my chamber:

has impelled the poem, in two lines, deep into its long-cadenced music and all the night-time, bitter and regretful change.

A modern opening, that of Crane's *The Broken Tower,* may be analyzed further. The first image dispatches, not only the "me" of the poem, but the poem itself:

The bell-rope that gathers God at dawn
Dispatches me as though I dropped down the knell
Of a spent day—

and the ringing irregular sway of the poem, its "steps from hell," the hiving of the stars and the broken world, follow until the tower becomes flesh and word; until the lake and tower of the ending take on their full meaning after many reverberations, sound after sound and image after image hunting back— not only to the beginning, but to each successive image and each successive sequence of sound.

The images of a poem have so curious a motion. This is certainly more apparent in a short poem—one of the length, say, of *The Broken Tower,* which can be held easily by the memory or the page. (It occupies two pages as I have it in print before me; to scan the full effect, I suggest you copy it out so that you can have it all on a sheet.) The relationships in sound are dense in the first stanza: "The bell-rope" evoking the syllables in "dispatches," "dropped down the knell," "spent day," "pit to crucifix," "feet chill on steps from hell." "Gathers" turns us back to "rope" in the novelty of its idea of the bell-rope gathering God; "dawn" and "spent day" set up a ripple of context, and "dispatches" and "dropped down" tie both idea and music more tightly to the meaning.

One cannot say, of course, tie both idea and music more tightly to the meaning. The idea, the music, and the meaning are identified. Nothing here is "tied." The bonds are those of imaginative and musical relationship. I use the word "bonds," and think of the disappointment of Orpheus before the sibyl, to whom he went in mourning, for an oracle. The sibyl said only

The Furies are the bonds of men

giving to Orpheus an unsuspected presage of his death, and speaking of the ties that at once chain and connect human beings.

The bonds of poetry, that make for form and development, are those of growth within the poem. And if the poem grows by means of its images, what do these images resemble and reflect in our lives?

It seems to me that the gestures we may compare are the images of history, and those symbols which carry through many levels of training and background to reach us imaginatively. Certain lives do that, so that the whole life becomes an image reaching backward and forward in history, illuminating all time. The life of Jesus; the life of Buddha; the life of Lincoln, or Gandhi, or Saint Francis—these give us the intensity that should be felt in a lifetime of concentration, a lifetime which seems to risk the immortal meanings every day, pure in knowledge that the only way to realize them is to risk them. Think, too, of Beethoven's life, of the Curies and Father Damien; or of that living person whose daily meanings carry most to you. These lives, in their search and purpose, offer their form, offer their truths. They reach us as hope.

At the "singular points" in history—to return to Clerk Maxwell's phrase—certain gestures provide expression. Heroes are made. That is, a man or woman allows many people to feel the moment of crisis, and to understand that it is common to all imaginations ready to receive its meaning.

In this country, one man who cut through to the imagination of all was John Brown, that meteor, whose blood was love and rage, in fury until the love was burned away. That crazy murderous old man, he must be called by Lincoln, and he must be hanged, condemned in agony. But that precipitating stroke, like the archaic bloody violence of the Greek plays, spoke to many lives.

In Belgium, during the last war, the Jews were required by edict to wear the yellow Star of David which would mark them and set them apart. On the first day of the edict's validity, nobody appeared in the street without the yellow badge. In a great simple act of love and identification, the Belgian people had cancelled the power of a ruling that, without the acceptance of the majority, could not force any group apart from the rest of the people.

And in fascist Germany, one first-rate poet stayed. He was rumored by the exiles to be one thing and another. He was a man of good will, a doctor and a poet, who had written, all his life, against war and against the masks of evil, saying, "God give us each his sin to awaken him!" Now he was writing the poems of the newborn, and myths of many returnings, of the pure coming home, stronger, more beautiful than before, after destruction. He was reading publicly, to the Hitler Youth; and a storm of hatred arose from his old friends. He did accept, it was true, the invitations that others refused in pride. He did go and read, to packed meetings; and what he said in his defense was "I cannot withhold my gentle voice." He was against them, and they wanted him. They seemed to want what he had to say. The offering of his parables, his gentleness that allowed himself to give these words of renewal and peace to whomever asked them of him—they are part of a gesture which, I believe, reaches softly and graciously to the imagination.

These gestures speak to many lives. They give hope and impetus to many kinds of people.

They are infinitely multiplied. You will know those who risked themselves and died in the Resistance movements of many lands; little children, who in a far-reaching moment of consciousness, made their gifts; miners, anonymous women, those suffering and poor, and the privileged of all functions in life, those gifted with insight so that they understand the beauty of unconditional love, and live and make their gifts. The gestures of the individuals are not history; but they are the images of history.

*   *   *

A poem is not its images any more than a symphony is its themes.

A poem is not its words any more than a symphony is its notes.

The image, the word, the note—those are methods by which the imaginative experience is presented and received.

"The image," says C. Day Lewis in *The Poetic Image,* "is a method of asserting or reasserting spiritual control over the material." And he makes a very suggestive definition of what the critics have called "pure poetry" as "poetry whose meaning is deliberately concentrated within its images."

But behind these notions of control lies, every time, belief.

Faith is found here, not in a destiny raiding and parcelling out knowledge and the earth, but in a people who, person by person, believes itself. Do you accept your own gestures and symbols? Do you believe what you yourself say? When you act, do you believe what you are doing?

*   *   *

Facing and communicating, that will be our life, in the world and in poetry. Are we to teach this? All we can show to people is themselves; show them what passion they possess, and we will all have come to the poetry. This is the knowledge of communication, and it is the fear of it which has cut us down.

Our lives may rest on this; and our lives are our images.

CHAPTER 4

If our imaginative response to life were complete, if we were fully conscious of emotion, if we apprehended surely the relations that make us know the truth and the relations that make us know the beautiful, we would be—what? The heroes of our myths, acting perfectly among these faculties, loving appropriately and living with appropriate risk, spring up at the question. We invented them to let us approach that life. But it is our own lives of which they remind us. They offer us a hope and a perspective, not of the past in which they were made—not that alone—but of the future. For if we lived in full response to the earth, to each other, and to ourselves, we would not breathe a supernatural climate; we would be more human.

The tendency of art and religion, and the tendency of poetic meaning, is toward the most human.

*   *   *

How can a group of many people, bound in a balance of statehood, with its fundamental hope a tendency toward democracy, realize its full humanity? Has any group—any culture—ever done this?

We think of the Greek society, its lifetime, its limitations, and its effects, of the many contributive societies, known and little known, whose gifts and interpenetrations and conflicts reach our custom. What background is there for a criterion of imaginative maturity, in our society?

Our education molds us toward conduct, the outward and ethical are given lip-service, the outward and predatory are glorified by business society, and the young are brought up in conduct leading toward aggression surrounded by strict tabus. We know from the movies, the radio, and from every ad in the morning paper, what behavior is expected. We know what approvals are required from us; every day that knowledge is borne in on a flood of words.

Few enough among us who consider our society have spoken openly of the power to live. In his most plain and passionate book, John Collier writes:

> If the primitive group molded its members toward conduct alone (which is tacitly assumed by most anthropologists as well as most laymen), then the group's significance to modern life would not be great. But if there is anything written clear across the almost infinite diversity of primitive society, it is that the group molds its members toward emotion, toward the experience of crises of realization and of conscience. . . . For the tribe to survive, even for the world to survive, requires intensity—intensity within form—in man. Hence, to a degree hardly imaginable in our modern society and state, the ultimate concentration of the primitive group is upon education—upon personality development. Every experience is used to that end, every specialized skill and expression is bent to that end. There results an integration of body-mind and of individual-group which is not automatic, not at the level of conformity and habit, but spontaneous, essentially spiritual, and at the level of freedom.

*   *   *

What is the fear of poetry? To a great extent it is a fear produced by a mask, by the protective structure society builds around each conflict. The conflict, here, is a neurotic one, a false conflict based on a supposed antithesis of fact and relationship, of inner and outer effectiveness; it is a conflict upheld by the great part of organized society. The fear is a fear of disclosure, but, in this instance, of disclosure to oneself of areas within the individual, areas with which he is not trained to deal, and which will only bring him into hostile relationships with his complacent neighbor, whose approval he wants.

At this point he denies one of his most important functions and resources. What must follow?

"Through the eclipse of large areas of the self," says Karen Horney in *Our Inner Conflicts*, "by repression and inhibition as well as by idealization and externalization, the individual loses sight of himself; he feels, if he does not actually become, like a shadow without weight and substance."

The individual is likely to think that he has actually become a richer personality during this amputation—it is really closer to an attrition of a major attribute. You have seen American men pride themselves on their aversion to art in general, feeling that this aversion gives them greater solidity, in fact greater reality. It is likely that the entire process is the attempt of a creature, stunted in one member, to become more whole by casting off the member. But this attribute, the poetic imagination, does not resemble the eye, which can be put out for its offense, so much as it resembles the blood, which must be strengthened by feeding.

*   *   *

The one difference between the artist and the audience is that the artist has performed upon his experience that work of acknowledging, shaping, and offering which is the creative process. The audience, in receiving the work of art, acknowledges not only its form, but their own experience and the experience of the artist.

Both artist and audience create, and both do work on themselves in creating.

The audience, in fact, does work only on itself in creating; the artist makes himself and his picture, himself and his poem. The artwork is set to one side with a word, then, as we look at the common ground, the consciousness and imagination of artist and audience.

It may be said here in objection that the corruption of consciousness effects an impoverishment upon the artwork, and that there is good art and bad art. Of course there is an effect, a direct effect, for better or for worse. But I cannot acknowledge the way of thought that has given us so many double definitions of "good art" and "bad art."

A work of art is one through which the consciousness of the artist is able to give its emotions to anyone who is prepared to receive them. There is no such thing as bad art.

There is art and non-art; they are two universes (in the algebraic term) which are exclusive. We are considering art, its nature and the nature of its power for good; and we are fortunate in not having to be concerned with non-art.

It seems to me that to call an achieved work "good art" and an unachieved work "bad art" is like calling one color "good red" and another "bad red" when the second one is green.

And what about rewriting, you may ask, or correcting the line of a drawing? What about the work of the creative editor or critic? Improvement is sometimes conceivable, I would answer. It is possible to change a work of art in degree. But I doubt that it is possible to revise "bad art" into "good art" (and I renounce the terms). That would require not a change of degree but of kind, and it could not be done unless you changed the phase of the work, by as radical a process as changes water to steam: you would be making a new work.

The charge of obscurity, however, must be looked at very closely. It is one of the major charges brought against contemporary poetry, and it must always be taken as a declaration by the audience, which says "I find this poem obscure," and which tells us, at first, very much about the audience and nothing about the poem. It should rank with the complaint, "I do not understand this poem," as a statement descriptive only of the one who makes it. *Nothing has yet been said about the poem,* in either charge. If you are going to follow up this challenge, you must then inquire into the consciousness of the challenger. Is the challenger prepared to receive the poem? Or is this merely another way of disowning imaginative experience?

*   *   *

Writing is only another way of giving—a courtesy, if you will, and a form of love.

But does one write in order to give?

One writes in order to feel: that is the fundamental mover.

The more clearly one writes, the more clearly will both the writer and the reader feel. But there must be imaginative truth—truth which is the health and strength and richness of imagination before poet or reader can approach the poem.

If that truth exists, and we are not locked away in defenses and denials, we move toward it, and it finds us.

Is there a risk of intensity, in this culture? Then, if we take that risk, the psychiatrists might declare we were adjusted to reality.

In another language, the word is not "adjusted," which implies a static condition to be adjusted to; the word is "full-valued," which accepts a world of process, a dynamic universe of time and growth relations.

The full-valued human being is capable of the total imaginative response. There is no threat to the self; the truth of the poem is taken

PART TWO
BACKGROUNDS AND SOURCES

CHAPTER 5

American poetry has been part of a culture in conflict.

It is not the variety of our life, for that is easy to draw abundance from; I speak of the tearing that exists everywhere in Western culture. We are a people tending toward democracy at the level of hope; on another level, the economy of the nation, the empire of business within the republic, both include in their basic premise the concept of perpetual warfare. It is the history of the idea of war that is beneath our other histories. There we acknowledge the dynamic, and there many of our people see relationships tending toward equilibrium. In our periods of armistice, you hear everywhere, among the big-businessmen, the café owners, the untrained workmen, the unemployed, talk of another war—a next equilibrium toward which some efforts course, toward which all their inertia flows. This equilibrium is death. But around and under and above it is another reality; like desert-water kept from the surface and the seed, like the old desert-answer needing its channels, the blessing of much work before it arrives to act and make flower. This history is the history of possibility. Not vaguer than the other principle, it leads to definite things; but since these are future things, they cannot be described under the present daylight, the present poems are not their songs but will be their old ballads, anonymous, and their traditional tunes. All we can do is believe in the seed, living in that belief.

Indications are here.

*   *   *

Outrage and possibility are in all the poems we know, the long line from the first magic and the rituals of the heart and hero. Indeed, our poets are in their dread and music heroes of possibility as Shelley was, or of outrage as Rimbaud was, or of the process and relationship between the two—transformed by Dante into the soul's journey, and by Shakespeare annealed into every speech almost, almost into every breath.

In the early, Colonial poetry, not much is acknowledged of the conflicts spreading to the general scene. Freneau's "restless Indian queen" is queen of "a ruder race"—Edward Taylor makes the bread of life cry "Eat, eat me, soul, and thou shalt never die," with no particularization of individual consciousness; Anne Bradstreet takes up the endless dialogue of Western thought between the flesh and the spirit—the dialogue of separation which begets separation; Bryant glides over all, water-strider of that verse. Only with Emerson do we come to the "hope beyond hope," to Surface and Dream; and to the statement of the half-gods and the gods. Perhaps these conflicts are the old same war— I believe so—and truth or reality, process or moment, gods or half-gods, are the terms for immortal necessities, which are not checks and balances, but phases, if you will, of essence—all to be fought for, realized, and sung.

Surely they have their poets in our background. I do not think of Poe here, although in his disowning, in his selective fantasy, he spoke for something native to all of us—some appetite for life and permanence that could be threatened, partly by the conflict of the age, the machine-rigid cities, the brutal power which was an end in itself. So threatened, the appetite turns to violence and the grave—in Poe, in Fitz-James O'Brien, and much later, in our writers of violence and the romantic hunt of criminals.

It is not until we reach, in our history, the poems of Melville—and I always except here the Indian chants, unknown to earlier times than this—that the conflict is open, and turned to music. All of Melville's prose announces the problem of evil—evil white-skinned and humped, one-legged and blasted, racing through the seas; or carried dumbly through ships and prisons and the hereditary tainted doom, or in the factories that are parables of woman's sexual life, or in the "spiritual inveteracies and malices" that enter every novel and every story. Innocence—Ishmael—is set with the others, and is sometimes saved.

But in the poems, the oppositions turn to music. The first draft of *Art* says

> *In him who would evoke—create,*
> *Contraries must meet and mate*

This is close to the center of the matter (as close as it is to Blake's "where opposites meet"). Simply, the line of culture was begun in America at a point of open conflict. All the wars of European thought began us, and Eastern balance has not yet come in. Melville knew both; his rejection of both was for the sea, and the future, perhaps. But it is outrage, the problem of evil, that is both on the surface, and deep, as in *Pebbles:*

> *Implacable I, the old implacable sea:*
> *Implacable most when most I smile serene,—*
> *Pleased, not appeased, by myriad wrecks in me.*

The Civil War turned him into a poet who saw aspects of wars to come, veteran of a knowledge in some ways strange to his time, like the veterans in our own age of the war in Spain. "Now save thyself," he writes, "Who wouldst rebuild the world in bloom."

From the brilliant masked symbol in *The Portent* he draws the future and the war:

> *The cut is on the crown*
> *(Old John Brown!)...*
> *... Hidden in the cap*
> *Is the anguish none can draw;*
> *So your future veils its face,*
> *Shenandoah!*
> *But the streaming beard is shown*
> *(Weird John Brown),*
> *The meteor of the war.*

In the threats of the first winter, 1860–1861, he spoke clearly, writing *The Conflict of Convictions:*

> *The People spread like a weedy grass,*
> *The thing they will they bring to pass,*
> *And prosper to the apoplex.*
> *The rout it herds around the heart,*
> *The ghost is yielded in the gloom;*
> *Kings wag their heads—Now save thyself*
> *Who would rebuild the world in bloom.*

He speaks of this conflict as "Tide-mark / And top of the ages' strife . . ." and leads into the refrain, a virile resolution,

> *The Ancient of Days forever is young,*
> *Forever the scheme of Nature thrives;*
> *I know a wind in purpose strong—*
> *It spins against the way it drives. . . .*

> YEA AND NAY—
> EACH HATH HIS SAY;
> BUT GOD HE KEEPS THE MIDDLE WAY.

In *Misgivings,* the war has become "The tempest bursting from the waste of Time," and in *The March into Virginia,* written in 1861, Melville writes "All wars are boyish, and are fought by boys."

*　　*　　*

The poet of the full consciousness, in prose and verse, [Melville] mourns; but his mourning is the true image-making work that is part analysis still. In *America,* he describes:

> *So foul a dream upon so fair a face,*
> *And the dreamer lying in that starry shroud. . . .*

This conflict penetrates. In the individual, it is sexual conflict; and, in any person, it can be seen in the search for a matching half of that human integral of two people; of whom any one is a fraction whose estimate comes through in the word "shied"—"And shied the fractions through life's gate"—

At the end of *After the Pleasure Party,* with its overpowering sense of sexual threat, the prayer is to Urania, the "armed virgin," the "helmeted woman"—

> *O self-reliant, strong and free,*
> *Thou in whom power and peace unite,*
> *Transcender! raise me up to thee,*
> *Raise me and arm me!*

Before these lines the effort is described, for which the speaker is to be raised and armed: it is the longed-for remaking of self, or the setting free of the sexless component in order to pierce the mystery. The telling image works against itself, in a passage intended to be about sexlessness and at the same time to establish the selfhood of the *couple.* Here are the lines in full:

> *Could I remake me! or set free*
> *This sexless bound in sex, then plunge*
> *Deeper than Sappho, in a lunge*
> *Piercing Pan's paramount mystery!*
> *For, Nature, in no shallow surge*
> *Against thee either sex may urge,*
> *Why hast thou made us but in halves—*
> *Co-relatives? This makes us slaves.*
> *If these co-relatives never meet*
> *Selfhood itself seems incomplete.*
> *And such the dicing of blind fate*
> *Few matching halves here meet and mate.*
> *What Cosmic jest or Anarch blunder*
> *The human integral clove asunder*
> *And shied the fractions through life's gate?*

Perhaps the clearing dealing with the parts of conflict are to be found in the short poem *Art,* whose first draft was thrown away in favor of this:

> *Instinct and study; love and hate;*
> *Audacity—reverence. These must mate,*
> *And fuse with Jacob's mystic heart,*
> *To wrestle with the angel—Art.*

*   *   *

Melville knew the sea, its poising and somnambulism, its levels of revery, the dive to blackness and the corposants, the memories of shore and sleep and love among disaster. Abstract among detail, he finds and finds; in his unresolved Clarel, his Pierre who acts and is doomed, and above all in *Moby-Dick,* everything is essential, and more essential than it seems. But it is what is seems: the myth of tragedy rises up, world-shaped and enormous; Ahab is Ahab, and the Whale the Whale. If there is evil in whalehood; if there is evil in the chase; if darkness leaps from light; even so, there is redemption, and it lies in sympathy with another human being, in the arrival of a touch, and beyond that touch, of "the centre and circumference of all democracy," God our divine equality.

Whitman faced the same period and problem. His critics say that he does not discriminate between good and evil. F. O. Matthiessen in his full and powerful *American Renaissance,* declares of Whitman's "indiscriminate acceptance" that "it becomes real only when it is based on an awareness of the human issues involved, when it rises out of tenderness over man's struggle and suffering, and says:

I moisten the roots of all that has grown.

This awareness of Whitman's is a process, lifelong, and whatever acceptance was finally reached expressed itself in an identification with America as a people, multitudinous and full of contradictions.

But, first, Whitman needed to accept himself. In the testimony of the poems, this most decisive step was the most difficult. Every trap was ready, just here. His idealized image was far from what he knew he was, in the late 1840s. Deeper than the acts of his living or the image-making of himself, his conflicts tore him: truth and reality were both at stake, and unless he could find them both, he would be lost to himself. His struggle was a struggle for identity.

He faced, not only good, but the *problem* of good.

Among his many faces, how was he to reach and insist on the good? How was he to be enough for himself, and take the terrible forms of earth also to be his own? How was he to identify, to talk of the expression of love for men and women, and see flashing that America—with its power, war, Congress, weapons, testimony, and endless gestation? America is what he identified with: not only the "you" in his lifelong singing of love and identification, but "me" also.

It was harder for Whitman to identify with himself than with the "you" of the poems.

To discover his nature as a poet and to make his nature by knowing it is the task before every poet. But to Walt Whitman, crowded with contradictions, the fifteen-year-old large as a man, the conventional verse-maker who learned his own rhythms at the sea-edge, the discovery of his nature was a continual crisis. He speaks of himself as ill-assorted, contradictory. His readers reacted violently from the beginning to his writing about sex—and of course it is not writing *about* sex, it is that physical rhythms are the base of every clear line, and that the avowals and the secrecy are both part of the life of a person who is, himself, a battleground of forces.

In the short conventional meter of *After the Pleasure Party,* Melville's bitter pain at

The human integral clove asunder

makes its cry. Melville, however, was speaking of a couple—of himself as half, needing to mate with the "co-relative," and crying out for the power to free sex by setting free the sexless essential man, or by remaking himself. Whitman, also, used these terms of need; but the "halves" he fought to bring together were in himself, and he chose, early in his life as a poet, not to allow himself the concept of a central sexless man, but to take the other way: to remake himself.

It is in the remaking of himself that Whitman speaks for the general conflict in our culture. For, in the poems, his discovery of himself is a discovery of America; he is able to give it to anyone who reaches his lines.

*   *   *

[Whitman] wrote of the terrible doubt of appearances, and of himself among the shows of the day and night. He spoke of

the sense of what is real, the thought if after all it should prove unreal . . .

This struggle was not a struggle for conformity in the "normal," but for the most intense reality which the individual can achieve, a struggle of process and hope and possibility which we all make when we desire to include our farthest range and then extend the newly-created self into the new again, when we base our desire in the belief that the most real is the most subtle, in art and in life.

It was Whitman's acceptance of his entire nature that made the work possible. The line of a man full of doubt is

I never doubt whether that is really me. . . .

Will went into this work on the self, and there are signs of the achievements here as well as the scars. Whitman is accused by many of showing too much will, and we know how unlikely it is for the efforts of will to lead alone to form. The form of Whitman does not arrive as a product of will, line by line. Each poem follows the curves of its own life in passion; it stands or falls, dies or grows, by that. The form is there, but it is a form of details. For the large work is a double work, and we must seek form in its two expressions: the entire collection of *Leaves of Grass,* and the life-image of Whitman as he made himself, able to identify at last with both the people in their contradictions and himself in his. Able to identify—and this is his inner achievement—with his own spirit, of which his body, his life, his poems are the language.

For Whitman grew to be able to say, out of his own fears,

Be not afraid of my body,

and, out of his own scattering,

I am a dance.

He remembered his body as other poets of his time remembered English verse. Out of his own body, and its relation to itself and the sea, he drew his basic rhythms. They are not the rhythms, as has been asserted, of work and love-making; but rather of the relation of our breathing to our heartbeat, and these measured against an ideal of water at the shore, not beginning nor ending, but endlessly drawing in, making forever its forms of massing and falling among the breakers, seething in the white recessions of its surf, never finishing, always making a meeting-place.

     *   *   *

Forced by his own time to see the industrial war, the war of the States, the disavowal of death (one of the deepest sources, in our culture, of the corruption of consciousness), Whitman's fight for reconciliation was of profound value as a symbol. The fight was the essential process of democracy: to remake and acknowledge the relationships, to find the truth and power in diversity, among antagonists; and a poet of that democracy would have to acknowledge and make that truth emerge from the widest humanity in himself, among the horizons of his contradicted days and nights. The reconciliation was not a passive one; the unity was not an identification in which the range was lost (although "Identify" is a key word in his work); the peace toward which his poems tended was not simply a lack of war. He put away the war he had known, in the hospitals, as a pioneer in what is now called psychiatric nursing. He did that as he put away, in writing a dirge for Lincoln, the fact of the murder. It was simply that, to Whitman, the life, the fact of Lincoln's death, and the "debris and debris of all the slain soldiers of the war" were more immediate in this "victorious song, death's outlet song." In a minor poem of four lines, he uses one line to call the assassination

The foulest crime in history known in any land or age—

and we can see that the line is thrown away. It is a "bad line," and with it Booth is dismissed. So, this poet will say, of slavery,

> *On and on to the grapple with it—Assassin! then your life or ours be at*
>   *stake, and respite no more.*

These are flat lines, the power of music is lost. On these, and on the "catalogues," charges are made that Whitman is full of "bad lines," and that he is a "bad influence."

Whitman is a "bad influence"; that is, he cannot be imitated. He can, in hilarious or very dull burlesques, be parodied; but anyone who has come under his rhythms to the extent of trying to use them knows how great a folly is there. He cannot be extended; it is as if his own curse on "poems distill'd from poems" were still effective (as it forever is); but what is always possible is to go deeper into one's own sources, the body and the ancient religious poetry, and go on with the work he began.

As for the "cataloguing" lines: it seems to me that they stand in a very clear light, not only among his poems entire, but also in regard to present techniques.

There has been a good deal of regret over the printed poem, since first the press was used; and recently, with the mourning over a supposed breakdown in communication, I have heard simple people and college presidents complain that the function of the poet is past, that the bard is gone.

*   *   *

But whether a poem is approached through the eyes in a book, or through the ears, the eyes within the eyes, the visual imagination, are reached; and this in itself is a way of reaching the total imagination. This visual summoning may be made often or very seldom, depending on your poet; if the occurrence is well prepared, the impact is unforgettably strong. The visual imagination may be spoken of as including the eyes. The imaginative function includes the senses. It includes, perhaps most easily, a kind of seeing; we are perhaps most used to having sight invoked in the telling of stories and poems.

Whitman draws on this continually, sometimes with a word at a time—

> *The birth, the hasting after the physician, the beggar's tramp, the drunk-*
>   *ard's stagger, the laughing party of mechanics,*
> *The escaped youth, the rich person's carriage, the fop, the eloping couple,*

The early market-man, the hearse, the moving of furniture into the town,
the return back from the town,
They pass, I also pass—

sometimes these visual summonings are accomplished in a procession of short phrases:

Passage to more than India!
O secret of the earth and sky!
Of you O waters of the sea! O winding creeks and rivers!
Of you O woods and fields! of you strong mountains of my land!
Of you O prairies! of you gray rocks!
O morning red! O clouds! O rain and snow!
O day and night, passage to you!

sometimes they follow each other line after line:

With the fresh sweet herbage under foot, and the pale green leaves of the
trees prolific,
In the distance the flowing glaze, the breast of the river, with a wind-
dapple here and there,
With ranging hills on the banks, with many a line against the sky, and
shadows,
And the city at hand with dwellings so dense, and stacks of chimneys,
And all the scenes of life and the workshops, and the workmen home-
ward returning.

These successions are not to be called catalogues. That name has thrown readers off; it is misleading. What we are confronted with here, each time, is not a list, but a sequence with its own direction. It is visual; it is close to another form, and its purpose is the same as the purpose which drives this passage:

And Sutter, on his way home—
—passes through the prosperous landscapes of a happy countryside.
Wealth, fertility and contentment can be sensed everywhere.
The rain has ceased . . . Myriads of raindrops shimmer in the sunshine.
Suddenly, he meets a group of working people with picks, and pans for
gold-washing.
Astonished, Sutter follows them with his eyes, then turns his horse and
gallops towards the fort.

*The store-keeper from near the fort comes up to Sutter to show him gold
    dust in the palm of his hand.
He asks Sutter if this is really gold or not.
Sutter nods slowly.*

That sequence describes a key action; in the next few lines,

*The dams are taut with their heavy loads, the canal locks are shattered,
    and the waters rush through their old courses.*

You will recognize the form of that passage, if you imagine it with your eyes.
It is typical, and it is very like Whitman. But it is a fragment of the script of a
movie called *Sutter's Gold.*

Whitman, writing years before the invention of the moving picture camera,
has in his poems given to us sequence after sequence that might be the detailed
instructions, not to the director and cameramen only, but to the film editor
as well. The rhythm of these sequences is film rhythm, the form is montage;
and movies could easily be made of these poems, in which the lines in the
longer, more sustained speech rhythms would serve as sound track, while
these seemingly broken and choppy descriptive lines would serve well as
image track.

*　　*　　*

Melville is the poet of outrage of his century in America, Whitman is the
poet of possibility; one cannot be repeated more than the other. But Whitman's significance is based on the possibility realized in his period, as Dante's
is based on the system of his religion in his time. As far as their imagination
of *possibility* outranges their time, their systems live; for their images are deep
in their belief. Melville's outrage lives; he touched perpetual evil, the perpetual hunt, and sea-images, world-images gave these their language. They speak
for the backgrounds of our present. In our history, our open history, we
know the gifts of many poets: in our buried history are the lost poems and
songs; but these two master-poets, in all their work, stand at the doors of
conflict, offering both courage and possibility, and choosing, emphasizing
one or the other according to the ways in which forces that work in all of us
drove them, and were driven, as they lived toward their forms.

CHAPTER 6

There is also, in any history, the buried, the wasted, and the lost.

In the life of this people, we have seen some of that submerged continent of song surface and take its place. But in this society, perhaps more than in any other, because of all the arrivals which brought its people to it determined to live differently from before, there is and has been a great submergence. In many families, we were parented by the wish to move differently, to believe differently—that is, more intensely—from the past and the past place. Many came freely, inviting all the risk. I think of those others—stolen from beside African rivers, seduced by promises of land and work, who reached harbor and found the homestead underwater, the work a job of conscription; and those in Mexico who were promised an American education, and arrived to find themselves signed to four years at the hottest place in the assembly line; and those newly come from the camps of Europe who wake in the Louisiana swamp. Their awakening is sharp, and we can tell their dreams. They do not long for home; they long for America. What of the others? born to mine-towns and the cave-in under the house-floor? driving the night trucks packed with high explosive? anonymous in the school-rooms, the outcast teacher among the very young? Their songs have been lost as the songs of the unborn. Or the happy, who kiss lying in the park? who dive in the clear branchwater, and rise dripping to April in the South? and sing their lost songs among the green of our seasons as well as among our freezing rigid power. Dead power is everywhere among us—in the forest, chopping down the songs; at night in the industrial landscape, wasting and stiffening the new life; in the street of the city, throwing away the day. We wanted something different for our people: not to find ourselves an old, reactionary republic, full of ghost-fears, the fears of death and the fears of birth. We want something else.

We see the symptoms and the symbols of the conflicting wishes in our poetry.

They are among us, the voices of the present, the famous voices and the unacknowledged, and the voices of the past. We may choose; we are free to choose, in the past as well as now, and there is a tradition at our hand.

Behind the past of any of us is that moment of arrival, with its song.

The tribes do not have that: their creation myths are based on this continent. In their relation to our culture, which had denied them and starved them at the root, they tell us that they still live, and that we may rise to full life at any time. * * *

The buried voices of the Indian chants have hardly reached our written literature. Rafinesque, Mary Austin, John Neihardt, have translated some ceremonial poetry; a few others have forced Indian images on poems of their own, with as choppy and unabsorbed a set of results as we have seen, during the last few years, in those poets who have used Lorca, whole and unassimilated, corrupting the fiery purities of his Spanish into a grotesque of English.

A few songs carry over. In recording Hasteen Klah's singing of the Navajo Ceremonial Songs, Dr. Harry Hoijer translates the *There Are No People Song*, with its refrain

> *You say there were no people*
> *Smoke was spreading*
> *You say there were no people*
> *Smoke was spreading—*

and the *Second Song of the Flood*, which begins

> *They are running from the water, I came up with it*
> *When my spiritual power was strong, I came up with it*
> *When it was holy, I came up with it—*

and the *Song of the Sun and Moon,* here in full:

> *The first man holds it in his hands*
> *He holds the sun in his hands*
> *In the center of the sky, he holds it in his hands*
> *As he holds it in his hands, it starts upward.*
>
> *The first woman holds it in her hands*
> *She holds the moon in her hands*
> *In the center of the sky, she holds it in her hands*
> *As she holds it in her hands, it starts upward.*
>
> *The first man holds it in his hands*
> *He holds the sun in his hands*
> *In the center of the sky, he holds it in his hands*
> *As he holds it in his hands, it starts downward.*
>
> *The first woman holds it in her hands*
> *She holds the moon in her hands*
> *In the center of the sky, she holds it in her hands*
> *As she holds it in her hands, it starts downward.*

These are the dance rhythms brought into poetry; the footbeat is heard, even through translation; the repetition gives us at once the ritual and bare strength.

In the Indian culture, the songs had religious presence. We have the spectacle of a culture which values its poetry driven into captivity and repression by a power-culture which sets no store on this art.

*   *   *

On work gangs, prison gangs, in the night-clubs, on the ships and docks, our songs arise. From the Negroes of this country issues a wealth of poetry. * * *

The continent in its voices is full of song; it is not to be heard easily, it must be listened for; among its shapes and weathers, the country is singing, among the lives of its people, its industries, its wild flamboyant ventures, its waste, its buried search. The passion is sung, beneath the flatness and the wild sexual fevers, contorted gothic of the Middle West; the passion is sung, under the regret and violence and fiery flowers of the South; the passion is sung, under the size and range and golden bareness of the Western Coast, and the split acute seasons of the cities standing east.

Children sing their games, work gangs their hammer-measures: meaningless rhymes, some say, but it is not so. The meaning is here; it is the game of the work, their rhythms set by songs. And in the hospitals, poems arrive, and in the quiet rooms at home; the little book in the hand, the long perceptive gaze; in the t.b. ward, at lunch hour in the shop, in the bunk-house of the lumber camp, and in the extremity of the mental institution, the poems rise; and on the battlefield, lost and forgotten, as truth is found—sharp emotional truth in a flash of life—the poems rise.

One may speculate about the lost poems. The folklore scholars, the anthropologists, have found many of them again; the teachers of children, men like Hughes Mearns, have discovered and instigated many, and kept us from their loss; poets and editors like Louis Untermeyer have, again and again, taken up the first work of new poets, as he the privately-printed first book of Stephen Spender; the little magazines, for a while flourishing (so that Cecil Day Lewis could say to me, "There is a place for poetry in America as long as the little magazines survive—"), could save many more. However, what of the dream-singing and its songs? I think of California in 1870, when the Indian tribes, after their final subjugation, turned to dream-singing, sang their hope that the ghosts of their fighters would come back riding, to fight again and this time have the victory. Then, in the next season, they lost that hope, and dreamed—like the Europeans in the camps—singing of how they themselves would save themselves, and would rise and fight; and then, losing that promise, began to tell, to sing their dreams, fusing their wishful dreaming.

Belief has its structures, and its symbols change. Its tradition changes. All the relationships within these forms are interdependent. We look at the symbols, we hope to read them, we hope for sharing and communication. Sometimes it is there at once, we find it before the words arrive, as in the gesture of John Brown, or the communication of a great actor-dancer, whose gesture and attitude will tell us before his speech adds meaning from another source. Sometimes it rises in us sleeping, evoked by the images of dream, recognized in the blood. The buried voices carry a ground music; they have indeed lived the life of our people. In times of perversity and stress and sundering, it may be a life inverted, the poet who leaps from the ship into the sea; on the level of open belief, it will be the life of the tribe. In subjugated peoples, the poet emerges as prophet.

"The artist must prophesy," writes Collingwood, "not in the sense that he foretells things to come, but in the sense that he tells his audience, at risk of their displeasure, the secrets of their own hearts."

The dreaming Indians, then, in the spring of the next year, found they were dreaming in patterns. This, the most private, the most "obscure" of makings, was shared; they were dreaming the same dreams.

Acknowledging that, the core of prophecy in loss and exile, they made their new religion. They began to sing their dreams.

*   *   *

"Whom do you write for?" Gertrude Stein was asked. "Myself and strangers," she answered.

Where is the stranger, the reader, in the half-light of the buried life?

*   *   *

PART THREE
THE "USES" OF POETRY

CHAPTER 7

*   *   *

There are ways in which poetry reaches the people who, for one reason or another, are walled off from it. Arriving in diluted forms, serving to point up an episode, to give to a climax an intensity that will carry it without adding heaviness, to travel toward the meaning of a work of graphic art, nevertheless poetry does arrive. And in the socially accepted forms, we may see the response and the fear, expressed without reserve, since they are expressed during enjoyment which has all the sanctions of society.

Close to song, poetry reaches us in the music we admit: the radio songs that flood our homes, the juke-boxes, places where we drink and eat, the songs of work for certain occupations, the stage-songs we hear as ticketed audience.

Even before music, in the rhythm-songs of children, the change-about of key words makes the texture of song. Music is not separated from non-music, in the large world of childhood; the running of the word, the imitative noises, the early groupings and *portamento* sounds are part of an experience which is fluid. In a study of the music of young children, Gladys Evelyn Moorhead and Donald Pond say that over and over again they have seen a child's activities take their course, speech becoming song or chant or speech once more, movement merging into rhythmic sound and returning again to movement, musical instruments being played and discarded without any break or change in the essential character of the activity. It is not possible for the observer to make a sharp distinction between speech and song.

In the same way, certainly, it is not possible while watching children to make a distinction between play and work; and, from Vico on, this lack of distinction has reminded the perceptive of poetry. The little child I watch will take a car that fits his hand and run it up the long hill of a chair-back, making an uphill sound, and then a babble of syllables signifying "car" and "up" and signifying his pleasure most of all. That this is work and learning is so; but to anyone listening who is willing to put away the grown-up distinctions and impatiences, it is also, and primarily, an expression: the sound and the act both "meaning" car-and-up; or, perhaps, something like up-sounds-car.

These little children will let you feel the pleasure with which they prolong the syllables when they know, say, thirty of them. Later, their statements will be sung; and the statement of one, "I have a red chair," will be taken up, and repeated by others in chant form, as the pleading and response will gather against the hum and mutterings of a Virginia congregation, raised to a religious and creative moment and joining to form a song, to make flower—rather than compose—a spiritual.

Neither among the children nor in the congregation—devoted and mature—is there a question of composition, nor of a split between work and play, devotion and form. With the children, form is unknown. None of the limits are acknowledged; one cannot speak in terms of freedom, T. S. Eliot would say. "There is no freedom in art," he believes; "freedom is only freedom when it appears against the background of an artificial limitation."

If the children are expressing possibility and not limitation, may not the congregation be seen as expressing spiritual limitation? And may not the background of art be precisely that consciousness of spiritual limitation?—which can be translated into formal terms at any moment?

Now the songs which children are taught to sing are unlike the songs they make. We learn that a four-line, rhymed verse, carrying some narrative, is the first. Songs that are fit: measured, "story," songs:

> *Early in the morning, down by the station,*
> *See the little puffer-billies all in a row;*
> *See the little driver turn his little engine;*
> *Piffity-piff! Choo-choo! Off we go!*

is closer, in its feeling, and sound imitation, and pointing "See" than most of the small ballads. But the children's own music is likely to sing:

> *Da da da da da da da da. Pea-nuts.*

or

> *You can't catch me. You can't catch me.*

or

> *Along comes the steamboat and the*
> *person comes walking down the street. And the*
> *water comes right down and shows the man.*
> *Ah . . . man. Yah yah yah dow ha*
> *bee oh ah bah ah oh ah nay nay*
> *yow oh nah nah.*

The child's sense of simplicity, his complex consciousness of rhythm, and in fact his concepts, cannot be satisfied or judged by adult standards. He is interested in things as themselves, he requires that rhythms "be dynamic and generated by impulses which he can feel," in the words of Moorhead and Pond. The child is not concerned with what he should feel. Adults look for melodic unsophistication, rhythmic uncomplexity, and lack of harmonic subtlety, and long to impose a program on the music. They serve as middlemen; and the function of the middleman is to select so that the audience conform to his ideas, whether his position be as movie executive, publisher, advertising art director, or a grown-up introducing his early songs to a child.

There is no tradition of the songs of children from two to six. We do know many of the songs that have been sung to babies and little children; the Provençal songs, and the Spanish lullabies, as Lorca transcribed them, and the sacred lullabies of Europe are timeless and evocative, and one may understand a great deal, in singing them, about early music; and also why the French say instead of "go to sleep," "make sleep."

*   *   *

Clearest among the traditions of poetry in our music is that of the blues. In Abbe Niles' classic introduction to Handy's book, the illiteracy of their makers is mentioned first: they were barroom pianists, careless nomadic laborers, watchers of trains and steamboats, streetcorner guitar players, and whores. They were outcasts, says the book. What must first be said is that they were Negroes in the South. They had known the spirituals and work songs, John Henry and Joe Turner were their important people and their songs were the background. So was the Mississippi, Storyville and Beale Street. So also were the French and Italian operas, and Beethoven. You have to remember W. C. Handy, not old and fêted as I saw him, but after the panic of 1893, leading the orchestra in selections from Beethoven's Fifth in the afternoon, and numbers by Paul Dresser and Charles K. Harris at night. In 1903, Handy got his own band together, and, one of those days, outside a country station, he heard somebody playing a guitar with a knife-blade and singing something about "where the Southern cross the Dog." That bit and his jotting of the tune turned into *Yellow Dog,* with its ending:

> *Easy Rider's got to stay away, so he*
> *Had to vamp it, but the hike ain't far,—*
> *He's gone where the Southern cross the Yellow Dog.*

If the song were printed verse, a cry of "obscurity!" would rise. There is one kind of "obscurity"—that is, a reference to private images, which are private only because the poem is badly written and the image in question has not been prepared for, in any of the ways of musical or verbal approach which can be achieved in a poem. Another complaint will come from an audience either outside of a group culture or not wishing to be exposed to a novelty which might for a moment cause them to lose their equilibrium. Syntax can be as great a novelty here as any other. But, in these songs, the references are very plain, and known to an entire—whether or not "outcast"—society. It would be easy for a visiting lecturer to ask what the title *Tiger Rag* or *Rum Boogie* means; and he might very well be told. In the same way, it would be easy enough to find out that an easy rider is the pimp who is the whore's true lover, that "to vamp" refers to shoes and means "to walk," and that the ending describes Morehead, Mississippi, where the Yazoo Delta Railroad crosses the Southern lines.

The blues is a method. It represents a treatment of songs, first by W. C. Handy, and then by a great line of singers and musicians. That it includes its minor thirds, its subdominant modulations, its tragic despair and its edge of sharpened humor—all of this is true; it also includes its own verse form and, by now, a rich uncollected literature of song. On the records and in the song-books, in the sheets and the critiques, you will find every riff, every trumpet solo and break, every detail of orchestration, analyzed. Almost nothing has been said about the words. Both Sterling Brown and Langston Hughes have written, in their own poems and in prose, about the blues and their scenes and significance; but the amazing mixture of keen poetry and vulgarization has never come into our texts, either for what it is or for its influence on our poetry.

It is easy to see the colors of other song-literature on our poems. The Border ballads above all have set their magic and their formal base into the foundation of English and American poetry. The *lieder* and Heine's lyrics have entered our tradition; and the Elizabethan lyric as Shakespeare, Peele and Jonson knew it. Lorca, particularly in translation, has left an odd, unassimilated trace on images and lines of poets writing English without any real idea of what the *romancero* was to him, or the *cante jondo*. But these songs which are deep in our years and memories—with the *St. Louis Blues* as fountain-head—are hardly recorded as influence.

They are present to us, and the poetry is in the lines of these blues and folksongs, from *TB Blues* with its timeless

> *Too late, too late, too late, too late, too late;*

and Lead Belly's *New York City:*

> *When I get to Louisiana, gonna walk and tell,*
> *New York City is a burnin' hell.*

The ballad that Lead Belly made about Bill Martin and Ella Speed lets the description in, with its moments of talk among the verses. His shouts about Washington, his talkin' blues, like *Roberta,* in which he sings:

> *Way up de river, far as I can see,*
> *I thought I spied my ol-time used-to-be.*

and then, speaking:

> *He looked, an' he thought he spied de steamboat comin'.*
> *But it wasn' nothin' but a cypress tree.*

or the song *Blind Lemon,* about Blind Lemon Jefferson, the early singer and guitar-player who taught Josh White, and Lead Belly himself, and many others.

Another singer whose blues enter into our tradition is Jelly Roll Morton, whose

I'm the winin' boy, don't deny my name

has one of the most subtle and haunting effects of all our songs.

Bessie Smith is the great voice of this song. *Young Woman's Blues,* with

See that long lonesome road—
Lord, you know it's got to end—

is one of the monuments of those seasons and their people. Her blues, too, is the one beginning

He left me at midnight, clock was striking twelve—

and the countless others which have been carried on by singers now living, or preserved among the many records Bessie Smith made, which today are reissued or collectors' items. Her life acts out these songs; with her Tennessee childhood, the discovery by Ma Rainey and the nights singing in barns and tents; the bronze, full woman, pushing away the microphone, her power and implacable richness matched only by the great singers—the wealth in New York, the stage shows and floods of drink, the despair in her songs and in her failures, and the final agony when after an accident in Mississippi in 1937, the hospital turned her away because she was not white, and she bled to death after the frantic ride and the waiting for her turn at the second hospital. In full possession of their triumph and their song, their powers realized, these singers in a moment are surrounded by the doorless walls of an ambivalent society. When a door is made,and the unnumbered eyes shine from behind the wall, the song is proved. We have seen it, as we look in dread away from that hospital, to a courtroom in San Francisco or to that day before the Lincoln Memorial in Washington when Marian Anderson, denied a hall, sang human realization in the open air. The poetry is in these songs, not only the art-songs, but the spirituals and the blues. In the *Death Sting Me Blues* that Sara Martin sings, which opens

O come all you women and listen to my tale of woe.

It is impossible, surely, to separate these songs from their music. In some of them, the words are nothing—as the words of many of the best songs are—

without the unity of song. But Robert Goffin has said that jazz music is "pure and clean," and that the lyrics are "impure and dirty." The truth is otherwise.

Descended as they are from spirituals, they do not have the sacred declaration of

> *Well, they pierced him in the side and the blood come*
> *a-twinkalin down,*
> *Well, they pierced him in the side, and the blood come*
> *a-twinkalin down.*
> *Then he hung down his head, and he died.*

But from those peaks of devotional song, we get the transition into daily fact of this:

> *Our Father, who art in heaven, White man owe me 'leven,*
> *and pay me seven,*
> *Thy Kingdom come, Thy will be done, And if I hadn't*
> *tuck that, I wouldna' got none.*

*   *   *

The syllabic singing which has been called "scat" and "bop" is extremely popular now, and, as far as I know, always has been. There are examples of the same syllabic songs in mediaeval students' notes, and I am sure we are on the road back to incantation—or, full circle, to the game-songs of children, used to set a rhythm in motion. The repetition of tones, or of syllables, does produce a trance-like condition, as does the watching of a rhythmic motion such as perfect oscillation. Helmholtz says, in his basic study of tone, that water in motion has an effect similar to that of music; the motion of waves, rhythmic and varied in detail, produces the feelings of repose or weariness—and, he adds, reminds us of order and power and the fine links of life.

Meter, in poetry, is allied to these effects and the long search for their causes. We begin to believe that there are resonances according to which the body responds, in its rhythms, to external motion and rhythm. Beyond that, the connections by which we may identify because of rhythm are beginning to be made. In a series of tests, it was discovered that very few people recognized their own hands or feet or profile views, but that when they were shown a film in which they could see themselves walking (even when the face was not shown), they could identify with their own rhythms, and recognize themselves. In this recognition, both empathy and memory present new possibilities. We know that memory has a great deal to do with the power of poetry. We know that verse has a certain value as a mnemonic device. This value depends partly on the rhythm itself; partly on the meter, the segmenting of rhythm into measurable parts; and partly on the sounds, not even of the words this time, but of the syllables.

In prose, the search may be for the *mot juste;* if you allow the concept of the ideal, in poetry you will have to search for the right word, yes, but you will have to go farther, and find the sound *juste.*

*   *   *

The silences, here, are part of the sound. In the melodic music. Working on film, one deals with time; part of the data is the rate at which the projector functions, the number of seconds per foot of film at which the image-track and the sound-track are shown. When one is transcribing sound for film, the pauses may be indicated by time. And in a song, too, the pauses are indicated.

In the printed poem, the punctuation has an importance which all too frequently has not been given it. Many poets, and of course many students, will say that they have no patience with punctuation: they "cannot punctuate" as they "cannot spell." But, as you realize when you hear a poet read his own work, the line in poetry—whether it be individual or traditional—is intimately bound with the poet's breathing. The line cannot go against the breathing-rhythm of the poet.

Punctuation is biological. It is the physical indication of the body-rhythms which the reader is to acknowledge; and, as we know it, punctuation in poetry needs several inventions. Not least of all, we need a measured rest. Space on the page, as E. E. Cummings uses it, can provide roughly for a relationship in emphasis through the eye's discernment of pattern; but we need a system of pauses which will be related to the time-pattern of the poem. I suggest a method of signs equivalating the metric foot and long and short rests within that unit. For spoken poetry, for poems approaching song, and indeed for the reading of any of these—since we are never without the reflection of sound which exists when we imagine words—a code of pauses would be valuable.

To receive from song all that it may give would be to bring new gifts to poetry. Even in commercial song-writing, with its continual appraisal of an artificial target—"the public" thought of as apart from "the people"—flickers of imagery and lyricism rise, and make themselves felt. * * *

But all our arts of song offer this: a young poetry not yet born. The vitality and sense of triumph in our singing have this promise; the emptiness of its relation to the needs of the people have turned it away again and again. The singing arts are ready for poetry. Perhaps it is their joy that will invite the poems.

I think of a story about a holy day, at the end of which a blessing on the new moon must be made. Once, at the end of Yom Kippur, the sky was cloudy, the moon could not be seen. The Baal Shem Tov tried in his holiness with all his powers of concentration to make the moon come out. Outside, the chassidim were celebrating: they danced and rejoiced, until they burst into the room of the Baal Shem Tov, at first dancing before him, and then drawing him into the dance. Suddenly, in the dance, someone called "The moon is out!" They all ran out to bless the new moon.

And the holy man said, "What I could not do through my concentration, they have done through their joy."

* * *

CHAPTER 9

* * *

The cutting of films is a parable in the motion of any art that lives in time, as well as a parable in the ethics of communication. * * *

There you sit, in a bright cubicle, with a stack of shallow cans of film at your elbow, a red china-pencil in your hand, your face bent to the viewer of the Movieola, where the film is passing, enlarged to the plainness of a snap-shot. You stop the machine; run it backwards for a moment or two; send the sequence through again, and mark a suggested ending with your red pencil. You copy the number of feet counted by the meter. That is the end of a crucial sequence in a film. What has been done? And what is the audience going to see? For the externals of the studio do, in the end, have something to do with the finished film. But to speak of the externals of the cutting-room is as if I were to say, about the writing of a poem: I sit at this table with the light held in the bottle of ink and glancing off the paper; I draw a sheet of white paper where my right hand may easily move on it and I lead the flow of ink across the page. Paper, ink, words are no more the material of poetry than the film, the marks on the sound-track, the shears, are the material of movies. Yet they enter in. But the editor in the cutting-room is dealing in time, in rhythms of length and relationship. * * * The single image, which arrives with its own speed, takes its place in a sequence which reinforces that image.

This happens most recognizably in films and in poetry. If you isolate certain moments in Hitchcock films, you have the illustration of the reinforced image that is used in poetry constantly. There was a point in *The Thirty-nine Steps* at which a landlady opened the door of an apartment, walked in, and saw a corpse flung across the bed, with a knife-handle rising fiercely from the dead back. The landlady turned to you, and opened her mouth with a scream of horror which was pure horror, and somehow more than a scream. The sound was not identified until a moment later, when you saw the train (carrying the hero away from the scene of the crime) as it hurled out of a black tunnel, still screaming, and you knew that the blast of its whistle had served for both voices.

Again, in *A Woman Alone* (which was shown under several names), there is a moment at the aquarium, when looking into a fish-tank with two conspirators, safely meeting in this public and shadowy place, you see the water troubled by the motion of swimming, until a distortion is produced which makes the little streets and structures of the tank shudder and seem to lean. Suddenly it is clear, not only that the bomb that these conspirators have plotted has gone off, and that this fish-tank is Piccadilly Circus, and the walls are falling down; but also a comment on the nature of explosion is made clear. An explosion, says the image in the fish-tank, is distortion, is maximum derangement from the human being's point of view, is a warping of reality that becomes more unbearable as you see it more clearly; in this case, as you see it more slowly. That comment is the reinforcement, the gift adding to our experience when an image is well-placed in a work of art which lives in time.

In the Russian film, *Life Is Beautiful,* the ending of war is shown in the form of earlier sequences *in reverse:* great explosions of earth are gathered back into the ground as you watch, melons push through the soil-surface; in the ironic and moving quickness of wishful thinking.

In another Hitchcock film, *Foreign Correspondent,* one of the most exciting and melodramatic sequences ever made, the airplane crash in mid-ocean is accomplished with a minimum of reference, in the speed and economy of image that is to be found in concentrated poems. The only continuity is the screaming of the planes' engines in their fall. The first shot is one of the plane from outside; then the camera draws closer to the fuselage and we go in the window with it. From then on we are inside the plane, trapped in the fall. All we see are the fragmentary images of disaster: an end of the wing ripped; fear stamped on a face seen for a second; the posture of bodies braced in fall; the end of the wing breaking; the tense stubborn attitudes of the pilot and radio operator, staying at their posts at the more dangerous nose of the ship; the crowding of passengers toward the tail of the plane; the stump of wing; the water hurling into the cabin as the plane crashes in the sea. These are all fragments assembled; it is easy to reconstruct the way in which they were shot and joined; but we make the continuity in the theatre. With one constant, the constant of sound,—and, threaded on that, a group of related but broken images, we make imaginatively an experience so satisfying and convincing and melodramatic that it is completely achieved within its own definition.

That definition does not expect very much. In *Alexander Nevsky,* the great scene of the battle on the ice; in *Paisan,* the great scenes in the marshes, slow and purposive and tragic in their risk; in *The Passion of Joan of Arc,* the turning of faces seen close; the stairs in *Potemkin;* these are all examples which have their parallels in poetry.

*   *   *

To understand the possibilities of language moving against, as well as with, a flow of images, will be to understand new values in film as well as in poetry. The combination of narrator, the voices of dialogue, music, sound, and beyond these voices from anywhere—as the images may be images from anywhere for which we are prepared—will give us a new function. We are the age to develop this function, and the film is a matrix for the new form.

To move through this door, however, will require a sense of revelation as well as a steady and human grasp of reality and meaning. The door itself is there. It is real.

In India, in the caves of Ajanta, generations of painter-monks left on the rocky walls a series of frescoes painted according to a method lost, after the sixth century A.D., to the Eastern world and never known in the West. The method was a religious one.

In our tradition of representational painting, the frame is a window; through it we see these landscapes, this room, these men and women under the lights we know. The canvas of the picture is denied, or rather a double attitude is taken. The painter, classically, draws figures on the plane of the picture—on the canvas; the beholder knows he is meant to look *through* the canvas at the painted scene. Cézanne paints solids, but we reach them beyond the canvas. The trickiest of the trompe-l'oeil paintings disregard the plane entirely.

The school of Buddhist painter-monks at Ajanta believed a different principle. They felt that the sensation of space within ourselves is the analogy by which the world is known. The rocks of the cave-walls were real; they emphasized their crystals and prisms; these boulders, it is said, have the energy of a locomotive on the screen. Painting is not to lead away from reality. Against the walls, for there is no background as we know, start the figures, the holy figures of the life of Buddha, dancing, taking their ease, moving against flowered lawns, palaces, processions, the carnal scenes of the world. Everything is bathed in light; there is no shadow cast. There is no distortion except for movement and meaning: this red cow is elongated, neck, back, and flanks, for she is running.

There is a web of movement, in which these pillars, like candles, are co-ordinates. The Western idea of still life is unknown. There is no still life, there is life, and all life shares the movement of the mind. In living reality, all is movement. This is the dance, and it is to be acknowledged in art.

"No object is isolated," Kramrisch says of the Ajanta paintings. Each is carried by its origin. They are strung together by their rhythm; they yield themselves to the connections.

Here are you, in the cave. The walls are real, and they are accepted. You are confronted by the figures of your consciousness. They start out of the real walls, filling the space of the cave.

In this life, in this living contemplation, there is no sound. To it its language may be brought.

Our experience, set in our time in the world, may be shared through any art. We are ready for the pictures of our true life, we are ready for the poems of our true life.

All the forms wait for their full language. The poems of the next moment are at hand.

Art is not in the world to deny any reality. You stand in the cave, the walls are on every side. The walls are real. But in the space between you and the walls, the images of everything you know, full of fire and possibility, life appearing as personal grace, says Kramrisch. Dancing: creating, destroying, taking possession.

There is here a reciprocal reality. It is the clue to art; and it needs its poetry.

PART FOUR
THE LIFE OF POETRY

CHAPTER 10

In time of the crises of the spirit, we are aware of all of need, our need for each other and our need for ourselves. We call up our fullness; we turn, and act. We begin to be aware of correspondences, of the acknowledgment in us of necessity, and of the lands.

And poetry, among all this—where is there a place for poetry?

*   *   *

If there were no poetry on any day in the world, poetry would be invented that day. For there would be an intolerable hunger. And from that need, from the relationships within ourselves and among ourselves as we went on living, and from every other expression of man's nature, poetry would be—I cannot here say invented or discovered—poetry would be derived. As research science would be derived, if the energies we now begin to know reduced us to a few people, rubbing into life a little fire.

However, there is this poetry. There is this science. The farther along the way we go in each, the more clearly the relationship may be perceived, the more prodigal the gifts.

The definitions of Western culture have, classically, separated these two disciplines. When Darwin wrote of Humboldt that he displayed the rare union between poetry and science, he set the man in a line of heroes of that meeting-place—a line which includes Lucretius and Goethe and Leonardo, but which for the last centuries has been obscured in the critical structure which insists that the forms of imagination are not only separate, but exclusive.

The scientist has suffered before the general impoverishment of imagination in some of the same ways as the poet. The worker in applied science and the inventor might be thought of as the town crackpots, but there was always the reservation of an audience, like children lined up before a holiday conjuror, waiting to be shown. The theoretical scientist, like the poet, could never "show" his audience: they lacked language, and in another way, so did he. Unless the law could be translated into an image, it kept the pure scientist in a position remote from his society. He would be called "abstract," "obscure": he would be a freak of intellect, even to the members of his house.

The explosion of a bomb ended that period. The function of science was declared, loudly enough for the unborn to hear. The test on the bombing range at Alamogordo proved one series of devoted researches; Hiroshima, Nagasaki, Bikini, Eniwetok, acted out others. Only the human meanings were left to explore: the power for life.

That dramatizing of poetry, in a shock of annunciation, can never take place. For poetry is, at every instant, concerned with meaning. The poet—of the kind of poetry for which I hope—knows that consciousness and creation are linked, and cannot be postponed. The scientist of the science I hope for knows that too. And more than this recognition is shared, even in our flawed reality.

*   *   *

Kronecker said of mathematicians, "We are all poets!" The remark provoked assent and sneers; it was noticed.

To believe any of these statements, one must believe, with Clerk Maxwell, that science must turn to the "singular point" and the unique; in a structure of probabilities, he must hunt out the improbable. The conventional scientist, schoolbound, disavows everything but measurement and classification; he breaks his science into countries; he excludes what he considers inexact. He becomes more and more the reactionary, working for a uniform world. The dogma is one of repetition; a ritual nonsense is uttered, in a loud voice; and suitable tests for the conforming of other scientists and the rest of the citizenry are performed by these, who—working scientists, educators, politicians, critics of all forms—now will swear they are behaving scientifically.

William James met one such, in the person of a lady from Boston. As F. O. Matthiessen tells it, James was presenting one of his lucid, cogent arguments, and paused to say ironically, "That is like asking 'What holds the world up?' " The lady from Boston, impatient with all the talk, answered with clipped decision, "A rock." James wanted to take this farther—"What holds the rock up?" he asked. The lady said, "Another rock." "And *that* rock," James pursued, "what holds *it* up?" The lady stiffened. "Young man," she said in a voice that a doghater might use on an off-bounds Pekinese, "let me make myself clear: it's rocks, all the way!"

*　　*　　*

Science is a system of relations.

Poincaré, saying so, says also, "... It is before all a classification, a manner of bringing together facts which appearances separate, though they are bound together by some natural and hidden kinship. . . .

"It is in the relations alone that objectivity must be sought; it would be vain to seek it in beings considered as isolated from one another. . . .

"External objects ... for which the word *object* was invented, are really *objects* and not fleeting and fugitive appearances, because they are not only groups of sensations, but groups cemented by a constant bond. It is this bond, and this bond alone, which is the object in itself, and this bond is a relation.

"Therefore, when we ask what is the objective value of science, that does not mean: Does science teach us the true nature of things? but it means: Does it teach us the true relations of things?"

The search of man is a long process toward this reality, the reality of the relationships. One meaning of that search is love; one meaning is progress; one is science; and one is poetry.

For there is no human level on which the search does not exist. It may be objected, here, that the whole notion is a mirror of the mind. It is that; and of the emotions, too; of one situation regarding ourselves and each other; it is the expression which a total response to any experience evokes.

In science, the relationships may be expressed symbolically, using symbols designed for specific work.

The use of language involves symbols so general, so dense emotionally, that the life of the symbols themselves must continually be taken into consideration. In poetry, the relations are not formed like crystals on a lattice of words, although the old criticism (which at the moment is being called, of course, the New Criticism) would have us believe it so. Poetry is to be regarded according to a very different set of laws. I hope shortly to offer you a preliminary suggestion of these.

A long work is now being devoted to research based on the conviction that "poetry is words"; research that is of value in classifying according to one theory of criticism. That theory is fashionable now, I believe; and fashions in words are interesting to know. I have a high regard for some of the poets who are setting up these structures: dissecting poetry into ideas and things, and letting the life escape; or counting words as they might count the cells of a body; or setting the "impression" against the "scientific truth" in order to dismiss them both. But I cannot accept what they say. It seems to me that something is dragging at their words. They seem to be ignoring the most apparent facts of our condition in this period. What produces this sense of drag? These are cultivated people; yet, in all of their statements, one evidence after another shows that they are thinking in terms of static mechanics. Their treatment of language gives away their habit of expecting units (words, images, arguments) in which, originating from certain premises, the conclusion is inevitable. The treatment of correspondence (metaphor, analogy) is always that of a two-part equilibrium in which the parts are self-contained.

When Emerson said that language was fossil poetry, he was leading up to some of these contemporary verdicts. If we can think of language as it is, as we use it—as a process in which motion and relationship are always present—as a river in whose watercourse the old poetry and old science are both continually as countless pebbles and stones and boulders rolled, recognized in their effect on the color and the currents of the stream—we will be closer. To think of language as earth containing fossils immediately sets the mind, directs it to rigid consequences. The critics of the "New" group, going on from there, see poetry itself as fossil poetry. It will simplify the amending of these ideas—which tend with more and more of a list of error toward a wretched and static condition, to which nothing is appropriate but anguish and forgiveness—if we dismiss every static pronouncement and every verdict which treats poetry as static.

Truth is, according to Gibbs, not a stream that flows from a source, but an agreement of components. In a poem, these components are, not the words or images, but the relations between the words and images. Truth is an accord that actually makes the whole "simpler than its parts"; as he was fond of saying.

* * *

D'Arcy Wentworth Thompson, whose book *On Growth and Form* is a source and a monument, says that organic form is, mathematically, a function of time. There is, in the growth of a tree, the story of those years which saw the rings being made: between those wooden rippled rings, we can read the wetness or dryness of the years before the charts were kept. But the tree is in itself an image of adjustment to its surroundings. There are many kinds of growth: the inorganic shell or horn presents its past and present in the spiral; the crocus grows through minute pulsations, each at an interval of twenty seconds or so, each followed by a partial recoil.

A poem moves through its sounds set in motion, and the reaction to these sounds, their rhymes and repetitions and contrast, has a demonstrable physical basis which can be traced as the wave-length of the sounds themselves can be traced. The wave-length is measurable; the reaction, if you wish such measurements, could be traced through heartbeat and breath, although I myself do not place much value on such measurement.

The impact of the images, and the tension and attraction between meanings, these are the clues to the flow of contemporary poetry. Baudelaire, Lawrence, Eliot have been masters here, and well have known the effects and the essences they offered. But to go on, to recognize the energies that are transferred between people when a poem is given and taken, to know the relationships in modern life that can make the next step, to see the tendencies in science which can indicate it, that is for the new poets.

In the exchange, the human energy that is transferred is to be considered.

Exchange is creation; and the human energy involved is consciousness, the capacity to produce change from the existing conditions.

Into the present is flung naked life. Life is flung into the present language.

* * *

When the poem arrives with the impact of crucial experience, when it becomes one of the turnings which we living may at any moment approach and enter, then we become more of our age and more primitive. Not primitive as the aesthetes have used the term, but complicated, fresh, full of dark meaning, insisting on discovery, as the experience of a woman giving birth to a child is primitive.

I cannot say what poetry is; I know that our sufferings and our concentrated joy, our states of plunging far and dark and turning to come back to the world—so that the moment of intense turning seems still and universal—all are here, in a music like the music of our time, like the hero and like the anonymous forgotten; and there is an exchange here in which our lives are met, and created.

CHAPTER 11

Exchange is creation.

In poetry, the exchange is one of energy. Human energy is transferred, and from the poem it reaches the reader. Human energy, which is consciousness, the capacity to produce change in existing conditions.* * *

Fenollosa, writing of the Chinese written character as a medium for poetry, says this: "All truth is the transference of power. The type of sentence in nature is a flash of lightning. It passes between two terms, a cloud and the earth."

This is the threshold, now the symbols are themselves in motion. Now we have the charge, flaming along the path from its reservoir to the receptive target. Even that is not enough to describe the movement of reaching a work of art.

One of our difficulties is that, accepting a science that was static and seeing the world about us according to the vision it afforded, we have tried to freeze everything, including living functions, and the motions of the imaginative arts.

We have used the term "mind" and allowed ourselves to be trapped into believing there was such a *thing,* such a *place,* such a locus of forces. We have used the word "poem" and now the people who live by division quarrel about "the poem as object." They pull it away from their own lives, from the life of the poet, and they attempt to pull it away from its meaning, from itself; finally, in a trance of shattering, they deny qualities and forms and all significance. Then, cut off from its life, they see the dead Beauty: they know what remorse is, they begin to look for some single cause of their self-hatred and contempt. There is, of course, no single cause. We are not so mechanical as that. But there was a symptom: these specialists in dying, they were prepared to believe there was such a thing as Still Life. For all things change in time; some are made of change itself, and the poem is of these. It is not an object; the poem is a process. * * *

Charles Peirce takes Fenollosa's lightning flash, sets it away from the giving.

Peirce writes: "All dynamical action, or action of brute force, physical or psychical, either takes place between two subjects . . . or at any rate is a resultant of such actions between pairs." It is important here to understand what Peirce means by *semiosis*. ". . . By semiosis I mean, on the contrary, an action, or influence, which is, or involves, a coöperation of *three* subjects, such as a sign, its object, and its interpretant; this tri-relative influence not being in any way resolvable into actions between pairs. . . ."

The giving and taking of a poem is, then, a triadic relation. It can never be reduced to a pair: we are always confronted by the poet, the poem, and the audience.

The poet, at the moment of his life at which he finished the poem.

The poem, as it is available, heard once, or in a book always at hand.

The audience, the individual reader or listener, with all his life, and whatever capacity he has to summon up his life appropriately to receive more life. At this point, I should like to use another word: "audience" or "reader" or "listener" seems inadequate. I suggest the old word "witness," which includes the act of seeing or knowing by personal experience, as well as the act of giving evidence. The overtone of responsibility in this word is not present in the others; and the tension of the law makes a climate here which is that climate of excitement and revelation giving air to the work of art, announcing with the poem that we are about to change, that work is being done on the self.

These three terms of relationship—poet, poem, and witness—are none of them static. We are changing, living beings, experiencing the inner change of poetry.

*   *   *

In reading poems with groups of people, doing what is called "teaching poetry," I have found that I can best proceed if I can offer an experience first. * * *

I have called for a volunteer in workshop, and asked the intrepid one whether he could make a poem—quality set aside for the moment—on the spot. After his moment of blankness, we could see his face change, and soon he said he had something. I asked him whether he could remember it; and he said Yes, he could. Then I asked him to leave the room, to wait in the hall and after a while, to write the poem down; I would come out for him a little later.

When he left the room, there was a stir. I asked the group whether there was a poem; with a few dissenters at first, they agreed that there was. Where did the poem exist? There was some discussion here; one angry person said the poem did not exist until it was on paper; the rest said it existed in the poet's mind, in the poet's imagination.

What was the poem made of, what was its material? I listed the answers on the blackboard. Sensations, impressions, ideals, response to immediate stimuli, memory, rhythm, rhyme, divine light, inspiration—what was it made of?—words, images, sounds. A few people hazarded guesses based on their assumptions of the bias of the volunteer—his poem would mean this, it would have that social content, its structure might be such—

I went out into the hall, where the volunteer waited with a slip of paper in his hand. Briefly, I told him what had happened in the room since he left.

He came back to his place, and read his poem. Yes, it was exactly as he had composed it, while we watched. Well, perhaps one word was different.

Would he tear up the slip of paper? He tore it into small bits, a little random heap on the table before him.

Now where was the poem?

At this point the discussion takes a new direction and impetus. The poem exists in the imagination of the poet and the group; but are there as many poems as there are witnesses? What is the role of the words on the paper? Even, as a professor at the University of California asked, what would have happened if the volunteer had died in the hall—would there have been a poem?

We are on the way to answers. The nature of this reality has been established. We have all *gone through* an experience to which the questions and answers may now refer. We have seen the difference between art,—which is not destroyed when the paper is torn, because its material is not print on paper, but the imagination of the artist and the witnesses—and craft, whose material is otherwise. We have seen something come into existence, and be diffused—and, incidentally, we have seen how mistaken were the prejudices of the group concerning the prejudices of the poet. More has been acted out about point of view than a dozen lectures could describe—the difficult matter of the individual attitude, an "original relation to the universe," so elusive to the emotionally insecure. * * * More has been acted out, in this workshop experiment, about the creative process, than any exposition could declare.

CHAPTER 12

My one reader, you reading this book, who are you? what is your face like, your hands holding the pages, the child forsaken in you, who now looks through your eyes at mine?

●

Let me tell some of the childhood elements that have come into these pages, into this night with its intense sidelong moon and the fast seafog flying over the city, this brilliant day with its unique light in the streets and parks, its light shed down to the Bay and to the red bridge, the hours sloping again to evening, when I knew I must write these words to you.

●

The curious thing is that whatever I wrote in early life has come true. Or is beginning to come true. The death of the lover, the son, the secret wound, the homesickness for New York, the reconciliation with everything evaded, even the poems that would lead to poems, and the moments of illumination followed by immeasurable setback, the Red Sea always followed by the Desert. And then there is the Promised Land. No, I do not believe in any Eden of the past. That garden is the future. Every year since my childhood has been better, in spite of the losses and mistakes. At least the questions have been clearer. As for the answers—But even they have come as questioning.

●

The early days in the city. Stone, water, light. But also, the steep slope down to the river, the cattle-cars bellowing in soft-colored morning. The water-truck slanting a fountain, hard, on the black avenue. Sledding down snow on the slope. The sand-quarries of my father, raw and yellow, far out of town, in the fields. The first public day, whose crowds filled the streets. They kissed each other and seemed to cry. I went out, yes I took a drum and it was a pleasure to beat it hard. Bong, bong. The old lady walked down the center of the traffic-lane on Broadway; she was crying. My father and mother were out. Paper rained down.

That day was the False Armistice. The war was not yet over.

●

You put your head back very far. There it was! The plane. With its double wings and a frail body. You could feel it in the back of your neck.

●

The sands of summertime, the long ocean and sandbar. The Yacht Club, with its baitboxes at the end of the pier. Killies. Summer after summer, the pale hotels, yellow and white, the boardwalks with the light striking down through the wet planking. Iodine smells, the breaker curling and down, seething away, the little fish in the tide-pools, and summer past summer, the sandbar dissolving away. When the tide came in, you could still run for the beach, ankle-deep in the deceptive foam.

•

The streets and the life of the child. Each of these apartment houses, standing like dead trunks along the avenue, has its army of children. Each gang, formed arbitrarily in one twelve-storey house, is set against all other gangs on the block and on the next block. You fight the neighbor gang, on the brownstone stoops between apartment houses; in winter, with snowballs. Ice may be centered in the snowball. On Hallowe'en, particularly, the toughies from two avenues away. You must run; they have stockings filled with flour; they will club you down.

•

You are a part of the city. New York is a part of you. For your father is in the building business, and the skyscrapers are going up. Your father can climb these skeletons, he laughs with the men who are the bravest, the men who throw red-hot rivets with an easy hook of the tongs, and the men who catch the rivets in a bucket. In a tin can. High over the avenues, over the two rivers.

•

First reading, first music. The Victrola, the upright piano. A book about a rabbit. The headlines: ALLIES ADVANCE SIX MILES SOUTH TO SOISSONS.

•

The school at the corner, chosen so that you need not cross the street and be in danger. The fire-drill. We go down the stairs with our geography book, the drill waits until the book is balanced once more on the head.
Preparation for life.

•

The maids and nurses and chauffeurs, those who most talk to you, who give you books to read. B, who comes from the Pyrenees, where they play jacks with knucklebones. H and her mother, peaceable, Hungarian. The man who drives for us is Evelyn Nesbit's brother; you hear the details of the murder. Harry K. Thaw. The Woolworth Building.

•

When your sister is born, you are seven. All your Oz books have disappeared to make room for the baby. They were the most important: those countries of magic, those immense living dolls, the adventure and decency, the implacable witches, and the endless travelling dreams.

•

The city rises in its light. Skeletons of buildings; the orange-peel cranes; highways put through; the race of skyscrapers. And you are a part of this.

•

Before your birth, your parents knew the smaller cities. Father from Milwaukee, a Wisconsin whose cities were founded in 1848, the year his grandfather arrived; the violent legendary winters, ice-boats on the Lake, the newspaper route and all those hot fresh rolls. And the hard boyhood and difficult young manhood, turning into a salesman, alone, attached to his family, in New York, forming a partnership with Generoso Pope, and going on to identify with the building—the contracting for the building—of New York. And behind that, Bohemia, the river, the towns near Prague, the interview with Metternich of some unknown grandfather, who then must leave, overnight, for America.

Behind my mother, the simple Yonkers childhood, the years of clerical work, the ancestors. A silver goblet, hearsay of a cantor's songs, is all you know; then a gap of two thousand years until the Ancestor, Akiba, who fought to include the Song of Songs in the Bible, who was smuggled out of Jerusalem in a coffin by his disciples, who believed in Bar Cochba's revolution, who was tortured to death by his Roman friend, the general Rufus, until he said smiling: "The commandment says: Thou shalt love the Lord thy God with all thy heart, with all thy soul, and with all thy might. I have always loved Him with all my heart and with all my soul; now I know that I love Him with all my life." And he died.

•

The books. The translations Longfellow made. Poe's stories. Oscar Wilde's essays and fairy tales. All of Victor Hugo, and particularly *The Man Who Laughed*. Dickens, Dumas, the Book of Knowledge, and behind them all the Bible.

•

Knife and a fork.
A bottle and a cork.
And that's the way to
Spell New York—

•

Ibbety bibbety sibbety sab,
Ibbety bibbety kanaba,
Upsiderry,

Down the ferry,
Out goes Y—o—u.

•

Those are counting-out rhymes, and jump-rope rhymes. Their meaning is the rhythm of the game. (Years later, you see that "kanaba" was "canalboat," and "upsiderry" should have been "dictionary," or had been, but was no longer.) "Kaiser, Kaiser, turn around," is too close to your own name for comfort. There was some feeling against Germans in the recent war. Now, for your stamp-collection, you acquire a new set of portrait stamps, all of men with flaring beards. Do their faces frighten you? You are told to be frightened. They are Bolsheviki. What are Bolsheviki?

•

One Saturday morning, you are late, and your father leaves for the office without taking you along. Usually, you walk with him for a few blocks, and then the car meets you, and you drive down to Fiftieth Street and the River, where The Office stands, with its garages filled with green-and-white trucks, and at the foot of the street, the great white or corn-yellow or grey mountains of sand and crushed rock.

This morning you are too late to catch up. You go on walking, determined not to be abandoned. You know you were not ready; and now you can not meet the car. The car has already somehow passed you; but you go on, ready to cry, unwilling to turn back. Suddenly the avenue changes, and you are half-afraid, half caught up in excitement at a city where you had never walked. Here are the broken pavings of a wild, noisy, other world. Wide doors with welders' forges burning inside; the black caves of industrial garages; the autumn-colored trains bearing down the center of the street, clanging in red and brown and black, firing clouds up and behind; the barley-smelling tenements, shackled with fire escapes; the hard children running past you; and the harshness and clarity of this new city, the bitter marvellous struggle of a dream.

Now here is The Office, and you a different child.

•

The heroes are the Yankee baseball team, the Republican party, and the men who build New York City.

•

And Joan of Arc. In Domremy, as a little girl, she began to know what she had to do. Now you go to another school, a fine school, full of pictures on the walls, maps unrolled over the blackboard, many possible friends.

Silence in the courtroom!
The judge wants to spit.

•

Fire on the mountain.
Fire on the sea.
You can't catch me.

•

Potsie is a hopscotch game played with a bit of slate. On certain days in the city, a wind turns back from Downtown, the sea flows over these parks and buildings, you know again you live in a harbor, you know your place is where a river meets the sea and a city is built.

Your nurses have their ways. They vanish quickly, as you begin to love them. One sits all day long on Riverside Drive while you play. Her head is back, her mouth is open. She is letting the sun shine down her throat. She used to be a singer, and she wants her lost voice to come back.

One punishes you because you have called her name out loud in the street. That brings bad luck.

One accuses your father of hypnotizing your mother's friend to death. She leaves quickly; she is in love with her doctor, who has been "giving her pills."

•

You were born in the house where Gyp the Blood lived. The people you know in this house are the janitor's son, who helps you raise your one-eyed chick; Ted Lewis, the bandleader; the neighbors' children, who are very heroic in the house gang. From cellar to cellar of the enormous buildings, interminable war; one day you are locked into the cellars of a strange house, and must work your way through the tunnels, past the intense furnaces, to the court and over the iron gates to the open street.

•

Nobody suspects that there are living artists and living poets. All are dead: the musicians, the poets, the sculptors. This is a world of business. Reality is the city; real men go to The Office.

Poetry does not enter the life of anyone you see, except as spoken bits of Owen Meredith, Bryant, Robert Service, Elizabeth Barrett Browning. Except in the servants' rooms: what do you hear there? *The Man with the Hoe, The Ballad of Reading Gaol.* The little five-cent books, smelling of castor oil, are read and reread. In the families you know, the sets of books in the front, bought as furniture—the piano is furniture of the same order—are rarely opened. No reading, in these houses, or in yours, until, at a stroke, your mother begins to read Emerson and the Bible, to revive a lost interest in her religion, and slowly to move, without direction, and years later, after the family breaks, to move forward in her development, as so many of these women move, at their first chance, in their fifties or their sixties.

•

Building is booming. The highways reach out, skyscrapers begin in these deep-cut foundations, down to Manhattan bedrock and beyond, bridges are planned. Concrete must contain expansion joints, the strips of material that allow the forcing heat of these summers, the forcing cold of these violent white winters, to do their work. The principle of the expansion joint, you learn, runs through all.

There is a terrible moment in *The Blue Bird* when the graves are about to open.

The river, and the city, and the sea. They are always beautiful, in their many lights and in their darknesses.

•

But there are living poets!

And now the poems that you have been making, ever since the beginning, have their sense, they can be shown. Now I can say "I," although in the unguarded moments, in the questioning, the "you" is the one asked. I show the best poems of my tenth year, in a little notebook, to my teacher. There is a picture of a Buddha under the glass of her desk; she calls us to quiet by ringing a gong shaped like a dark bowl; when I come to school with red eyes she speaks to me very kindly.

She has a scuffle with D, the bad boy of the class; she cuffs him—she who is always contained, and gentle!—and leads him out, howling. She comes back. "Write what you saw," she said. We do write; and no two accounts agree. "That was staged," she says after we read our reports. "Now we will begin our study of the American Revolution. These are the sources we will use . . ."

•

We are asked about a clock which many of us pass on the way to school. We are asked to vote: are the figures on the clock Roman numerals or Arabic numerals. All those who take that road to school vote: we are almost evenly divided. "Now look at the clock, on your way home." I walk up Broadway. The clock's dial is legible: its hands tell the time by pointing to the letters HOTEL ALAMAC.

A teacher asks: "How many of you know any other road in the city except the road between home and school?" I do not put up my hand.

These are moments at which one begins to see.

•

I have always been well, and always been strong. The maids and chauffeurs who were my friends told me their stories before they married or committed suicide. All the time, I was writing poems. There were the red-headed boy C, the black-haired boy J, the beautiful girl J; all these I loved wordlessly from afar.

•

Now there are cars, and country clubs: the long trimmed fields edged with tall grass, sand traps, interrupted by little lakes.

The two sacred things, tabu, never to be discussed, are money and sex. A young girl is supposed to know these facts about the people she meets: what sex they are, whether they have money, how old they are. Everybody else knows facts, popular songs, jokes.

An aunt defends me to my parents. There is constant need of defense. We seem physically close, in our family, although nobody is supposed to be "demonstrative"; it is conversation that is lacking. For a long time I imagine the farthest intimacy in terms of perfectly open talk at the dinner-table.

But the days of crowding in the baby's room with the nurse, and going to school in the Pierce, are over. There is a different apartment, high over the river. The far plains and domes of New Jersey, the train-barges on the river, the moving lights of the river-signs, are all clear as glass in this air.

There is deep estrangement in all the houses I know. Money is seen as the estranger.

Now the skyscrapers go up, my cousin sells out to Hearst, Valentino is dead and the women push over the cars in a blast of grief; Sacco and Vanzetti are dead, and something is signified by this that can not be put aside; Caruso is long dead, but we remember, and Gatti-Casazza gives us his book of carica-tures. The B.P.M. plate goes up on the car, and we are privileged to drive through lights.

The winter afternoons, waiting in front of the car entrance to Altman's, with the pale ivory-cool tab in one's hand, as the numbers flash on the board of lights. Going to the Museum, along the row of cat-headed deities, to the Gian-pietrino Madonna, to the *Descent into Hell,* to the Contemporary Design show, and the Spanish show. Listening to sermons every week, or reading the Bible during these sermons, among a congregation whose watered-down faith leaves hardly anything besides business custom, and camouflage, except during one month of turning and renewal.

There are Shelley and Keats, every word of their poems.

There are Mantegna and Pollaiuolo.

There is the Park with its groves and lakes, its little capes of stone.

There are the cement-mixers, turning and turning as they ride through the streets, and the broad metal strips which read: SERVICE. And the murdering years of this business, the competitors outdone, the leap up with the Walker rule, the questions that Carlo Tresca later asked me, which never were answered.

And a few friends, their homes in the afternoons, the music. The Ravel *Pavane,* the *Jeune Fille aux Cheveux de Lin.* And, at home, governesses, violin practice of H. while I read Chesterton and Chaucer and *Of Human Bondage,* and *The Romance of Leonardo da Vinci.*

•

The dead vagrant, killed by hunger, found starved to death outside the full locked warehouse.

•

Subway, the hurling of lights in the curved blackness, the passengers' acquiescence, the beating yellow dimness in the trains. An open wound outside the school building, where they dug and blasted for a new line. Stones shattering the braced window of a classroom. No, this is not a wound: this is an origin.

•

The building of the Bridge, past which we drove to the new school at Fieldston every day. The towers, which were never covered, which rose in their driven naked beauty, and the hundreds of hooks inverted in the concrete piles. Finally, cables, a slender roadbed, the long arc across the Hudson.

A moment at which I knew there would always be poetry. The quarrel with M; how she threatened never to speak to me again except on one condition: that I promise not to write these poems. I do not remember the quarrel; I remember that she wrote far better than I, and that the threat to be cut off seemed a real threat. I promised. For four weeks, I was not troubled. A promise given becomes so binding that there is no difficulty in keeping it. But, at the end of that time, a poem began, and the trouble with it. For two weeks, I wrestled with my word, with the poem, with all the risks, and I did not know who I was. At the end of six weeks, there was no longer any choice. I got up in the night, and wrote the poem down. The next day I told M that I could no longer keep the promise. "What promise?" she asked.

•

I think there is choice possible at any moment to us, as long as we live. But there is no sacrifice. There is a choice, and the rest falls away. Second choice does not exist. Beware of those who talk about sacrifice.

•

And first death seen. The great winds blowing along the River, singing in the windows on the Drive, holding their high notes through the keyholes, with all the rooms of our protected houses exposed to death and the wind.

•

The books being Blake, D. H. Lawrence, Proust.
The flaming torch of the Sherry-Netherlands Tower.
The race between the Chrysler and Empire State Buildings.
Movies: *Metropolis, The Crowd.*
The symphony as a regular function, first a river of sensation, then the boredom of a habit, and then, with an adaptive gesture, a coming into focus, a sudden opening to music.
And the bookshop of Mr. O'Malley a cool, cavernous, traditional second-hand bookstore on Amsterdam Avenue near Seventy-Fifth Street, where I began to spend many afternoons, for the O'Malley family adopted me, and let me listen, and read, and soon help a little.

•

Contemporary poetry is reached, in the fresh anthologies by Untermeyer and Aiken, in the Modern Library, and then in all the books at school and here. MacLeish's *Hamlet* is new, and Jeffers' *Tamar* and *Roan Stallion* and *The Tower Beyond Tragedy*. McKnight Black is publishing, and D. H. Lawrence, and we read *Prufrock* together.

•

To have loved the caddy at the country club, Russell, and listened to his stories as we lounged in the high sea-grass. And, filled with love and worship and helplessness, to have pitied him as his father drank his earnings down. And made plans as we told our fortunes in the clouds, or swam in the weedy Bay, or walked over the docks of oyster-shells. And have left him at the end of summer.

•

As I tell about it now, they alternate, the sense of excitement and the sense of discomfort, in memory. The bare branches and the poems; the man in the little railroad hut and his love affair with a schoolteacher up the river; the two whores on our block, Black Chiffon and Yellow Hat; the grocery stores where the respectable unconscious women and the kept women and the madams marketed together; the drugstore where we drank our sodas, which I later, at the Luciano trial, learned was the all-night center—during all those years—of the narcotics and prostitution industries of New York; the clumsiness, in the face of their families' hopes for a quiet, eligible, bridge-playing future, of the gifted girls and boys. There was a sense of discomfort in some of us, sunk deep in the nap of the "comfortable life"; all we knew was that we were not comfortable.

All I knew was that. The first gestures were the clumsy, groping ones of protest, in my first poems as at my first dance.

There were the marvellous chances: the hours near the river in the country, when my school moved just outside the city. The discovery, late, of school libraries and public libraries. The first hearing of *Sacre du Printemps.* The excellent physics lab, and Frank Oppenheimer working at the next table, and the explosive splash on the ceiling of which we used to say: "See that? That's Frank." Janice Loeb, bursting with all the concerns which would lead her to film, talking Jeffers and Despiau, Renoir, Matisse, Stravinsky; she took her temperature before and after reading certain poems; she could send it up one degree, Fahrenheit; that impressed us inordinately.

when the world rode in, as in the poems rode

And Elinor Goldmark, teaching English; and Henry Simon, teaching English and Sonata Form. And Dudley Fitts, coming to school to take apart *Trees:* . . . it is nursing, its arms are up, it is looking at God, it is living-with rain, this nursing creature has snow on its bosom. . . . Do you see it? And John Lovejoy Elliott and Felix Adler showing us Father Damien, and Pasteur, and Stevenson, and *The Dream of John Ball,* and *The Harbor.* And the productions of *Midsummer Night's Dream* and *Everyman.* There were the moments of perception.

•

Then after one summer at a camp in Maine, I visited the family of the F. sisters, and for the first time saw a household in which all the members shared these excitements. We went to the theatre and Mr. F. spoke of his latest case, a labor case he was to win well; and Mrs. F. as we drove that night to Westchester, let down her hair in the car; it streamed back, near my face, colored in the night. I had never seen anyone's mother do that. The next day, they showed me the book of D. H. Lawrence's paintings for the first time. We went back to the city, and I learned that people lived below Fifty-Seventh Street, below Fourteenth Street. I learned that I had been brought up as a protected, blindfolded daughter, who might have finally learned some road other than that between school and home, but who knew nothing of people, of New York, or of herself. Everything was to be begun; not only that, but unlearned, and then at last begun.

•

To come to college was to enter the world of people. Locked-in, with the keyword *protection,* asking too much of friends. I had kept myself away. The first day at college ended childhood.

Then I began to write the poems that are in my first book.

•

The images of personal love and freedom, controlled as water is controlled, as the flight of planes is controlled. The images of relationship, in which the ancestor carried out of Jerusalem and the unborn son may meet; the music of the images of relationship.

Experience taken into the body, breathed-in, so that reality is the completion of experience, and poetry is what is produced. And life is what is produced.

To stand against the idea of the fallen world, a powerful and destructive idea overshadowing Western poetry. In that sense, there is no lost Eden, and God is the future. The child walled-up in our life can be given his growth. In this growth is our security.

"A poet has to undergo a process of birth and growth: he does not discover himself until he has rejected the alternate selves represented by the poetry already existing in the world," says Herbert Read. These selves are represented by all the idols ringing our childhood: we can make autobiographies of a parade of symbols. The drum, the sidewalk, the river, the tower, the father, the car, the aunt, the chauffeur, the sister, the mother, the book, the piano, the harbor, the slum, the sand-hill, the lake, the cement-mixer, the sacred dome, the school door, the museum stair, the field of coarse grass, the golf green, the Bridge, the poem written in the dark, the unsolved murder, the corner whore, stain on the lab ceiling, the granite mountain under whose cliff the adolescent all night lay, waiting to climb in the morning light.

Have I spoken of Baldface? of Emerald Pool?

Of the climb up Mount Washington?

How can I look back and not speak of the stupid learning about birth? Of the stupid learning that people make love, and how it seemed the reason for all things, the intimacy of my wondering, the illumination that—to an adolescent—was the cause for life around me, the reason why the unhappy people I knew did not kill themselves?

Looking back from what I knew in Spain, I must remember the silent storms of puberty, the unleashed marvel of power that could only wreck what I knew, a world of constriction and fear, a materialist world that exposed the American danger, in materialism, to be mystical about material values.

The real estate crash and the stock market crash ripped open the veils of that world.

Our drive was not for the old unity. We had entered the age of the long war and the circular traps: unemployment which branded these children with a sense of waste that dragged back each drop of blood; silence among all the shouting and the floods of print that renewed a distrust of all beliefs and all poetry; and beyond all of this, a sense of human possibility that would not let us rest in defeat ever, or admit the notion of defeat. In art, of course, the mysticism of success and failure will not hold. The world of business is open warfare, cold iron through every throat, and the battle-shriek "Success!" But in art, these terms cannot apply. One works on oneself; one writes the poem, makes the movie, paints; and one is changed in the process.

The work is what we wanted, and the process. We did not want a sense of Oneness with the One so much as a sense of Many-ness with the Many. Multiplicity no longer stood *against* unity. Einstein, Picasso, Joyce, gave us our keys; the nature of motion reached us from Proust as from the second-run movie; the Hippodrome girls went down into the eternal lake, Lindbergh had conquered time, Roosevelt had at last spoken openly to us of the demon of our house, and he had named it: fear.

Against this would always stand the sense of wonder and range in New York, of both my parents, and of my childhood. The world could find an image, infinite as the flower, in this city; the city could find an image, eternal as change, in this meeting-place of sea and river, with their magnificence and filth among the growing.

But our youth and our time had shown us that images were only one beginning. The century had shown us that there were many ways of selling out, many careers for the corrupted consciousness.

Those of us whose imaginations had been reached would not sell out: we would not stop at the images, or at "sincerity," at security, or at any one field. There are relationships, we said, to be explored; and in our weakness and limitation, in ignorance and several poverties and doubt and disgust, we thought of possibility.

CHAPTER 13

The identified spirit, man and woman identified, moves toward further identifications. In a time of long war, surrounded by the images of war, we imagine peace. Among the resistances, we imagine poetry. And what city makes the welcome, in what soil do these roots flourish?

For our concern is with sources.

The sources of poetry are in the spirit seeking completeness. If we look for the definitions of peace, we will find, in history, that they are very few. The treaties never define the peace they bargain for: their premise is only the lack of war. The languages sometimes offer a choice of words: in the choice is illumination. In one long-standing language there are two meanings for peace. These two provide a present alternative. One meaning of peace is offered as "rest, security." This is comparable to our "security, adjustment, peace of mind." The other definition of peace is this: peace is completeness.

It seems to me that this belief in peace as completeness belongs to the same universe as the hope for the individual as full-valued.

In what condition does poetry live? In all conditions, sometimes with honor, sometimes underground. That history is in our poems.

In what climate, poetry? Some will say, the climate of slavery, where the many feed the few, and the few explore their arts and their sciences. Fashionable now again, the talk of the elite reaches politics and education.

Some will say, in the wide-open boom times of a patron system: the historic heights of a building Church, the Renaissance of the small acquisitive states, the times when the bankers founded their galleries, and the prize of nations is their art.

Some will say, in the pit of suffering, when all is lost but the central human fire, when the deliverers come, speaking in the holy symbols of risk and life and everything made sacred.

But we know the partial truth in each of these. We know the slaveholder minds among us, contriving their elite, copying and multiplying natural waste, and believing that meaning can always be put off. These people insist, "He is so great a poet, you need not hear what he says." They are, in their contempt for value, armed. They have whips in their hands. I shall not say they are enemies of poetry; although they are. Only see the effect of their poets on these men: the literature of aversion, guilt, and the longing for forgiveness does its work on the writers and on the witnesses. Its work is tragic; contempt is bred here, and remorse, the dead scatterings. At its best, the poems are those of power and love.

We know the men who need the times of profit; the moment these years fade, they tell us there is no place now for humor, there is no place for poetry. They try to make humor and rage and poetry luxury products. But this cannot be done. At its best, the poems are those of vitality and love.

We know, too, those who are warped until suffering is what they need. We have seen an "occasional verse" grow up of depression and of war. One of the worst things that could happen to our poetry at this time would be for it to become an occasional poetry of war. A good deal of the repugnance to the social poetry of the 1930s was caused by reactionary beliefs; but as much was caused, I think, because there were so many degrees of blood-savagery in it, ranging all the way from self-pity,—naked or identified with one victim after another—to actual blood-lust and display of wounds, a rotten sort of begging for attention and sympathy in the name of an art that was supposed to produce action. This was not confined to "social" literature; you may see the style of self-pity in many of the "realistic" novels and confessions of these years. But, fundamentally, this literature is purified to compassion. At its best, the poems are those of offering and love.

We need a background that will let us find ourselves and our poems, let us move in discovery. The tension between the parts of such a society is health; the tension here between the individual and the whole society is health. This state arrives when freedom is a moving goal, when we go beyond the forms to an organic structure which we can in conscience claim and use. Then the multiplicities sing, each in his own voice. Then we understand that there is not meaning, but meanings; not liberty, but liberties.

*   *   *

For the last time here, I wish to say that we will not be saved by poetry. But poetry is the type of the creation in which we may live and which will save us.

The world of this creation, and its poetry, is not yet born.

The possibility before us is that now we enter upon another time, again to choose. Its birth is tragic, but the process is ahead: we must be able to turn a time of war into a time of building.

There are the wounds: they are crying everywhere. There are the false barriers: but they are false. If we believe in the unity and multiplicity of the world, if we believe in the unity and multiplicity of man, then we believe too in the unity and multiplicity of imagination. And we will speak across the barriers, many to many. The great ideas are always emerging, to be available to all men and women. And one hope of our lives is the communication of these truths.

To be against war is not enough, it is hardly a beginning. And all things strive; we who try to speak know the ideas trying to be more human, we know things near their birth that try to become real. The truth here goes farther, there is another way of being against war and for poetry.

We are against war and the sources of war.

We are for poetry and the sources of poetry.

They are everyday, these sources, as the sources of peace are everyday, infinite and commonplace as a look, as each new sun.

As we live our truths, we will communicate across all barriers, speaking for the sources of peace. Peace that is not lack of war, but fierce and positive.

We hear the saints saying: Our brother the world. We hear the revolutionary: Dare we win?

All the poems of our lives are not yet made.

We hear them crying to us, the wounds, the young and the unborn—we will define that peace, we will live to fight its birth, to build these meanings, to sing these songs.

Until the peace makes its people, its forests, and its living cities; in that burning central life, and wherever we live, there is the place for poetry.

And then we will create another peace.

San Francisco
July 1949

SELECTED POEMS

By 1941, the poet John Crowe Ransom had given a name to a literary theory that was to become the dominant point of view in American universities for the next two decades: "The New Criticism." In some respects, Rukeyser's The Life of Poetry *was her personal manifesto against the New Criticism, which defined the poem as a world in itself; a self-contained organization of words and sounds, of formal negotiations of irony and ambiguity. To look into the poem or to use it to look into the world in which it was written, the New Critics said, was to fall prey to the "personal heresy." (The term is Cleanth Brooks's.)*

Throughout the '40s and '50s, Rukeyser's work was dismissed by more and more reviewers and readers who marched in step with The New Critics. (Rukeyser was one of a number of poets disdained by the New Critics; among them were Walt Whitman and William Carlos Williams.) Her poetry was deemed amorphous, vague, sloppy, self-indulgent. Her social concerns were considered passé, or, in an era marked by McCarthy's scare tactics and black-listing, "un-American." Her singular courage in writing about pregnancy and motherhood—during years when the worst thing a woman poet could do was to claim and celebrate that "feminine" (hence, trivial) experience—increased her isolation.

"Night Feeding," for example, from Rukeyser's Selected Poems, *(1951), gives us the mother in the night, waking to the cry of her child's call for milk. "Night Feeding" is a terrifying and poignant lullaby in that staple of English verse, the iambic pentameter. At odds with the measured lines, though, it teems with personal heresy, and with the return of sounds, like a heartbeat, that Rukeyser called her rhymings. "Rhyme itself, as it has come down to us through European tradition," she explained to her audience at a lecture in 1968, "is one returning of sound. One return has never been enough for me. I wanted sound established and recurring many times, as the recurrences in our lives come many times."*

Here, full-bodied and full-voiced, Rukeyser follows her own voice and the voice of her child, refusing to privilege the destination over the journey.

.   .   .   .   .

NIGHT FEEDING

Deeper than sleep but not so deep as death
I lay there sleeping and my magic head
remembered and forgot.   On first cry I
remembered and forgot and did believe.
I knew love and I knew evil:
woke to the burning song and the tree burning blind,
despair of our days and the calm milk-giver who
knows sleep, knows growth, the sex of fire and grass,
and the black snake with gold bones.

Black sleeps, gold burns;   on second cry I woke
fully and gave to feed and fed on feeding.
Gold seed, green pain, my wizards in the earth
walked through the house, black in the morning dark.
Shadows grew in my veins, my bright belief,
my head of dreams deeper than night and sleep.
Voices of all black animals crying to drink,
cries of all birth arise, simple as we,
found in the leaves, in clouds and dark, in dream,
deep as this hour, ready again to sleep.

ONE LIFE

How to describe the 330-page One Life? *Is it biography? Is it poetry? Is it myth-making or myth-debunking? Rukeyser called it "a story and a song, based on episodes in the life of Wendell Willkie." (Willkie was the Republican candidate who ran against Roosevelt in the 1940 presidential election.)*

It's a difficult undertaking to excerpt from One Life. *When Rukeyser published her* Collected Poems *in 1978, she included all the poems, but none of the prose material that surrounded them—an expedient and appropriate decision for a book that was called* Collected Poems, *but a real problem in giving a grasp of* One Life *as a book in which poems grow out of prose, and vice versa. Here, however, are two brief excerpts—they might be called prose poems—that have not been reprinted since the book was originally published.**

   •   •   •   •   •

*That's not exactly true. On Nov. 2, the day before the 1992 presidential election, the *New York Times* published "Submit Your Own Answer" (under the title "A Quiz for Candidates") on its Op-Ed page.—Ed.

[COLLEGE RADICALS]

College radicals, a term meaning, in the United States, the young who have not surrendered.

Many surrender early everywhere, forgetting their birth.

Forgetting the origin in bravery and full relationship. The surrender is made easy. There is a foam of rewards; you may float along stag lines, festivals and ball games, like the songs. Before they know it, they are surrendered—the spectacular boys, the long adventurous girls, talented, shining. All are surrendered, and then pretending coldness, or pretending they are used to the world. Walling themselves in, from their first adolescence. Beginning at puberty to forget. They begin when they are troubled by what they suppose they should be feeling. The wound is there; the consciousness, which is variety, which is the need for growth and form as well as their perception, the consciousness has begun its own corruption. The rites of change become a memory of jungle, and these—the next people, the most beautiful—have forgotten animal and plant and mud, and nebula; they know only the floors of their own forgetting.

The icicles and the assassins have begun.

How do they conspire to keep from growing? How can you keep the great tree down, force the great thick trunk to open at the top to a dwarf crown? These energies are then driven in.

A faint drumming, in the walls of the room. For the rest of their lives.

Q: Why should anyone seek to assume the burden of the Presidency?

WILLKIE: I am 48 years old. I've done a lot of thinking on our problems. I have certain ideas about our government. I want to do something about it.

Q: Why should anyone seek to assume the burden of the Presidency?

ROOSEVELT: Somebody has to face it.

Q: Which do you consider the better answer? Give your reasons. On a separate sheet, you may submit your own answer. Write legibly. In marking these papers, spelling will be taken into consideration, as well as neatness, family background, religious practices, sexual practices, superstitions, penmanship, color of hair, color of eyes, color of skin (area visible when fully clothed), color of skin (area invisible when fully clothed), color of distinctive body markings, color of political beliefs at the following ages: 7, 13, 18, 20½, 24, 29, 35, 41, 50, 80; color of political beliefs one month after start of first remunerative position, color of political beliefs one month after loss (for whatever reason) of fifth remunerative position, color of fifteen typical friends, color of employee (present), color of five typical enemies, color of landlord (present); color of campaign backers: (1) over $5,000, (2) under $5,000; attitude toward England, attitude toward twenty selected corporations, attitude toward U.S.S.R.; attitude toward any four of the following: (1) children, (2) the tariff, (3) baseball, (4) Charles Chaplin, (5) hybrid corn, (6) old age, (7) the movies, (8) theater in Washington, (9) vice in Washington: (9a) financial, (9b) sexual, (9c) supernatural, (10) regular church attendance, (11) your nearest Chamber of Commerce, (12) spirituous liquors, (13) quiet evenings at home, (14) human burial, (15) masturbation, (16) mothers, (17) group games for growing children, (18) the party system in the U.S.

Write an essay of not more than 200 words on any of the following: (a) New England and the South, (b) mining and farming, (c) oil wells and relief, (d) war and peace, (e) male and female, (f) brandy and Scotch, (g) good and evil, (h) God.

BODY OF WAKING

Rukeyser began teaching on a regular basis at Sarah Lawrence College in Bronx-
ville, New York, in 1954. Her responsibilities there, coupled with caring for her
young child, left less time for writing. There were additional worries. Throughout
the '50s, Rukeyser was the target of investigation by several McCarthyite groups.
Nevertheless, write she did. Finances were tight, and she often took on projects
that promised extra income—articles, children's books, screenplays. Sifting through
pages and pages of some of these works in her papers at the Library of Congress,
one is struck by Rukeyser's unwavering "Rukeyserness." No matter the genre, every
project bears the stamp of her distinctive, iconoclastic imagination.

Perhaps that's part of the reason (a subtle form of blacklisting may be another)
that many of these projects did not pan out. "Oh my God," one can almost hear
a film studio editor crying in alarm, "all we wanted was a standard boy-meets-
girl with a little war motif for background."

But it all kept coming—the projects, the poems, the ideas. In Body of Waking,
Rukeyser continues her exploration and celebration of "the power that shines past
storm." For those who think of her as exclusively an urban poet, here are lyrics
whose attention to the specificities of the natural world are marvelous and assured.

More and more, we find poems that can be read as evocations of the power
and possibility derived from loving another woman. "King's Mountain" and " 'Long
Enough,' " for example, are richly suggestive lyrics of sexual and political wak-
ening. " 'Long Enough,' " particularly, suggests that the woman who "too long
lived in "the empire / Of his darkened eyes / Bewildered in the grey silver / Light of
his fantasies" may be writing of her emergence into a country where male fanta-
sies no longer rule her.

Rukeyser's biography will have to be written for us to know when she first fell
in love with a woman. We do, however, know this: she did have women lovers,
love for women was central in her life and work, and she did speak out, whenever
it was threatened, for love in all its forms and all its expressions.

.   .   .   .   .

KING'S MOUNTAIN

In all the cities of this year
I have longed for the other city.

In all the rooms of this year
I have entered one red room.

In all the futures I have walked toward
I have seen a future I can hardly name.

But here the road we drive
Turns upon another country.

I have seen white beginnings,
A slow sea without glaze or speed,
Movement of land, a long lying-down dance.

This is fog-country. Milk. Country of time.

I see your tormented color, the steep front of your storm
Break dissipated among limitless profiles.

I see the shapes of waves in the cross-sea
Advance, a fog-surface over the fog-floor.
Seamounts, slow-flowing. Color. Plunge-point of air.

In all the meanings of this year
There will be the ferny meaning.

It rises leaning and green, streams through star-lattices;
After the last cliff, wave-eroded silver,
Forgets the limitations of our love,
These drifts and caves dissolve and pillars of these countries
Long-crested dissolve to the future, a new form.

F. O. M.*

the death of Matthiessen

It was much stronger than they said. Noisier.
Everything in it more colored. Wilder.
More at the center calm.
Everything was more violent than ever they said,
Who tried to guard us from suicide and life.
We in our wars were more than they had told us.
Now that descent figures stand about the horizon,
I have begun to see the living faces,
The storm, the morning, all more than they ever said.
Of the new dead, that friend who died today,
Angel of suicides, gather him in now.
Defend us from doing what he had to do
Who threw himself away.

HAYING BEFORE STORM

This sky is unmistakable. Not lurid, not low, not black.
Illuminated and bruise-color, limitless, to the noon
Full of its floods to come. Under it, field, wheels, and
      mountain,
The valley scattered with friends, gathering in
Live-colored harvest, filling their arms; not seeming to hope
Not seeming to dread, doing.
                        I stand where I can see

*F. O. (Francis Otto) Matthiessen (1902–1950) was a highly respected literary critic. His 1941
American Renaissance, produced during a distinguished teaching career at Harvard, is still considered a classic. Some have suggested that Matthiessen's homosexuality helped him understand
the oppression of economic and social outsiders, an understanding reflected in both his critical
writing and his political activism. Matthiessen's death by suicide in the spring of 1950 (he took
his own life by leaping from the twelfth floor of a Boston hotel) was a stunning blow to the
literary community of the left.—Ed.

Holding a small pitcher, coming in toward
  The doers and the day.
                    These images are all
  Themselves emerging: they face their moment: love or go
down.
  A blade of the strong hay stands like light before me.
  The sky is a torment on our eyes, the sky
  Will not wait for this golden, it will not wait for form.
  There is hardly a moment to stand before the storm.
  There is hardly time to lay hand to the great earth.
  Or time to tell again what power shines past storm.

"LONG ENOUGH"

"Long enough. Long enough,"
I heard a woman say—
I am that woman who too long
Under the web lay.
Long enough in the empire
Of his darkened eyes
Bewildered in the greying silver
Light of his fantasies.

I have been lying here too long,
From shadow-begin to shadow-began
Where stretches over me the subtle
Rule of the Floating Man.
A young man and an old-young woman
My dive in the river between
And rise, the children of another country;
That riverbank, that green.

But too long, too long, too long
Is the journey through the ice
And too secret are the entrances
To my stretched hidingplace.
Walk out of the pudorweb

And into a lifetime
Said the woman; and I sleeper began to wake
And to say my own name.

THE SIXTH NIGHT: WAKING

That first green night of their dreaming, asleep beneath the
    Tree,
God said, "Let meanings move," and there was poetry.

TREE

It seemed at the time like a slow road and late afternoon
When I walked past a summery turning and saw that tree in the sun
That was my first sight of it. It stood blasted open,
Its trunk black with tar on its unsealed destruction.
You could see blue through that window, endless sky in the
    wound
Bright blue past the shining of black harm. And sound
Fresh wood supported branches like judge's arms,
Crutch under branch, crutch where the low hand leaned,
Strong new wood propping that apple-tree's crown.

And the crown? World-full, beneficent, round,
Many-branching; and red, apple-red, full of juices and color-ripe,
The great crown spread on the hollow bark and lived.
Lavish and fertile, stood on her death and thrived.

For three years remembering that apple-tree,
I saw in it the life of life in crisis,
Moving over its seasons, meeting death with fruition.
I have been recognizing all I loved.

Now, after crisis of day and crisis of dream,
That tree is burning and black before my years.
I know it for a tree. Rooted and red it bears.
Apple and branch and seed.
Real, and no need to prove, never a need
For images: of process, or death, or flame; of love, or
    seeming, or speed.

WATERLILY FIRE

Rukeyser was on her way to the Museum of Modern Art on a spring day in 1958 to meet her friend Richard Griffith, who was a curator there. It was on that day that a huge fire broke out, reaching the museum and destroying one of the large paintings from Monet's Waterlily *series.*

That event served as the starting point for her long poem "Waterlily Fire," the poem that May Swenson called "the crown piece" of Rukeyser's selection of works spanning the years 1935–1962. The Museum of Modern Art was supposedly "fireproof," Rukeyser later explained in an interview. Yet the fire was raging, the waterlilies were burning. ("Whatever can happen in a city of stone, / Whatever can come to a wall can come to this wall," she realizes.) Rukeyser asks herself: what does that say about my *life? And what does that say about what can happen to the people I know and the people I don't know?*

John Donne's "No man is an island" becomes Muriel Rukeyser's "I know in myself an island," and "whatever can happen to a woman can happen to me."

.   .   .   .   .

WATERLILY FIRE

FOR RICHARD GRIFFITH

1 / The Burning

Girl grown woman   fire   mother of fire
I go to the stone street turning to fire.   Voices
Go screaming   Fire   to the green glass wall.
And there where my youth flies blazing into fire
The   dance   of sane and insane images, noon
Of seasons and days.   Noontime of my one hour.

Saw down the bright noon street the crooked faces
Among the tall daylight in the city of change.
The scene has walls   stone   glass   all my gone life
One wall a web through which the moment walks
And I am open, and the opened hour
The world as water-garden   lying behind it.
In a city of stone, necessity of fountains,
Forced water fallen on glass, men with their axes.

An arm of flame reaches from water-green glass,
Behind the wall I know waterlilies

The time of this poem is the period in New York City from April 1958, when I witnessed the destruction of Monet's *Waterlilies* by fire at the Museum of Moden Art, to the present moment.

The two spans of time assumed are the history of Manhattan island and my lifetime on the island. I was born in an apartment house that had as another of its tenants the notorious gangster Gyp the Blood. Nearby was Grant's Tomb and the grave of the Amiable Child. This child died very young when this part of New York was open country. The space with its memory of amiability has been protected among all the rest. My father, in the building business, made us part of the building, tearing down, and rebuilding of the city, with all that that implies. Part 2 is based on that time, when building still meant the throwing of red-hot rivets, and only partly the pouring of concrete of the later episodes.

Part 4 deals with an actual television interview with Suzuki, the Zen teacher, in which he answered a question about a most important moment in the teachings of Buddha.

The long body of Part 5 is an idea from India of one's lifetime body as a ribbon of images, all our changes seen in process.

The quote "island of people" was the group who stayed out in the open in City Hall Park in April of 1961, while the rest of the city took shelter at the warning sound of the sirens. The protest against this nuclear-war practice drill was, in essence, a protest against war itself and an attempt to ask for some other way to deal with the emotions that make people make war.

Before the Museum of Modern Art was built, I worked for a while in the house that then occupied that place. On the day of the fire, I arrived to see it as a place in the air. I was coming to keep an appointment with my friend the curator of the museum's film library, Richard Griffith, to whom this poem is dedicated.—MR

Drinking their light, transforming light and our eyes
Skythrown under water, clouds under those flowers,
Walls standing on all things stand in a city noon
Who will not believe a waterlily fire.
Whatever can happen in a city of stone,
Whatever can come to a wall can come to this wall.

I walk in the river of crisis toward the real,
I pass guards, finding the center of my fear
And you, Dick, endlessly my friend during storm.

The arm of flame striking through the wall of form.

2 / The Island

Born of this river and this rock island, I relate
The changes : I born when the whirling snow
Rained past the general's grave and the amiable child
White past the windows of the house of Gyp the Blood.
General, gangster, child.   I know in myself the island.

I was the island without bridges, the child down whose blazing
Eye the men of plumes and bone raced their canoes and fire
Among the building of my young childhood, houses;
I was those changes, the live darknesses
Of wood, the pale grain of a grove in the fields
Over the river fronting red cliffs across—
And always surrounding her the river, birdcries, the wild
Father building his sand, the mother in panic her parks—
Bridges were thrown across, the girl arose
From sleeping streams of change in the change city.
The violent forgetting, the naked sides of darkness.
Fountain of a city in growth, an island of light and water.
Snow striking up past the graves, the yellow cry of spring.

Whatever can come to a city can come to this city.
Under the tall compulsion
                              of the past
I see the city
                  change like a man changing

I love this man   with my lifelong body of love
I know you

        among your changes

                wherever I go
Hearing the sounds of building

                the syllables of wrecking
A young girl watching

           the man throwing red hot rivets
Coals in a bucket of change
How can you love a city that will not stay?
I love you

        like a man of life in change.

Leaves like yesterday shed, the yellow of green spring
Like today accepted and become one's self
I go, I am a city with bridges and tunnels,
Rock, cloud, ships, voices.   To the man where the river met
The tracks, now buried deep along the Drive
Where blossoms like sex pink, dense pink, rose, pink, red.

Towers falling.   A dream of towers.
Necessity of fountains.   And my poor,
Stirring among our dreams,
Poor of my own spirit, and tribes, hope of towers
And lives, looking out through my eyes.
The city the growing body of our hate and love,
The root of the soul, and war in its black doorways.
A male sustained cry interrupting nightmare.
Male flower heading upstream.

Among a city of light, the stone that grows.
Stigma of dead stone, inert water, the tattered
Monuments rivetted against flesh.
Blue noon where the wall made big agonized men
Stand like sailors pinned howling on their lines, and I
See stopped in time a crime behind green glass,
Lilies of all my life on fire.
Flash faith in a city building its fantasies.

I walk past the guards into my city of change.

3 / Journey Changes

Many of us   Each in his own life waiting
Waiting to move   Beginning to move   Walking
And early on the road of the hill of the world
Come to my landscapes emerging on the grass

The stages of the theatre of the journey

I see the time of willingness between plays
Waiting and walking and the play of the body
Silver body with its bosses and places
One by one touched awakened into into

Touched and turned one by one into   flame

The theatre of the advancing goddess   Blossoming
Smiles as she stands intensely being in stillness
Slowness in her blue dress advancing standing I go
And far across a field over the jewel grass

The play of the family stroke by stroke acted out

Gestures of deep acknowledging on the journey stages
Of the playings the play of the goddess and the god
A supple god of searching and reaching
Who weaves his strength   Who dances her more alive

The theatre of all animals, my snakes, my great horses

Always the journey   long   patient   many haltings
Many waitings for choice and again easy breathing
When the decision to go on is made
Along the long slopes of choice and again the world

The play of poetry approaching in its solving

Solvings of relations in poems and silences
For we were born to express   born for a journey
Caves, theatres, the companioned solitary way
And then I came to the place of mournful labor

A turn in the road and the long sight from the cliff

Over the scene of the land dug away to nothing and many
Seen to a stripped horizon carrying barrows of earth
A hod of earth taken and emptied and thrown away
Repeated farther than sight.   The voice saying slowly

But it is hell.   I heard my own voice in the words
Or it could be a foundation   And after the words
My chance came.   To enter.   The theatres of the world.

4 / Fragile

I think of the image brought into my room
Of the sage and the thin young man who flickers and asks.
He is asking about the moment when the Buddha
Offers the lotus, a flower held out as declaration.
"Isn't that fragile?" he asks.   The sage answers:
"I speak to you.   You speak to me.   Is that fragile?"

5 / The Long Body

This journey is exploring us. Where the child stood
An island in a river of crisis, now
The bridges bind us in symbol, the sea
Is a bond, the sky reaches into our bodies.
We pray : we dive into each other's eyes.

Whatever can come to a woman can come to me.

This is the long body : into life from the beginning,
Big-headed infant unfolding into child, who stretches and finds
And then flowing the young one going tall, sunward,
And now full-grown, held, tense, setting feet to the ground,
Going as we go in the changes of the body,
As it is changes, in the long strip of our many
Shapes, as we range shifting through time.
The long body : a procession of images.

This moment in a city, in its dream of war.
                    We chose to be,
Becoming the only ones under the trees
                              when the harsh sound
Of the machine sirens spoke. There were these two men,
And the bearded one, the boys, the Negro mother feeding
Her baby. And threats, the ambulances with open doors.
Now silence. Everyone else within the walls. We sang.
                    We are the living island,
We the flesh of this island, being lived,
Whoever knows us is part of us today.

Whatever can happen to anyone can happen to me.

Fire striking its word among us, waterlilies
Reaching from darkness upward to a sun
Of rebirth, the implacable.   And in our myth
The Changing Woman who is still and who offers.

Eyes drinking light, transforming light, this day
That struggles with itself, brings itself to birth.
In ways of being, through silence, sources of light
Arriving behind my eye, a dialogue of light.

And everything a witness of the buried life.
This moment flowing across the sun, this force
Of flowers and voices body in body through space.
The city of endless cycles of the sun.

I speak to you   You speak to me

THE SPEED OF
DARKNESS

(1 9 6 8)

In the early '60s, Rukeyser completed her prose work The Orgy, *published in 1965. She also translated selections on the work of Octavio Paz and Gunnar Ekelöf. Then, in 1964, at the age of fifty, she suffered her first stroke. Because the stroke attacked the right side of the brain, her powers of speech were affected. In the process of finding her way back to language, Rukeyser would produce a classic of feminist literature. The bold, breathtaking poems of* The Speed of Darkness, *stripped down to the essentials of "naked" urgency, tell us not only of one woman's struggle, but of all women's struggle to speak, to be heard, and to hear themselves.*

"No more masks! No more mythologies!" she cries out. So many of the doors that women poets can pass through today were first opened by those lines of Muriel Rukeyser's. Now, nothing is off limits for the poem—not sex, not family secrets, not the failures of imagination that produce human misery and war and that exile us even from ourselves. Now, nothing is illegitimate: not children, not mothers, not any of our loves or lovers.

"What would happen if one woman told the truth about her life? / The world would split open"—twenty-one syllables from Rukeyser's "Käthe Kollwitz" that, a quarter-century after they were written, still split the brain and heart like a bolt of lightning.

.   .   .   .   .

FOR MY SON

You come from poets, kings, bankrupts, preachers,
    attempted bankrupts, builders of cities, salesmen,
the great rabbis, the kings of Ireland, failed drygoods
    storekeepers, beautiful women of the songs,
great horsemen, tyrannical fathers at the shore of ocean, the
    western mothers looking west beyond from their
        windows,
the families escaping over the sea hurriedly and by night—
the roundtowers of the Celtic violet sunset,
the diseased, the radiant, fliers, men thrown out of town, the
    man bribed by his cousins to stay out of town, teachers,
        the cantor on Friday evening, the lurid newspapers,
strong women gracefully holding relationship, the Jewish girl
    going to parochial school, the boys racing their iceboats
        on the Lakes,
the woman still before the diamond in the velvet window, say-
    ing "Wonder of nature."
Like all men,
you come from singers, the ghettoes, the famines, wars and
    refusal of wars, men who built villages
that grew to our solar cities, students, revolutionists, the
    pouring of buildings, the market newspapers,
a poor tailor in a darkening room,
a wilderness man, the hero of mines, the astronomer, a white-
    faced woman hour on hour teaching piano and her
        crippled wrist,
like all men,
you have not seen your father's face
but he is known to you forever in song, the coast of the skies,
    in dream, wherever you find man playing his part
        as father, father among our light, among our darkness,
and in your self made whole, whole with yourself and whole
    with others,
the stars your ancestors.

THE BACKSIDE OF THE ACADEMY

Five brick panels, three small windows, six lions' heads with
      rings in their mouths, five pairs of closed bronze doors—
the shut wall with the words carved across its head
ART REMAINS THE ONE WAY POSSIBLE OF SPEAKING
      TRUTH.—
On this May morning, light swimming in this street, the
      children running,
on the church beside the Academy the lines are flying
of little yellow-and-white plastic flags flapping in the light;
and on the great shut wall, the words are carved across:
WE ARE YOUNG AND WE ARE FRIENDS OF TIME.—
Below that, a light blue asterisk in chalk
and in white chalk, Hector, Joey, Lynn, Rudolfo.
A little up the street, a woman shakes a small dark boy,
she shouts What's wrong with you, ringing that bell!
In the street of rape and singing, poems, small robberies,
carved in an oblong panel of the stone:
CONSCIOUS UTTERANCE OF THOUGHT BY SPEECH
      OR ACTION
TO ANY END IS ART.—
On the lowest reach of the walls are chalked the words: Jack is
      a object,
Walter and Trina, Goo Goo, I love Trina,
and further along Viva Fidel now altered to Muera Fidel.
A deep blue marble is lodged against the curb.
A phone booth on one corner; on the other, the big mesh
      basket for trash.
Beyond them, the little park is always locked. For the two
      soldier brothers.
and past that goes on an eternal football game
which sometimes, as on this day in May, transforms to
      stickball
as, for one day in May,
five pairs of closed bronze doors will open
and the Academy of writers, sculptors, painters, composers,
      their guests and publishers will all roll in and
the wave of organ music come rolling out into

---

the street where light now blows and papers and little children
      and words, some breezes of Spanish blow and many
            colors of people.
A watch cap lies fallen against a cellophane which used to hold
      pistachio nuts
and here before me, on my street,
five brick panels, three small windows, six lions' heads with
      rings in their mouths, five pairs of closed bronze doors,
light flooding the street I live and write in; and across the river
      the one word FREE against the ferris wheel and the roller
            coaster,
and here, painted upon the stones, Chino, Bobby, Joey, Fat-
      moma, Willy, Holy of God
and also Margaret is a shit and also fuck and shit;
far up, invisible at the side of the building:
WITHOUT VISION THE PEO
and on the other side, the church side,
where shadows of trees and branches, this day in May, are
      printed balanced on the church wall,
in-focus trunks and softened-focus branches
below the roof where the two structures stand,
bell and cross, antenna and weathervane,
I can see past the church the words of an ending line:
IVE BY BREAD ALONE.

POEM

I lived in the first century of world wars.
Most mornings I would be more or less insane,
The newspapers would arrive with their careless stories,
The news would pour out of various devices
Interrupted by attempts to sell products to the unseen.
I would call my friends on other devices;
They would be more or less mad for similar reasons.
Slowly I would get to pen and paper,

Make my poems for others unseen and unborn.
In the day I would be reminded of those men and women
Brave, setting up signals across vast distances,
Considering a nameless way of living, of almost unimagined
    values.
As the lights darkened, as the lights of night brightened,
We would try to imagine them, try to find each other.
To construct peace, to make love, to reconcile
Waking with sleeping, ourselves with each other,
Ourselves with ourselves. We would try by any means
To reach the limits of ourselves, to reach beyond ourselves,
To let go the means, to wake.

I lived in the first century of these wars.

THE OVERTHROW OF ONE O'CLOCK AT NIGHT

is my concern.   That's this moment,
when I lean on my elbows out the windowsill
and feel the city among its time-zones, among its seas,
among its late night news, the pouring in
of everything meeting, wars, dreams, winter night.
Light in snowdrifts causing the young girls
lying awake to fall in love tonight
alone in bed; or the little children
half world over tonight rained on by fire—that's us—
calling on somebody—that's us—to come
and help them.

                    Now I see at the boundary of darkness
extreme of moonlight.

                    Alone.   All my hopes
scattered in people quarter world away
half world away, out of all hearing.

                    Tell myself:

Trust in experience.   And in the rhythms.
The deep rhythms of your experience.

THE POEM AS MASK

ORPHEUS

When I wrote of the women in their dances and wildness, it
        was a mask,
on their mountain, gold-hunting, singing, in orgy,
it was a mask; when I wrote of the god,
fragmented, exiled from himself, his life, the love gone down
        with song,
it was myself, split open, unable to speak, in exile from myself.

There is no mountain, there is no god, there is memory
of my torn life, myself split open in sleep, the rescued child
beside me among the doctors, and a word
of rescue from the great eyes.

No more masks! No more mythologies!

Now, for the first time, the god lifts his hand,
the fragments join in me with their own music.

ORGY

There were three of them that night.
They wanted it to happen in the first woman's room.
The man called her; the phone rang high.

Then she put fresh lipstick on.
Pretty soon he rang the bell.
She dreamed, she dreamed, she dreamed.
She scarcely looked him in the face
But gently took him to his place.
And after that the bell, the bell.
They looked each other in the eyes,
A hot July it was that night,
And he then slow took off his tie,
And she then slow took off her scarf,
The second one took off her scarf,
And he then slow his heavy shoe,
And she then slow took off her shoe,
The other one took off her shoe,
He then took off his other shoe,
The second one, her other shoe,
A hot July it was that night.
And he then slow took off his belt,
And she then slow took off her belt,
The second one took off her belt . . .

KÄTHE KOLLWITZ

1

Held between wars
my lifetime
              among wars, the big hands of the world of death
my lifetime
listens to yours.

The faces of the sufferers
in the street, in dailiness,

The German artist Käthe Kollwitz (1867–1945) is best known for her black-and-white prints and woodcuts depicting victims of war and social injustice, particularly women and children.—Ed.

their lives showing
through their bodies
a look as of music
the revolutionary look
that says   I am in the world
to change the world
my lifetime
is to love to endure to suffer the music
to set its portrait
up as a sheet of the world
the most moving the most alive
Easter and bone
and Faust walking among the flowers of the world
and the child alive within the living woman, music of man,
and death holding my lifetime between great hands
the hands of enduring life
that suffers the gifts and madness of full life, on earth, in our
        time,
and through my life, through my eyes, through my arms and
        hands
may give the face of this music in portrait waiting for
the unknown person
held in the two hands, you.

    2

Woman as gates, saying   :
"The process is after all like music,
like the development of a piece of music.
The fugues come back and

                            again and again
interweave.
A theme may seem to have been put aside,
but it keeps returning—
the same thing modulated,
somewhat changed in form.
Usually richer.
And it is very good that this is so."

A woman pouring her opposites.
"After all there are happy things in life too.

Why do you show only the dark side?"
"I could not answer this. But I know—
in the beginning my impulse to know
the working life

had little to do with
pity or sympathy.
I simply felt
that the life of the workers was beautiful."

She said, "I am groping in the dark."

She said, "When the door opens, of sensuality,
then you will understand it too. The struggle begins.
Never again to be free of it,
often you will feel it to be your enemy.
Sometimes
you will almost suffocate,
such joy it brings."

Saying of her husband   :   "My wish
is to die after Karl.
I know no person who can love as he can,
with his whole soul.
Often this love has oppressed me;
I wanted to be free.
But often too it has made me
so terribly happy."

She said   :   "We rowed over to Carrara at dawn,
climbed up to the marble quarries
and rowed back at night. The drops of water
fell like glittering stars
from our oars."

She said: "As a matter of fact,
I believe
that bisexuality
is almost   a necessary factor
in artistic production; at any rate,
the tinge of masculinity within me
helped me
in my work."

She said   :   "The only technique I can still manage.
It's hardly a technique at all, lithography.
In it
        only the essentials count."

A tight-lipped man in a restaurant last night saying to me   :
"Kollwitz?   She's too black-and-white."

        3

Held among wars, watching
    all of them
    all these people
    weavers,
    Carmagnole

Looking at
    all of them
    death, the children
    patients in waiting-rooms
    famine
    the street
    the corpse with the baby
    floating, on the dark river

A woman seeing
    the violent, inexorable
    movement of nakedness
    and the confession of No
    the confession of great weakness, war,
    all streaming to one son killed, Peter;
    even the son left living; repeated,
    the father, the mother; the grandson
    another Peter killed in another war; firestorm;
    dark, light, as two hands,
    this pole and that pole as the gates.

What would happen if one woman told the truth about her life?
    The world would split open

4 / Song : The Calling-Up

Rumor, stir of ripeness
rising within this girl
sensual blossoming
of meaning, its light and form.

The birth-cry summoning
out of the male, the father
from the warm woman
a mother in response.

The word of death
calls up the fight with stone
wrestle with grief with time
from the material make
an art harder than bronze.

5 / Self-Portrait

Mouth looking directly at you
eyes in their inwardness looking
directly at you
half light   half darkness
woman, strong, German, young artist
flows into
wide sensual mouth meditating
looking right at you
eyes shadowed with brave hand
looking deep at you
flows into
wounded brave mouth
grieving and hooded eyes
alive, German, in her first War
flows into
strength of the worn face
a skein of lines
broods, flows into
mothers among the war graves
bent over death

facing the father
stubborn upon the field
flows into
the marks of her knowing—
Nie Wieder Krieg
repeated in the eyes
flows into
"Seedcorn must not be ground"
and the grooved cheek
lips drawn fine
the down-drawn grief
face of our age
flows into
Pieta, mother and
between her knees
life as her son in death
pouring from the sky of
one more war
flows into
face almost obliterated
hand over the mouth forever
hand over one eye now
the other great eye
closed

DOUBLE DIALOGUE:
HOMAGE TO ROBERT FROST

In agony saying　：　"The last night of his life,
My son and I in the kitchen　：　At half-past one
He said, 'I have failed as a husband. Now my wife
Is ill again and suffering.' At two
He said, 'I have failed as a farmer, for the sun
Is never there, the rain is never there.'
At three he said, 'I have failed as a poet who
Has never not once found my listener.

There is no sense to my life.' But then he heard me out.
I argued point by point. Seemed to win. Won.
He spoke to me once more when I was done:
'Even in argument, father, I have lost.'
He went and shot himself. Now tell me this one thing:
Should I have let him win then? Was I wrong?"

To answer for the land for love for song
Arguing life for life even at your life's cost.

THE OUTER BANKS

1

Horizon of islands shifting
Sea-light flame on my voice
                         burn in me
                                    Light
flows from the water from sands   islands of this horizon
The sea comes toward me across the sea.   The sand
moves over the sand in waves
between the guardians of this landscape
the great commemorative statue on one hand
    —the first flight of man, outside of dream,
            seen as stone wing and stainless steel—
and at the other hand
        banded black-and-white, climbing
the spiral lighthouse.

This country, the Outer Banks of North Carolina, is a strong country of imagination: Raleigh's first settlements, in which Thomas Hariot the scientist served a year in the New World, were here; the Wright Brothers flew from here; Hart Crane's "Hatteras" is set among these sand-bars, these waters. Several journeys here, the last one for the sake of the traces of Thomas Hariot (toward a biography I was writing) led me to this poem. The *Tiger,* in the last part of the poem, is one of the ships sent out by Raleigh. The quotations are from Selma, Alabama, in 1965. The truncated wing is a monument to the Wright Brothers. The spiral lighthouse is Hatteras light.—MR

2

Flood over ocean,
avalanche on the flat beach. Pouring.
Indians holding branches up, to
placate the tempest,
the one-legged twisting god that is
a standing wind.
Rays are branching from all things:
great serpent, great plume, constellation:
sands from which colors and light pass,
the lives of plants.   Animals.   Men.
A man and a woman reach for each other.

3

Wave of the sea.

4

Sands have washed, sea has flown over us.
Between the two guardians, spiral, truncated wing,
history and these wild birds
Bird-voiced discoverers : Hariot,   Hart Crane,
the brothers who watched gulls.
"No bird soars in a calm,"   said Wilbur Wright.
Dragon of the winds forms over me.
Your dance, goddesses in your circle
sea-wreath, whirling of the event
behind me on land as deep in our own lives
we begin to know the movement to come.
Sunken, drowned spirals,
hurricane-dance.

5

Shifting of islands on this horizon.
The cycle of changes in the Book of Changes.
Two islands making an open female line.
That powerful long straight bar a male island.

The building of the surf
constructing immensities
between the pale flat Sound
and ocean ever
birds as before earthquake
winds fly from all origins
the length of this wave goes from the great wing
down coast, the barrier beach in all its miles
road of the sun and the moon to
a spiral lighthouse
to the depth turbulence
lifts up its wave like cities
the ocean in the air
spills down the world.

6

A man is walking toward me across the water.
From far out, the flat waters of the Sound,
he walks pulling his small boat

In the shoal water.
A man who is white and has been fishing.
Walks steadily upon the light of day
Coming closer to me where I stand
looking into the sun and the blaze inner water.
Clear factual surface over which he pulls
a boat over a closing quarter-mile.

7

Speak to it, says the light.
Speak to it music,
voices of the sea and human throats.
Origins of spirals,
the ballad and original sweet grape
dark on the vines near Hatteras,
tendrils of those vines, whose spiral tower
now rears its light, accompanying
all my voices.

8

He walks toward me.   A black man in the sun.
He now is a black man speaking to my heart
crisis of darkness in this century
of moments of this speech.

The boat is slowly nearer drawn, this man.

The zigzag power coming straight, in stones,
        in arcs, metal, crystal, the spiral
in sacred wet

                schematic elements of
cities, music, arrangement
spin these stones of home

                        under the sea
return to the stations of the stars
and the sea, speaking across its lives.

9

A man who is bones is close to me
drawing a boat of bones
the sun behind him
is another color of fire,
the sea behind me
rears its flame.

A man whose body flames and tapers in flame
twisted tines of remembrance that dissolve
a pitchfork of the land worn thin
flame up and dissolve again

                        draw   small   boat
Nets of the stars at sunset over us.
This draws me home to the home of the wild birds
long-throated birds of this passage.
This is the edge of experience, *grenzen der seele*
where those on the verge of human understanding
the borderline people stand on the shifting islands
among the drowned stars and the tempest.

"Everyman's mind, like the dumbest;
claws at his own furthest limits of knowing the world,"
a man in a locked room said.

Open to the sky
I stand before this boat that looks at me.
The man's flames are arms and legs.
Body, eye, head, stars, sands look at me.

I walk out into the shoal water
and throw my leg over the wall of the boat.

10

At one shock, speechlessness.
I am in the bow, on the short thwart.
He is standing before me amidships, rowing forward
like my old northern sea-captain in his dory.
All things have spun.
The words gone,
I facing sternwards, looking at the gate
between the barrier islands.   As he rows.
Sand islands shifting and the last of land
a pale and open line   horizon
sea.

With whose face did he look at me?
What did I say?   or did I say?
in speechlessness
move to the change.
These strokes provide the music,
and the accused boy on land today saying
What did I say?   or did I say?
The dream on land last night built this the boat of death
but in the suffering of the light
moving across the sea
do we in our moving
move toward life or death

11

Hurricane, skullface, the sky's size
winds streaming through his teeth
doing the madman's twist

and not a beach not flooded

nevertheless, here
stability of light
my other silence
and at my left hand and at my right hand
no longer wing and lighthouse
no longer the guardians.
They are in me, in my speechless
life of barrier beach.
As it lies open
to the night, out there.

Now seeing my death before me
starting again, among the drowned men,
desperate men, unprotected discoverers,
and the man before me
here.
Stroke by stroke drawing us.
Out there? Father of rhythms,
deep wave, mother.
There is no *out there*.
All is open.
Open water. Open I.

12

The wreck of the *Tiger,* the early pirate, the blood-clam's
        ark, the tern's acute eye, all buried mathematical
                instruments, castaways, pelicans, drowned five-
                        strand pearl necklaces, hopes of livelihood,
                                hopes of grace,
walls of houses, sepia sea-fences, the writhen octopus and those
        tall masts and sails,
marked hulls of ships and last month's plane, dipping his salute
        to the stone wing of dream,

turbulence, Diamond Shoals, the dark young living people:
"Sing one more song and you are under arrest."
"Sing another song."
Women, ships, lost voices.
Whatever has dissolved into our waves.
I a lost voice
moving, calling you
on the edge of the moment that is now the center.
From the open sea.

THE CONJUGATION OF THE PARAMECIUM

This has nothing
to do with
propagating

The species
is continued
as so many are
(among the smaller creatures)
by fission

(and this species
is very small
next in order to
the amoeba, the beginning one)

The paramecium
achieves, then,
immortality
by dividing

But when
the paramecium

---

desires renewal
strength another joy
this is what
the paramecium does:

The paramecium
lies down beside
another paramecium

Slowly inexplicably
the exchange
takes place
in which
some bits
of the nucleus of each
are exchanged

for some bits
of the nucleus
of the other

This is called
the conjugation of the paramecium.

WHAT I SEE

Lie there, in sweat and dream, I do, and "there"
Is here, my bed, on which I dream
You, lying there, on yours, locked, pouring love,
While I tormented here see in my reins
You, perfectly at climax. And the lion strikes.
I want you with whatever obsessions come—
I wanted your obsession to be mine
But if it is that unknown half-suggested strange

Other figure locked in your climax, then
I here, I want you and the other, want your obsession, want
Whatever is locked into you now while I sweat and dream.

ANEMONE

My eyes are closing, my eyes are opening.
You are looking into me with your waking look.

My mouth is closing, my mouth is opening.
You are waiting with your red promises.

My sex is closing, my sex is opening.
You are singing and offering : the way in.

My life is closing, my life is opening.
You are here.

THE SPEED OF DARKNESS

1

Whoever despises the clitoris despises the penis
Whoever despises the penis despises the cunt
Whoever despises the cunt despises the life of the child.

Resurrection music,   silence,   and surf.

2

No longer speaking
Listening with the whole body
And with every drop of blood
Overtaken by silence

But this same silence is become speech
With the speed of darkness.

3

Stillness during war, the lake.
The unmoving spruces.
Glints over the water.
Faces, voices.   You are far away.
A tree that trembles.

I am the tree that trembles and trembles.

4

After the lifting of the mist
after the lift of the heavy rains
the sky stands clear
and the cries of the city risen in day
I remember the buildings are space
walled, to let space be used for living
I mind this room is space
this drinking glass is space
whose boundary of glass
lets me give you drink and space to drink
your hand, my hand being space
containing skies and constellations
your face
carries the reaches of air
I know I am space
my words are air.

5

Between   between
the man : act   exact
woman : in curve   senses in their maze
frail orbits, green tries,   games of stars
shape of the body speaking its evidence

6

I look across at the real
vulnerable   involved   naked
devoted to the present of all I care for
the world of its history leading to this moment.

7

Life the announcer.
I assure you
there are many ways to have a child.
I bastard mother
promise you
there are many ways to be born.
They all come forth
in their own grace.

8

Ends of the earth join tonight
with blazing stars upon their meeting.

These sons,   these sons
fall burning into Asia.

9

Time comes into it.
Say it.   Say it.

The universe is made of stories,
not of atoms.

10

Lying
blazing beside me
you rear beautifully and up—
your thinking face—
erotic body reaching
in all its colors and lights—
your erotic face
colored and lit—
not colored body-and-face
but now entire,
colors   lights   the world thinking and reaching.

11

The river flows past the city.

Water goes down to tomorrow
making its children   I hear their unborn voices
I am working out the vocabulary of my silence.

12

Big-boned man young and of my dream
Struggles to get the live bird out of his throat.
I am he am I?   Dreaming?
I am the bird am I?   I am the throat?

A bird with a curved beak.
It could slit anything, the throat-bird.

Drawn up slowly.   The curved blades, not large.
Bird emerges   wet   being born
Begins to sing.

13

My night awake
staring at the broad rough jewel
the copper roof across the way
thinking of the poet
yet unborn in this dark
who will be the throat of these hours.
No.   Of those hours.
Who will speak these days,
if not I,
if not you?

FIVE SONGS FROM

HOUDINI

·   ·   (1 9 7 3)   ·   ·

As early as the late '30s, Rukeyser first began thinking about a play based on the life of Harry Houdini (1874–1926). Houdini (born Erich Weiss) was the great American magician and escape artist, famous for such exploits as freeing himself from chained boxes submerged underwater. The great American hero as escape artist—it was a natural for Rukeyser's imagination. For the next three decades, she worked, on and off, on her play—many versions of it exist. It was finally performed at the Lenox Art Center in Massachusetts in 1973. (A relatively unknown young actor at the time named Christopher Walken played the role of Houdini.)

Though her sly wit is apparent in several of her later poems, and her delightful sense of the absurd came through often in her conversation, interviews, and public readings, these five ditties from Houdini *are examples of Rukeyser at her jazzy, jaunty, and sometimes bawdy, best.*

.　　.　　.　　.　　.

CONEY ISLAND

Coney Island, Coney Island,
No need to let me know,
No need to tell me so
I need you now to show me . . .

Some.   Show me what's under the counter,
         Show me what's under your skin,
         Show me the way to get out
         And I'll show you the way to get in.

Others. Show me life, show me lives, people in dives,
         Show me yells, show me smells, and grimy hotels,
         Clams, yams, lobster and shrimps,
         Sand, candy, panders and pimps,
         Show me bim, show me bam, bamboozle me,
         Booze me and use me and foozle me,
         Show me rides, show me slides, people in tides,
         Show me money, show me funny, show me the sea,
                                        You, show, me.

Houdini and Beatrice. Let me see,
                       Let me feel,
                       Let me know what is real,
                       Let me bel-
                                ieve.

BEER AND BACON

When you see a woman riding the air
Well, you see a woman playing with fire,

A woman made of storm and desire
And she loves the whole damn zoo.
But you can be sure, whatever I do,
That I need my beer and bacon too.

I wake every night at 4 A.M.
And I tell my dreams to the man who is there,
Dreams of animals not like him—
A woman who rides on fire and air
Loves to dream with the whole damn zoo.
But I need my beer and bacon too.

My dreams ride out from the highest wire
Bodies like bubbles of color down there,
The feel of people of flesh and fire
Streaming toward me along the air—
But I make it clear, whatever I do,
That I need my beer and bacon too.

YES

It's like a tap-dance
Or a new pink dress,
A shit-naive feeling
Saying Yes.

Some say Good morning
Say say God bless—
Some say Possibly
Some say Yes.

Some say Never
Some say Unless
It's stupid and lovely
To rush into Yes.

———————

What can it mean?
It's just like life,
One thing to you
One to your wife.

Some go local
Some go express
Some can't wait
To answer Yes.

Some complain
Of strain and stress
Their answer may be
No for Yes.

Some like failure
Some like success
Some like Yes Yes
Yes Yes Yes.

Open your eyes,
Dream but don't guess.
Your biggest surprise
Comes after Yes.

WHAT THE KING SAID

Today your ambassador said in fun,
"Things are tough in Washington—
Let's go see what Houdini has done."
With all the forms of American rape,
We need a good all-purpose escape,
    An all-purpose good economy escape . . .
Every President and king
Must be able to get out of everything,

So do it 'n' do it 'n' do it 'n' do it Houdini,
Do do do it for me.

His Majesty said to Houdini the Great:
"Just the thing for a head of state,
You can have all your locks and clocks
As long as I'm in the royal box;
I've too much sense to investigate.
    Do it as long as I can see,
From the orchestra or the balcony,
And all the princesses agree
    Whatever it is you do Houdini
    Do it 'n' do it 'n' do it 'n' do it for me—.
    Except for the wildest youngest of all princesses
    And she sings rapturously:
    Do it 'n' do it 'n' do it 'n' do it Houdini,
    Do do do it to me."

I MAKE MY MAGIC

I make my magic
of forgotten things:
night and nightmare and the midnight wings
of childhood butterflies—
and the darkness, the straining dark
underwater and under sleep—
night and a heartbreak try to keep
myself, until before my eyes
the morning sunlight pours
and I am clear of all the chains
and the magic now that rains
down around me is
a sunlight magic,
I come to a sunlight magic,
yours.

· · · F R O M · · ·
BREAKING OPEN
(1 9 7 3)

By 1967, Rukeyser had resigned from the faculty at Sarah Lawrence College ("I couldn't be a tenured professor at any college: it would make me very nervous," she said), but she continued to teach poetry workshops in New York City and around the country through a program of the Teachers and Writers Collaborative, an organization she helped found. In 1971, she published The Traces of Thomas Hariot, a speculative biography of the seventeenth-century astronomer, mathematician, and chronicler of the New World.

Then, in 1972, Rukeyser traveled to a world that was new for her. (Though, as she had reminded us in "The Outer Banks," every new world is our world, too: "There is no out there.") With Denise Levertov and Jane Hart, she went to North Vietnam on an unofficial peace mission. Later, back in the States, she was arrested and jailed in Washington, D.C., after participating in an antiwar demonstration just outside the Senate chambers.

Rukeyser's physical health had never been good, since a bout with typhoid in her early twenties. Now, there were still lingering effects of the stroke, and she had also been diagnosed with diabetes.

These experiences figure into Breaking Open. Rukeyser celebrates health and life with a mature-armed embrace in "Rondel" or gently parodies her own life choices in in "Gradus ad Parnassum." She flies to the war in "Flying to Hanoi" and the war flies to her in "Despisals," "What Do We See," and "Waking This Morning." Having called out "No more masks! No more mythologies!" in The Speed of Darkness, she goes back in "Icarus" and Myth" to revision the myths that leave women's voices out of the stories.

.   .   .   .   .

RONDEL

Now that I am fifty-six
Come and celebrate with me—

What happens to song and sex
Now that I am fifty-six?

They dance, but differently,
Death and distance in the mix;
Now that I'm fifty-six
Come and celebrate with me.

WAITING FOR ICARUS

He said he would be back and we'd drink wine together
He said that everything would be better than before
He said we were on the edge of a new relation
He said he would never again cringe before his father
He said that he was going to invent full-time
He said he loved me that going into me
He said was going into the world and the sky
He said all the buckles were very firm
He said the wax was the best wax
He said Wait for me here on the beach
He said Just don't cry

I remember the gulls and the waves
I remember the islands going dark on the sea
I remember the girls laughing
I remember they said he only wanted to get away from me
I remember mother saying   :   Inventors are like poets,

a trashy lot

I remember she told me those who try out inventions are
    worse
I remember she added   :   Women who love such are the worst
    of all
I have been waiting all day, or perhaps longer.
I would have liked to try those wings myself.
It would have been better than this.

GRADUS AD PARNASSUM

Oh I know
If I'd practised the piano
I'd never be so low
As I now am

Where's Sylvia Beerman?
Married, rich and cool
In New Rochelle
She was nobody's fool,

She didn't write in verse
She hardly wrote at all
She rose she didn't fall
She never gave a damn

But got up early
To practise Gradus
Ad Parnassum   —   she
Feels fine. I know.

BALLAD OF ORANGE AND GRAPE

After you finish your work
after you do your day
after you're read your reading
after you've written your say—
you go down the street to the hot dog stand,
one block down and across the way.
On a blistering afternoon in East Harlem in the twentieth
      century.

Most of the windows are boarded up,
the rats run out of a sack   —
sticking out of the crummy garage
one shiny long Cadillac;
at the glass door of the drug-addiction center,
a man who'd like to break your back.
But here's a brown woman with a little girl dressed in rose and
      pink, too.

Frankfurters frankfurters sizzle on the steel
where the hot-dog-man leans   —
nothing else on the counter
but the usual two machines,
the grape one, empty, and the orange one, empty,
I face him in between.
A black boy comes along, looks at the hot dogs, goes on
      walking.

I watch the man as he stands and pours
in the familiar shape
bright purple in the one marked ORANGE
orange in the one marked GRAPE,
the grape drink in the machine marked ORANGE
and orange drink in the GRAPE.
Just the one word large and clear, unmistakable, on each
      machine.

I ask him   :   How can we go on reading
and make sense out of what we read?   —
How can they write and believe what they're writing,
the young ones across the street,
while you go on pouring grape into ORANGE
and orange into the one marked GRAPE   —?
(How are we going to believe what we read and we write and
        we hear and we say and we do?)

He looks at the two machines and he smiles
and he shrugs and smiles and pours again.
It could be violence and nonviolence
it could be white and black   women and men
it could be war and peace or any
binary system, love and hate, enemy, friend.
Yes and no, be and not-be, what we do and what we don't do.

On a corner in East Harlem
garbage, reading, a deep smile, rape,
forgetfulness, a hot street of murder,
misery, withered hope,
a man keeps pouring grape into ORANGE
and orange into the one marked GRAPE,
pouring orange into GRAPE and grape into ORANGE forever.

SECRETS OF AMERICAN CIVILIZATION
FOR STAUGHTON LYND

Jefferson spoke of freedom but he held slaves.
Were ten of them his sons by black women?
Did he sell them? or was his land their graves?
Do we asking our questions become more human?

Are our lives the parable which, living,
We all have, we all know, we all can move?

Then they said   :   The earth belongs to the living,
We refuse allegiance, we resign office, and we love.

They are writing at their desks, the thinking fathers,
They do not recognize their live sons' faces;
Slave and slaveholder they are chained together
And one is ancestor and one is child.
Escape the birthplace; walk into the world
Refusing to be either slave or slaveholder.

FROM A PLAY : PUBLISHER'S SONG

I lie in the bath and I contemplate the toilet-paper:
Scottissue, 1000 sheets   —
      What a lot of pissin and shittin,
      What a lot of pissin and shittin,
Enough for the poems of Shelley and Keats   —
All the poems of Shelley and Keats.

LOOKING AT EACH OTHER

Yes, we were looking at each other
Yes, we knew each other very well
Yes, we had made love with each other many times
Yes, we had heard music together
Yes, we had gone to the sea together
Yes, we had cooked and eaten together
Yes, we had laughed often day and night

Yes, we fought violence and knew violence
Yes, we hated the inner and outer oppression
Yes, that day we were looking at each other
Yes, we saw the sunlight pouring down
Yes, the corner of the table was between us
Yes, bread and flowers were on the table
Yes, our eyes saw each other's eyes
Yes, our mouths saw each other's mouth
Yes, our breasts saw each other's breasts
Yes, our bodies entire saw each other
Yes, it was beginning in each
Yes, it threw waves across our lives
Yes, the pulses were becoming very strong
Yes, the beating became very delicate
Yes, the calling   the arousal
Yes, the arriving   the coming
Yes, there it was for both entire
Yes, we were looking at each other

DESPISALS

In the human cities, never again to
despise the backside of the city, the ghetto,
or build it again as we build the despised
backsides of houses.   Look at your own building.
You are the city.

Among our secrecies, not to despise our Jews
(that is, ourselves) or our darkness, our blacks,
or in our sexuality   wherever it takes us
and we now know we are productive
too productive, too reproductive
for our present invention   —   never to despise
the homosexual who goes building another

with touch   with touch   (not to despise any touch)
each like himself, like herself each.
You are this.

                                        In the body's ghetto
never to go despising the asshole
nor the useful shit that is our clean clue
to what we need.   Never to despise
the clitoris in her least speech.

Never to despise in myself what I have been taught
to despise.   Nor to despise the other.
Not to despise the *it*.   To make this relation
with the it   :   to know that I am it.

WHAT DO WE SEE?

When they're decent about women, they're frightful about
        children,
When they're decent about children, they're rotten about
        artists,
When they're decent about artists, they're vicious about
        whores,
        What do we see?   What do we not see?

When they're kind to whores, they're death on communists,
When they respect communists, they're foul to bastards,
When they're human to bastards, they mock at hysterectomy—
        What do we see?   What do we not see?

When they're decent about surgery, they bomb the Vietnamese,
When they're decent to Vietnamese, they're frightful to police,
When they're human to police, they rough up lesbians,
        What do we see?   What do we not see?

When they're decent to old women, they kick homosexuals,
When they're good to homosexuals, they can't stand drug
        people,
When they're calm about drug people, they hate all Germans,
        What do we see?   What do we not see?

Cadenza for the reader

When they're decent to Jews, they dread the blacks,
When they know blacks, there's always something   :   roaches
And the future and children and all potential.   Can't stand
        themselves
                Will we never see?   Will we ever know?

DESDICHADA

1

For that you never acknowledged me, I acknowledge
the spring's yellow detail, the every drop of rain,
the anonymous unacknowledged men and women.
The shine as it glitters in our child's wild eyes,
one o'clock at night.   This river, this city,
the years of the shadow on the delicate skin
of my hand, moving in time.
Disinherited, annulled, finally disacknowledged
and all of my own asking.   I keep that wild dimension
of life and making and the spasm
upon my mouth as I say this word of acknowledge
to you forever.   *Ewig.*   Two o'clock at night.

2

While this my day and my people are a country not yet born
it has become an earth I can

---

acknowledge.   I must.   I know what the
disacknowledgment does.   Then I do take you,
but far under consciousness, knowing
that under under flows a river wanting
the other   :   to go open-handed in Asia,
to cleanse the tributaries and the air, to make for making,
to stop selling death and its trash, pour plastic down men's
          throats,
to let this child find, to let men and women find,
knowing the seeds in us all.   They do say Find.
I cannot acknowledge it entire.   But I will.
A beginning, this moment, perhaps, and you.

          3

Death flowing down past me, past me, death
marvelous, filthy, gold,
in my spine in my sex upon my broken mouth
and the whole beautiful mouth of the child;
shedding power over me
death
if I acknowledge him.
Leading me
in my own body
at last in the dance.

FROM
BREAKING OPEN

          *   *   *

Written on the plane:

The conviction that what is meant by the unconscious is the same
as what is meant by history. The collective unconscious is the

living history brought to the present in consciousness, waking or sleeping. The personal "unconscious" is the personal history. This is an identity.

We will now explore further ways of reaching our lives, the new world. My own life, yours; this earth, this moon, this system, the "space" we share, which is consciousness.

Turbulence of air now. A pause of nine minutes.

.   .   .   .   .

Written on the plane. After turbulence:

The movement of life : to live more fully in the present. This movement includes the work of bringing this history to "light" and understanding. The "unconscious" of the race, and its traces in art and in social structure and "inventions"—these are our inheritance. In facing history, we look at each other, and in facing our entire personal life, we look at each other.

I want to break open. On the plane, a white cloud seen through rainbow. The rainbow is, optically, on the glass of the window.

*   *   *

FLYING TO HANOI

I thought I was going to the poets, but I am going to the
    children.
I thought I was going to the children, but I am going to the
    women.
I thought I was going to the women, but I am going to the
    fighters.
I thought I was going to the fighters, but I am going to the
    men and women who are inventing peace.

I thought I was going to the inventors of peace, but I am going
        to the poets.
My life is flying to your life.

WAKING THIS MORNING

Waking this morning,
a violent woman in the violent day
Laughing.
                Past the line of memory
along the long body of your life
in which move childhood, youth, your lifetime of touch,
eyes, lips, chest, belly, sex, legs, to the waves of the sheet.
I look past the little plant
on the city windowsill
to the tall towers bookshaped, crushed together in greed,
the river flashing flowing corroded,
the intricate harbor and the sea, the wars, the moon, the
        planets, all who people space
in the sun visible invisible.
African violets in the light
breathing, in a breathing universe.   I want strong peace, and
        delight,
the wild good.
I want to make my touch poems:
to find my morning, to find you entire
alive moving among the anti-touch people.

                I say across the waves of the air to you:
today once more
I will try to be non-violent
one more day
this morning, waking the world away
in the violent day.

MYTH

Long afterward, Oedipus, old and blinded, walked the
roads.   He smelled a familiar smell.   It was
the Sphinx.   Oedipus said, "I want to ask one question.
Why didn't I recognize my mother?"   "You gave the
wrong answer," said the Sphinx.   "But that was what
made everything possible," said Oedipus.   "No," she said.
"When I asked, What walks on four legs in the morning,
two at noon, and three in the evening, you answered,
Man.   You didn't say anything about woman."
"When you say Man," said Oedipus, "you include women
too. Everyone knows that."   She said, "That's what
you think."

· · · F R O M · · ·

THE GATES

· · (1 9 7 6) · ·

In an essay called "A Talk: Convocation 1972" published in In Search of Our Mother's Gardens, *Alice Walker wrote: "Another great teacher was Muriel Rukeyser, who could link up Fujiyama with the Spanish Civil War, and poetry to potty training. If you have ever talked with a person of cosmic consciousness, you will understand what I mean. . . . Afraid of little, intimidated by none, Muriel Rukeyser the Poet and Muriel Rukeyser the Prophet-person, the Truth-doer (and I must add the Original One-of-a-Kind, which would seem redundant if applied to anyone else) taught me that it is possible to live in this world on your own terms."*

The years between Breaking Open *and* The Gates *were full ones for this woman of cosmic consciousness. Despite another major stroke, Rukeyser continued leading poetry reading and writing workshops across the country. In 1975, she was elected President of the P.E.N. American Center, and when she learned about the imprisonment of the poet Kim Chi Ha in South Korea, she traveled there herself to stand outside the prison gates in eloquent protest.*

The Gates *would be Rukeyser's last full-length book of new poems, though she would live to see her* Collected Poems *published in 1978. In forty-five years of her writing life, she wandered freely but never wavered in a commitment she made to herself the year her first book was printed. In her journal from 1935, in an entry dated June 3, these words: "I want to write things down. I will, too. And I will rest my love on whom I love."*

. . . . .

ST. ROACH

For that I never knew you, I only learned to dread you,
for that I never touched you, they told me you are filth,
they showed me by every action to despise your kind;
for that I saw my people making war on you,
I could not tell you apart, one from another,
for that in childhood I lived in places clear of you,
for that all the people I knew met you by
crushing you, stamping you to death, they poured boiling
     water on you, they flushed you down,
for that I could not tell one from another
only that you were dark, fast on your feet, and slender.
     Not like me.
For that I did not know your poems
And that I do not know any of your sayings
And that I cannot speak or read your language
And that I do not sing your songs
And that I do not teach our children
       to eat your food
       or know your poems
       or sing your songs
But that we say you are filthing our food
But that we know you not at all.

Yesterday I looked at one of you for the first time.
You were lighter than the others in color, that was
     neither good nor bad.
I was really looking for the first time.
You seemed troubled and witty.

Today I touched one of you for the first time.
You were startled, you ran, you fled away
Fast as a dancer, light, strange and lovely to the touch.
I reach, I touch, I begin to know you.

PAINTERS

In the cave with a long-ago flare
a woman stands, her arm up. Red twig, black twig, brown
        twig.
A wall of leaping darkness over her.
The men are out hunting in the early light
But here in this flicker, one or two men, painting
and a woman among them.
Great living animals grow on the stone walls,
their pelts, their eyes, their sex, their hearts,
and the cave-painters touch them with life, red, brown, black,
a woman among them, painting.

ISLANDS

O for God's sake
they are connected
underneath

They look at each other
across the glittering sea
some keep a low profile

Some are cliffs
The bathers think
islands are separate like them

THE GATES

Scaffolding. *A poet is in solitary; the expectation is that he will be tried and summarily executed on a certain day in autumn. He has been on this cycle before : condemned to death, the sentence changed to life imprisonment, and then a pardon from his President during a time of many arrests and executions, a time of terror. The poet has written his stinging work—like that of Burns or Brecht—and it has got under the skin of the highest officials. He is Kim Chi Ha.*

An American woman is sent to make an appeal for the poet's life. She speaks to Cabinet ministers, the Cardinal, university people, writers, the poet's family and his infant son. She stands in the mud and rain at the prison gates—also the gates of perception, the gates of the body. She is before the house of the poet. He is in solitary.

1

Waiting to leave all day I hear the words;
That poet in prison, that poet newly-died
whose words we wear, reading, all of us. I and my son.

All day we read the words:
friends, lovers, daughters, grandson,
and all night the distant loves
and I who had never seen him am drawn to him

Through acts, through poems,
through our closenesses—
whatever links us in our variousness;
across worlds, love and poems and justices
wishing to be born.

2

Walking the world to find the poet of these cries.
But this walking is flying the streets of all the air.

Walking the world, through the people at airports,
this city of hills, this island ocean fire-blue and now this city.

Walking this world is driving the roads of houses
endless tiles   houses, fast streams, now this child's house.

Walking under the sharp mountains through the sharp city
circled in time by rulers, their grip; the marvelous
hard-gripped people silent among their rulers, looking at me.

3 / New Friends

The new friend comes into my hotel room
smiling.   He does a curious thing.
He walks around the room, touching
all the pictures hanging on the wall.
One picture does not move.

A new friend assures me   :   Foreigners are safe,
You speak for writers, you are safe, he says.
There will be no car
driving up behind you, there will be
no accident, he says.   I know these accidents.
Nothing will follow you, he says.
O the Mafia at home, I know, Black Hand
of childhood, the death of Tresca whom I mourn,
the building of New York.   Many I know.
This morning I go early to see the Cardinal.
When I return, the new friend is waiting.   His face
wax-candle-pool-color, he saying
"I thought you were kidnapped."

A missionary comes to visit me.
Looks into my eyes.   Says,
"Turn on the music so we can talk."

4

The Cabinet minister speaks of liberation.
"Do you know how the Communists use this word?"
We all use the word.   Liberation.

258

No, but look—these are his diaries,
says the Cabinet minister.
These were found in the house of the poet.
Look, Liberation, Liberation, he is speaking in praise.

He says, this poet, It is not wrong
to take from the rich and give to the poor.

Yes.   He says it in prose speech, he says it in his plays,
he says it in his poems that bind me to him,
that bind his people and mine in these new ways
for the first time past strangeness and despisal.

It also means that you broke into his house and stole his
        papers.

5

Among the days,
among the nights of the poet in solitary,
a strong infant is just beginning to run.
I go up the stepping-stones
to where the young wife of the poet
stands holding the infant in her arms.
She weeps, she weeps.
But the poet's son looks at me
and the wife's mother looks at me with a keen look
across her grief.   Lights in the house, books making every wall
a wall of speech.
                    The clasp of the woman's hand
around my wrist, a keen band
more steel than the words
Save his life.

I feel that clasp on my bones.

A strong infant is beginning to run.

6 / The Church of Galilee

As we climb to the church of Galilee
Three harsh men on the corner.
As we go to the worship-meeting of the dismissed,
three state police on the street.
As we all join at the place of the dispossessed,
three dark men asking their rote questions.
As we go ahead to stand with our new friends
that will be our friends our lifetime.
Introduced as dismissed from this faculty, this college,
this faculty, this university.
"Dismissed" is now an honorary degree.
The harsh police are everywhere,
they have hunted this fellowship away before
and they are everywhere, at the street-corner,
listening to all hymns,
standing before all doors,
hearing over all wires.
We go up to Galilee.
Let them listen to the dispossessed
and to all women and men who stand firm and sing
wanting a shared and honest lifetime.
Let them listen to Galilee.

7 / The Dream of Galilee

That night, a flute
across the dark, the sound
opening times to me, a time
when I stood on the green hillside
before the great white stone.
Grave of my ancestor
Akiba at rest over Kinneret.
The holy poem, he said to me,
the Song of Songs always;
and know what I know, to love
your belief with all your life,
and resist the Romans, as I did,
even to the torture and beyond.

Over Kinneret, with all of them,
Jesus, all the Judeans,
that other Galilee
in dream across war I see.

8 / Mother as Pitchfork

Woman seen as a slender instrument,
woman at vigil in the prison-yard,
woman seen as the fine tines of a pitchfork
that works hard, that is worn down, rusted down
to a fine sculpture standing in a yard
where her son's body is confined.
Woman as fine tines blazing against sunset,
wavering lines against yellow brightness
where her fine body becomes transparent in bravery,
where she will live and die as the tines of a pitchfork
that stands to us as her son's voice does stand
across the world speaking

The rumor comes that if this son is killed
this mother will kill herself

But she is here, she lives,
the slender tines of this pitchfork standing in flames of light.

9

You grief woman   you gave me a scarlet coverlet
thick-sown with all the flowers
and all the while your poet sleeps in stone

Grief woman, the waves of this coverlet,
roses of Asia,
they flicker soft and bright over my sleep

all night while the poet waits in solitary

All you vigil women, I start up in the night,
fling back this cover of red;

in long despair we work   write   speak   pray   call to others
Free our night   free our lives   free our poet

10

Air fills with fear and the kinds of fear:

The fear of the child among the tyrannical
unanswerable men and women, they dominate day and night.

Fear of the young lover in the huge rejection
ambush of sex and of imagination;
fear that the world will not allow your work.

Fear of the overarching wars and poverties,
the terrible exiles,
all bound by corruption until at last!   we speak!

And those at home in jail who protest the frightful war
and the beginning   :   The woman-guard says to me, Spread your
        cheeks,
the search begins and I begin to know.

And also at home the nameless multitude
of fears   :   fear in childbirth for the living child,
fear for the child deformed and love, fear
among the surgeries that can cure her, fear
for the child's father, and for oneself, fear.
Fear of the cunt and cock in their terrible powers
and here a world away fear of the jailers' tortures
for we invent our fear and act it out
in ripping, in burning, in blood, in the terrible scream
and in tearing away every mouth that screams.

Giant fears   :   massacres, the butchered that across the fields of
        the world
lie screaming, and their screams are heard as silence.
O love, knowing your love across a world of fear,
I lie in a strange country, in pale yellow, swamp-green, woods
and a night of music while a poet lies in solitary
somewhere in a concrete cell. Glare-lit, I hear,

without books, without pen and paper.
Does he draw a pencil out of his throat,
out of his veins, out of his sex?
There are cells all around him, emptied.
He can signal on these walls till he runs mad.
He is signalling to me across the night.

He is signalling.   Many of us speak,
we do teach each other, we do act through our fears.

Where is the world that will touch life to this prison?

We run through the night. We are given his gifts.

11

Long ago, soon after my son's birth
—this scene comes in arousal with the sight of a strong child
just beginning to run—
when all life seemed prisoned off, because the father's other son
born three weeks before my child
had opened the world
that other son and his father closed the world—
in my fierce loneliness and fine well-being
torn apart but with my amazing child
I celebrated and grieved.
And before that baby
had ever started to begin to run
then Mary said,
smiling and looking out of her Irish eyes,
"Never mind, Muriel.
Life will come will come again
knocking and coughing and farting at your door."

12

For that I cannot name the names,
my child's own father, the flashing, the horseman,
the son of the poet—
for that he never told me another child was started,
to come to birth three weeks before my own.

Tragic timing that sets the hands of time.
O wind from our own coast, turning
around the turning world.

Wind from the continents, this other child,
child of this moment and this moment's poet.
Again I am struck nameless, unable to name,
and the axe-blows fall heavy heavy and sharp
and the moon strikes his white light down over the continents
on this strong infant and the heroic friends
silent in this terrifying moment under all moonlight,
all sunlight turning in all our unfree lands.
Name them, name them all, light of our own time.

13

Crucified child—is he crucified?   he is tortured,
kept away from his father, spiked on time,
crucified we say, cut off from the man
they want to kill—
he runs toward me in Asia, crying.
Flash gives me my own son strong and those years ago
cut off from his own father and running toward me
holding a strong flower.

Child of this moment, you are your father's child
wherever your father is prisoned, by what tyrannies
or jailed as my child's father
by his own fantasies—
child of the age running among the world,
standing among us who carry our own time.

14

So I became very dark very large
a silent woman this time given to speech
a woman of the river   of that song
and on the beach of the world in storm given
in long lightning seeing the rhyming of those scenes
that make our lives.
Anne Sexton the poet saying

---

ten days ago to that receptive friend,
the friend of the hand-held camera:
"Muriel is serene."
Am I that in their sight?
Word comes today of Anne's
of Anne's long-approaching
of Anne's over-riding over-falling
suicide.   Speak for   sing for   pray for
everyone in solitary
every living life.

15

All day the rain
all day waiting within the prison gate
before another prison gate
The house of the poet
He is in there somewhere
among the muscular wardens
I have arrived at the house of the poet
in the mud in the interior music of all poems
and the grey rain of the world
whose gates do not open.
I stand, and for this religion and that religion
do not eat but remember all the things I know
and a strong infant beginning to run.
Nothing is happening.   Mud, silence, rain.

Near the end of the day
with the rain and the knowledge pulling at my legs
a movement behind me makes me move aside.
A bus full of people turns in the mud, drives to the gate.
The gate that never opens
opens at last.   Beyond it, slender
Chinese-red posts of the inner gates.
The gate of the house of the poet.

The bus is crowded, a rush-hour bus that waits.
Nobody moves.

"Who are these people?" I say.
How can these gates open?

My new friend has run up beside me.
He has been standing guard in the far corner.
"They are prisoners," he says, "brought here from trial.
Don't you see?   They are all tied together."

Fool that I am!   I had not seen the ropes,
down at their wrists in the crowded rush-hour bus.

The gates are open.   The prisoners go in.
The house of the poet who stays in solitary,
not allowed reading   not allowed writing
not allowed   his woman   his friends   his unknown friends
and the strong infant beginning to run.

We go down the prison hill.   On our right, sheds
full of people all leaning forward, blown on some ferry.
"They are the families of the prisoners.   Some can visit.
They are waiting for their numbers to be called."

How shall we venture home?
How shall we tell each other of the poet?
How can we meet the judgment on the poet,
or his execution?   How shall we free him?
How shall we speak to the infant beginning to run?
All those beginning to run?

ARTIFACT

When this hand is gone to earth,
this writing hand and the paper beneath it,
long gone, and the words on the paper forgotten,
and the breath that slowly curls around earth with
                        its old spoken words
gone into lives unborn and they too gone to earth—
and their memory, memory of any of these gone,

and all who remembered them absorbed in air and dirt,
words, earth, breeze over the oceans, all these now other,
there may as in the past be something left,
some artifact.   This pen.   Will it tell my?   Will it tell our?
This thing made in bright metal by thousands unknown to me,
will it arrive with that unnameable wish to speak a music,
offering something out of all I moved among?
singing for others unknown a long-gone moment in old time
      sung?

                                          The pen—
will some broken pieces be assembled by women, by guessing
      men
(or future mutations, beings unnamed by us)—
can these dry pieces join?   Again go bright?   Speak to you
      then?

RESURRECTION OF THE RIGHT SIDE

When the half-body dies its frightful death
forked pain, infection of snakes, lightning, pull down the
      voice.   Waking
and I begin to climb the mountain on my mouth,
word by stammer, walk stammered, the lurching deck of earth.
Left-right with none of my own rhythms.
the long-established sex and poetry.

                                I go running in sleep,
but waking stumble down corridors of self, all rhythms gone.

The broken movement of love   sex out of rhythm
one halted name   in a shattered language
ruin of French-blue lights behind the eyes
slowly the left hand extends a hundred feet
and the right hand follows follows
but still the power of sight is very weak

but I go rolling this ball of life, it rolls
and I follow it whole up the slowly-brightening slope

A whisper attempts me, I whisper without stammer
I walk the long hall to the time of a metronome
set by a child's gun-target   left-right
the power of eyesight is very slowly arriving
  in this late impossible daybreak
  all the blue flowers open

POEM WHITE PAGE
WHITE PAGE POEM

Poem   white page   white page   poem
something is streaming out of a body in waves
something is beginning from the fingertips
they are starting to declare for my whole life
all the despair and the making music
something like wave after wave
that breaks on a beach
something like bringing the entire life
to this moment
the small waves bringing themselves to white paper
something like light stands up and is alive

PARALLEL INVENTION

We in our season like progress and inventions.
The inventor is really the invention.

But who made the inventions?   To what uses
Were they put, by whom, and for what purposes?

You made an innovation and then
did you give it to me without writing it down?
Did you give it to her, too?
Did I develop it and give it to him,
or to her, or to them?

Did you quicken communication,
Did you central-control?   And war?   And the soul?

Let's not talk about communication
any more.

Did we deepen our integration ties
did we subsequently grow—
in strength?   in complexity?

Or did we think of doing the same things
at the same time and do them to each other?

And then out of our lovemaking
emergence of priests and kings,
out of our smiles and twists
full-time craft specialists,
out of our mouths and asses
division into social classes,
art and architecture and writing
from meditation and delighting
from our terrors and our pities
"of course," you say, "the growth of cities."

But parallels do not imply
identities—there is no iron law;
we are richly variable
levels of heaven and levels of hell;
ripples of change out from the center
of me, of you, of love the inventor.

NOT TO BE PRINTED,
NOT TO BE SAID,
NOT TO BE THOUGHT

I'd rather be Muriel
than be dead and be Ariel.

TRINITY CHURCHYARD
FOR MY MOTHER & HER ANCESTOR, AKIBA

Wherever I walked I went green among young growing
Along the same song, Mother, even along this grass
Where, Mother, tombstones stand each in its pail of shade
In Trinity yard where you at lunchtime came
As a young workingwoman, Mother, bunches of your days,
     grapes
Pressing your life into mine, Mother,
And I never cared for these tombs and graves
But they are your book-keeper hours.
You said to me summers later, deep in your shiniest car
As a different woman, Mother, and I your poem-making
     daughter—
"Each evening after I worked all day for the lock-people
"I wished under a green sky on the young evening star—
"What did I wish for?" What did you wish for, Mother?
"I wished for a man, of course, anywhere in my world,
"And there was Trinity graveyard and the tall New York
     steeples."

Wherever I go, Mother, I stay away from graves
But they turn everywhere in the turning world; now,
Mother Rachel's, on the road from Jerusalem.
And mine is somewhere turning unprepared

In the earth or among the whirling air.
My workingwoman mother is saying to me, Girl—
Years before her rich needy unreal years—
Whatever work you do, always make sure
You can go walking, not like me, shut in your hours.

Mother I walk, going even here in green Galilee
Where our ancestor, Akiba, resisted Rome,
Singing forever for the Song of Songs
Even in torture knowing. Mother, I walk, this blue,
The Sea, Mother, this hillside, to his great white stone.
And again here in New York later I come alone
To you, Mother, I walk, making our poems.

DOUBLE ODE
FOR BILL & ALISON

1

Wine and oil gleaming within their heads,
I poured it into the hollow of their bodies
but they did not speak.   The light glittered.
Lit from underneath they wre.   Water
pouring over her face, it
made the lips move and the eyes move, she
spoke:
Break open.
He did not speak.
A still lake shining in his head,
until I knew that the sun and the moon
stood in me with one light.

2

They began to breathe and glitter.   Moving
overflowed, gifts poured from their sex

upon my throat and my breast.
They knew.   They laughed.   In their tremendous games
night revolved and shook my bed.   I
woke in a cold morning.
Your presences
allow me to begin to make myself
carried on your shoulders, swayed in your arms.
Something is flashing among the colors.   I
move without being allowed.   I
move with the blessing of the sky and the sea.

3

Tonight I will try again for the music of truth
since this one and that one of mine are met with death.
It is a blind lottery, a cheap military trumpet
with all these great roots black under the earth
while a muscle-legged man
stamps in his red and gold
rough wine, creatures in nets, swords through their spines
and all their cantillation in our thought.

Glitter and pedestal under my female powers
a woman singing horses, blind cities of concrete, moon
comes to moonrise as a dark daughter.
I am the poet of the night of women
and my two parents are the sun and the moon,
a strong father of that black double likeness,
a bell kicking out of the bell-tower,
and a mother who shines and shines his light.

Who is the double ghost whose head is smoke?
Her thighs hold the wild infant, a trampled country
and I will fly in, in all my fears.
Those two have terrified me, but I live,
their silvery line of music gave me girlhood
and fierce male prowess and a woman's grave
eternal double music male and female,
inevitable blue, repeated evening
of the two.   Of the two.

4

But these two figures are not the statues east and west
at my long window on the river they are mother and father
but not my actual parents only their memory.
Not memory but something builded in my cells

Father with your feet cut off
mother cut down to death
cut down my sister in the selfsame way
and my abandoned husband a madman of the sun
and you dark outlaw the other one when do we speak
The song flies out of all of you the song
starts in my body, the song
it is in my mouth, the song
it is on my teeth, the song
it is pouring the song
wine and lightning
the rivers coming to confluence
in me entire.

5

But that was years ago.   My child is grown.
His wife and he in exile, that is, home,
longing for home, and I home, that is exile, the much-loved
        country
like the country called parents, much-loved that was, and exile.
His wife and he turning toward the thought
of their own child, conceive we say, a child.
Now rise in me the old dealings   :   father, mother,
not years ago, but in my last-night dream,
waking this morning, the two Mexican figures
black stone with their stone hollows I fill with water,
fill with wine, with oil, poems and lightning.
Black in morning dark, the sky going blue,
the river going blue.

Moving toward new form I am—
carry again
all the old gifts and wars.

6

Black parental mysteries
groan and mingle in the night.
Something will be born of this.

Pay attention to what they tell you to forget
pay attention to what they tell you to forget
pay attention to what they tell you to forget

Farewell the madness of the guardians
the river, the window, they are the guardians,
there is no guardian, it is all built into me.

Do I move toward form, do I use all my fears?

THE EDUCATION
OF A POET
(1 9 7 6)

Rukeyser originally delivered this lecture at The Academy of American Poets in December 1976. It was later adapted to appear in a collection of essays, The Writer on Her Work, *Volume I, edited and with an introduction by Janet Sternburg. Several poems are included in this essay; "The Return" is from* Body of Waking *(1958); "Recovering" and "Then" are from* The Gates *(1976).*

.   .   .   .   .

THE EDUCATION OF A POET

I was born in New York, in the house where a famous gangster lived, beside Grant's Tomb, very near the grave of the Amiable Child, at that corner of the Hudson River. And the life, both open and masked, first of the people of the city, and of the country, and of the world, opened itself to me. One opens, yes, and one's life keeps opening, and poets have always known that one's education has no edges, has no end, is not separated out and cannot be separated out in any way, and is full of strength because one refuses to have it separated out.

One wanted to be for the things of the world, and the way that they came to a young child, to a girl, to me, went like this: the excitement of the city and the excitements of my family, who came to this city from other places, these were very very strong. I came later to think that my whole generation, all my friends, thought that their imagination and fantasies were much stronger than their parents'. As we went on, we came to see that the imagination of our parents, however far underground, was strong and wild and fierce, and was acted out in history as well as in their private lives.

The child that I was then had nothing to do with the poetry of books. The poetry at home was only that of Shakespeare and the Bible. There were no books in the beginning. Later, there were the sets that were laughed at as pieces of furniture bought neither with discrimination nor taste. But these can also be seen in quite a different way, as the entire works of writers about whom one came to care. And so I was exposed to Dickens, Dumas, Victor Hugo, de Maupassant, Balzac. There was the Britannica, there was the Book of Knowledge, and My Book House, and Journeys Through Bookland. The popular history of art was there, as well as the popular history of science, and with the beginnings of science came the beginnings of pictures of nakedness. Nakedness was not shown at home. A great deal was done in secrecy, without open talk. There were three things that were never talked about: sex and money and death. They were taboo, and those giant taboos were powerful. The line that was on the wall beside my bed began "Where did you come from," and whether or not I was "Baby Dear" (and pretty soon I knew I wasn't), the "where did you come from" was very very strong.

We apartment children lived as gangs, with each gang set against every other, building by building all the way around the square block. There were the heroes: Ted Lewis, who lived in our house and asked "Is everybody happy?" and we didn't answer. There was Albert Payson Terhune and the collie Lassie who became the dog of our culture. D. H. Lawrence lived a block away at that time, but we didn't know that. When we could cross the street, we ran down the block to a certain window where the baseball scores would be held out on that art material used by everybody: the cardboards that came back from the laundry with the shirts. We would draw on them and write down the baseball scores, and discuss the exploits of heroes like Walter Johnson.

Form came in these ways. Form came in with the games, and a little later with golf, which had its own form and which technically one had to learn to perfection. I was expected to grow up and become a golfer. At a certain point, I stopped cold and never played again. But that was what I was supposed to be—a bridge-playing, golf-playing woman who if I wanted to write (and it was quite clear that I did) could write if I would do things that would let me write in the summer, teaching for instance. Or, it was suggested to me in my adolescence, it would be a good idea if I married a doctor, and when he was out on housecalls I could write my poems. Now of course we have no house-calls and we have women poets—the culture has changed to that extent.

But the preparation for poetry was strong. It was partly the silences of the house and the extreme excitement of the family. It was a building-business family, and the building was the building of New York. The method was the pouring of concrete, concrete that became the means of building—not the construction with stone and brick, but with the prestress concrete that involves a skeleton of metal. The riveters on those skeletons, and the throwing of redhot rivets, and the acrobatics and heroics impressed me, as did the pour-ing of concrete and that other use of form, the concrete being poured into forms.

My father was a young cement salesman who somehow got a chance at a sand quarry on Long Island. He needed somebody with a horse and wagon. He was given an introduction to a young Italian who lived in Jersey City. Together my father and the young, thin Generoso Pope formed a sand and gravel company, and the trucks of that company went around the city with their concrete mixers turning. The company never needed any advertising because those machines were the ads.

To a child, to a little girl whose family was coming up with the building of New York and who felt the astonishing ambition and pride that went with the building, to that child the pouring and its terms became part of life. I remem-ber being scolded in school when I said "orange peel crane," a technical term so obscure that nobody could possibly understand it. I remember being asked what grit was, and I said "number 4 gravel" when I was supposed to say "courage."

There were these things, and there were the questions of love and hate. The terrible silences among my mother, my father, and my much-loved aunt, my mother's older sister. They would have hot, passionate quarrels—forbid-den times as far as I was concerned. Once I was prevailed upon to copy

"Love's Old Sweet Song" and send it to my aunt so that she would talk to my mother again, and so that my father could see her again. This forbidden love was something that ran beneath the entire life of the family and went on and on until, just after my mother's death, my father married that aunt. Then, when they were in their late seventies, the whole relationship exploded into the cruelty and passion toward which it had been heading all along.

As a child I was not allowed to go across the street, and at one point my friends made a ring around me and pulled me across the street while I shouted, "But I promised I wouldn't cross." A promise was always unbreakable. It was through a promise that I knew really what writing poems meant to me. That didn't come until high school when my best friend said she wouldn't talk to me unless I would stop writing poems. I had to *promise* to stop writing. Not being talked to was the worst punishment I could imagine; I gave my promise at once. For four weeks I didn't question; it wasn't anything I would question. And then a poem began. I went into a great storm about that poem which was building and forming. I lived like that for two weeks, and finally one night I got up and wrote down the poem. At school the next morning I said to that friend, "I couldn't keep my promise," and she said "What promise?" I realized in a flash that it meant nothing to her and I knew what it meant to me. The pressure and the drivenness was in that moment, and has been there ever since.

The punishment of silence also came at home. Home was an apartment building on the West Side. The cellars of these buildings were places that the children made their own, and the roofs, and the sidewalks, and Riverside Drive, and the river itself. The river was quite different in those days. It was openly brutal: the cattle trains came down in the morning, and you could see the cattle going to the slaughterhouses; you could smell them. The whole city was open; the railroad tracks were not covered. Beyond the tracks was a place called Shantytown and, later, Hooverville. The people in the fine apartment houses insisted that Hooverville be destroyed because it spoiled their view. It was clear to a growing child that the terrible, murderous differences between the ways people lived were being upheld all over the city, that if you moved one block in any direction you would find an entirely different order of life. One morning I missed walking with my father to the car that took him to his office, which was on the edge of the river and the sandhills at Fiftieth Street. I went after him, and as I walked the neighborhood changed; the apartment houses and the residential blocks changed to the poor blocks with the smell of the poor, the smell of barley, the open doorways, the people lying against walls, the people working, the metalworkers, and finally the offices of the sand and gravel company. These changes were the clear statement of what we were willing to live among, what we see still everyday, and these were the beginnings.

Friends were the beginnings too. The boy Rusty Shaw, who was a caddy at a country club. We used to lie on the hills of oyster shells at Inwood Bay, Long Island, and talk and talk about how he could possibly manage to go on living at home where his father was drunk all the time and took whatever money Rusty made. There were the people who understood about sex. Sex was never talked about; my hands had been bound up at night for good reason. I didn't know about sex until I walked with a girlfriend through the Museum of Natural History underneath the great whale, and she told me about sex. It is curious, and one can't say silly, the way one first hears about it, but there it was and I thought Ah, *that's* why my parents don't commit suicide! That seemed to be the thing that would save the life of people in such misery and such silence.

The *feeling* life of my parents seemed to me to be in the world of opera and music. They went to the opera on Thursday evenings, and on certain Friday mornings the libretto would be on the hall table. When I came home from school on Friday I would read it, and it seemed strange but no stranger than anything else. From the librettos, I first learned about translations, and about lurid poetry and melodrama. From melodrama, Caruso gave them the worship of emotion. It was the kind of emotion that did come through to my parents, even though a great deal of emotion was cut off for reasons that I didn't know about then. Much later I read Jung, and when I went to Ireland I heard about an analyst who believed that what you are dominated by in your childhood is whatever your parents really love. I believe that now. I believe that I was dominated by what my father and my mother loved; it came through to me as deep sexuality centered in that forbidden aunt who was the figure of passion and sex in my early life, and through the opera singers and composers of the music that meant so much to them, and through the popular music of that time and the happiness of the young people who sat on the stoops and sang, and through the sadness my parents felt at that custom going out of the city.

I was beginning to write poems, and also to make up short piano pieces. But I didn't know what writing meant to me until that promise I gave in high school. The drivenness, the fact that the writing has to be done beyond all promises was there for a long time. There are promises to people one loves that take precedence at times. But one can trust—one knows that the poetry will come back, that it will resurrect. It's a risky thing; the poetry may come back on a different level. But it will come back. It came back to me. I never put it away completely. I was told by friends, for example, when it was a matter of deciding to go ahead and have a child, that I would have to choose between the child and poetry, and I said no. I was not going to make that choice; I would choose both.

It's very much a question of reinforcing choices as one makes them, of leaving one's life open to them, of going further in and confirming them, and also of clearing away, stripping away the masks. I said earlier that we thought that our imaginations were so much stronger than our parents', but I think that idea came from our not knowing how people with masked lives really lived. These were middle-class lives. There was no idea at that point of a girl growing up to write poems. That was a terrifying idea to my parents. Much later they said they thought they could have handled it if I had been a boy, but they were very strange in their feeling about anybody writing poems or doing anything serious in the arts.

How old were you when you know that there were living poets? Do you remember? In this culture a great many people don't know that there are living poets, or didn't know when I was growing up. I thought that real men went to the office everyday. The joy of learning that people wrote poems and that was what they could do with their lives was very great. I came to that knowledge through anthologies and single books of poems and through poets' collected poems, the fact that one could find the whole work of a person in one book and see how that spirit moves. I want to share with you some poems of mine, poems that have to do with the way my life has taken its shape.

THE RETURN

An Idea ran about the world
screaming with the pain of the mind
until it met a child
who stopped it with a word.

The Idea leaned over those newborn eyes
and dreamed of the nature of things:
the nature of memory and the nature of love;
and forgave itself and all men.

Quieted in a sea of sleeping
the Idea began its long return—
renewed by the child's sea-colored eyes
remembered the flesh, smiled and said:

I see birds, spring and the birthplace
unknown by the stable stone.
I know light and I know motion
and I remember I am not alone.

The Idea voyaged nearer my breathing, saying
Come balance come
into the love of these faces and forces
find us our equilibrium.

And the child stirred, asking his questions.
The Idea grew more fleshly and spoke:
Beaten down I was
Down I knew very long
Newborn I begin.

And the child went on asking his questions.

The Idea journeying into my body
returned, and I knew the nature of One,
and could forget One, and turn to the child,
and whole could turn to the world again.

Until the pain turns into answers
And all the masters become askers
And all the victims again doers
And all the sources break in light.

The child goes alive, asking his questions.

There are the questions of love and religion that have to enter, along with the social bonds between us, into everything we do. My mother had a story about recovery from illness that was central to her life. As she told the story, it went like this: "My mother was a heroic and noble woman. She saved my life. When I had diphtheria as a child and they gave me up for dead, she stayed all night feeding me cracked ice. By morning the fever had broken. If she hadn't fed me that ice all night long, I would never have come through." My mother also gave me a treasure that I believe has a great deal to do with the kind of poetry I think of as unverifiable fact. She told me we were descended from Akiba. Akiba was the martyr who resisted the Romans in the first century and who was tortured to death after his great work for the Song of Songs. He was flayed with iron rakes tearing his flesh until at the end he said, "I know that I have loved God with all my heart and all my soul, and now I know that I love Him with all my life." Now this is an extraordinary gift to give a child.

I've always thought of two kinds of poems: the poems of unverifiable facts, based in dreams, in sex, in everything that can be given to other people only through the skill and strength by which it is given; and the other kind being the document, the poem that rests on material evidence. So many parts of life have come into my poems. One recent poem that has formed over several years is called "Double Ode." I didn't know fully what the poem was when I began it. I thought it was a poem in which the figures of father and mother were represented both by the remembered parents and also by two small black Mexican statues that are on my windowsill. But as I went on with the poem, pieces came into it from my notebooks, pieces from Spain, from the bells in the towers of Florence, from the exile of my son and daughter-in-law during the Vietnam War. I realized that the doubleness of the ode was the doubleness of looking backwards and forwards, that it was not simply a poem of parents but of generations.

I need to speak also of my formal education, because at college everything was sharply intensified. I could spend long times in the library, I could take to bed for days, and I could also go to the coal mines in Pennsylvania (although when my parents came up and I said, "Do you want to go for a drive?" My mother said, "You mean the gate isn't locked? I never would have let you come here if I thought the gate wasn't locked.") There was so much more freedom, and an access to materials and to people who were more than I had thought people could be. It was there that everything opened again, but I left college because my father had gone bankrupt and could not afford to have a daughter at Vassar. I went ahead writing poems, the poems that were in my first book. It was a piece of luck that my first book was published, and an act of extreme generosity on the part of the editor of the Yale Series of Younger Poets. I sent my book in partly finished form the same year that James Agee's book entered the competition. Stephen Vincent Benet, the editor, wrote me that he'd had to choose between Jim Agee's book and mine, and he had chosen Jim's. He thought that my book could be published by a commercial firm, and he gave me letters of introduction. My book was turned down by eleven publishers during that year, and finally Benet asked me to put the book back in the Yale Series, saying of course it would have to stand in the competition. But he did publish it that year. A great deal of my life has involved that preliminary "no" and a final "yes," and I felt very lucky.

I could go on for days and talk about my entire life, but what I've begun to say here shows the direction, the strength of the poetry itself. I don't believe that poetry can save the world. I do believe that the forces in our wish to share something of our experience by turning it into something and giving it to somebody: that is poetry. That is some kind of saving thing, and as far as my life is concerned, poetry has saved me again and again. I don't know a lot of things. This year a friend asked me what direction my work was taking. I blurted out, as I do, and said I didn't know. I asked him if he knew where his work was taking him and he said yes, that it was going in a certain direction—socially, always. And for him that was one part and the other part was a mystery. I wish I had given that answer. I give it to you, and a poem as well:

RECOVERING

Dream of the world
speaking to me.

The dream of the dead
acted out in me.

The fathers shouting
across their blue gulf.

A storm in each word,
an incomplete universe.

Lightning in brain,
slow-time recovery.

In the light of October
things emerge clear.

The force of looking
returns to my eyes.

Darkness arrives
splitting the mind open.

Something again
is beginning to be born.

A dance is
dancing me.

I wake in the dark.

People have said that we contemporary poets are writing without form. I was brought up with forms and care very much about them. I care about the form in which the poems in the Bible are written, its parallelism that allows one to make one's own synthesis of whatever meanings one derives from opposites. But the idea that form has to be the forms of the past is nonsense. I was startled to read of Thurber's anger when he found out that the world wasn't necessarily round, that it might be pear-shaped. He said he couldn't stand it, he wanted to have form. I'd be very happy with the form of a pear. In order to give something to somebody there must be the form to shape the experience. It's difficult to make the equivalent of an experience, to make a poem that is so full of the resources of music and of meaning, and that allows you to give it to me, me to give it to you. All the forms of art come to us in their own ways and allow us to make more forms, and to make this exchange. I used to talk a great deal about communication. I don't anymore. I communicated badly with the people I was closest to, so I won't talk about it any longer. I'll try to do it. I think the exchange of energy is what happens in art. There are so many ways in which one is conducted to learning, so many ways in which one seeks, and ways in which one loves the people from whom one can learn. The passion with which one reaches to such people goes on forever and ever; it is in one's poems, and in the poems one reads, and in this poem:

THEN

When I am dead, even then,
I will still love you, I will wait in these poems,
When I am dead, even then
I am still listening to you.
I will still be making poems for you
out of silence;
silence will be falling into that silence,
it is building music.

NYQ: *Do you feel that the present time provides a fitting setting*
       for the poet? You have spoken about the Elizabethan age considered
       the much-vaunted age for poetry. But what about the present age?

MR: Well, one of the attacks on me for writing that
       Hariot book spoke of me as a she-poet—that I had no
       business to be doing this and I was broken for a
       while and looked out the window for a while. And
       then I thought, yes, I am a she-poet. Anything I bring
       to this is because I am a woman. And this is the thing
       that was left out of the Elizabethan world, the
       element that did not exist. Maybe, maybe, maybe
       that is what one can bring to life.

                                          — from an interview in
                                          The New York Quarterly,
                                          Summer 1972.

INDEX